Understanding and Regulating the Market at a Time of Globalization

Also by Hervé Dumez and Alain Jeunemaître

FINANCIAL MARKETS REGULATION (*co-authors*)
LA POLITIQUE DE CONCURRENCE EN EUROPE (*co-editors*)

Understanding and Regulating the Market at a Time of Globalization

The Case of the Cement Industry

Hervé Dumez
Researcher at the Centre de Recherche en Gestion
École Polytechnique
Paris

and

Alain Jeunemaître
Researcher
La Maison Française and Nuffield College
and
Associate
Regulatory Policy Research Centre
Hertford College
Oxford

Foreword by Suzanne Berger

First published in Great Britain 2000 by
MACMILLAN PRESS LTD
Houndmills, Basingstoke, Hampshire RG21 6XS and London
Companies and representatives throughout the world

A catalogue record for this book is available from the British Library.

ISBN 0–333–63383–0

First published in the United States of America 2000 by
ST. MARTIN'S PRESS, INC.,
Scholarly and Reference Division,
175 Fifth Avenue, New York, N.Y. 10010

ISBN 0–312–22622–5

Library of Congress Cataloging-in-Publication Data
Dumez, Hervé.
Understanding and regulating the market at a time of globalization
: the case of the cement industry / Herve Dumez and Alain
Jeunemaitre.
p. cm.
Includes bibliographical references and index.
ISBN 0–312–22622–5 (cloth)
1. Cement industries—Government policy—Case studies.   2. Foreign
trade regulation.   3. International trade.   4. Competition,
International.   I. Jeunemaître, Alain.   II. Title.
HD9622.A2D86   1999
338.4'766694—dc21   99–15385
                                                                     CIP

This book is printed on paper suitable for recycling and made from fully managed and sustained
forest sources.

10   9   8   7   6   5   4   3   2   1
09   08   07   06   05   04   03   02   01   00

Printed and bound in Great Britain by
Antony Rowe Ltd, Chippenham, Wiltshire

CONTENTS

ACKNOWLEDGEMENTS

We are deeply grateful to the many people we met in the course of our research. In particular our special thanks to:

The executives of Lafarge (France), Bertrand Collomb, Président Directeur Général and Bernard Kasriel, Directeur Général, Dominique Hooreman, Directeur d'affaires; Lafarge Corp. (Reston Virginia, and Dallas, Texas); Davenport Cement (Missouri); Calcia, then Ciments Français (France), Philippe Ronsin; Southdown (Houston, Texas), John Edgar Marston III, Vice President and General Counsel, John T. Bloom Junior, Manager Corporate Development;

The executives of the US Department of Justice, Paul Dennis; the Federal Trade Commission, Anne Malester, Claudia Higgins, Howard Morse, Benjamin Tahyar.

The Syndicat Français de l'Industrie Cimentière (SFIC), Renaud Lambert;

European lawyers, above all Henry Lesguillons (Jeantet et associés, Paris, Bruxelles), and US lawyers, Timothy MacCormick (Thompson and Knight, Dallas, Texas);

Douglas M. Queen (Douglas M. Queen Inc., Williamston, Massachussets);

John Lynch (Lynch Research and Investment, NY);

Michael Klass (National Economic Research Associates, Washington DC);

Jonathan Goldfarb (Merryl Lynch, New York).

We are also greatly indebted to our French colleagues of the École Polytechnique, from the Centre de Recherche en Gestion (CRG), particularly to Jacques Girin, his director, Michel Berry, the honorary director, Florence Charue-Duboc and Bertrand Nicolas, and from the Laboratoire d'Économétrie, to Jean Pierre Ponssard and Claude Henry.

We would also like to make particular mention of the Regulatory Policy Research Centre, George Yarrow, the Director, Susan Belton Jones, and Tim Keyworth. They all gave us invaluable advice. Tim managed to significantly improve our first English version. His guidance has been very helpful.

Our work has also benefited from the assistance of many in the search and the gathering of documents, Joyce Aicklen (Lafarge Corp.), civil servants at the US International Trade Commission, the Japanese Fair Trade Commission, Nathalie Moutot the librarian of ATHIL, Michel Multan, librarian at the École Polytechnique.

Finally, many thanks to Michèle Breton who helped in the editing process of the book.

The views expressed here are those of the authors and should not be ascribed to the above mentioned persons.

Hervé Dumez and Alain Jeunemaître

ABBREVIATIONS AND ACRONYMS

AD/CVD	Antidumping and Countervailing Duty
BKA	Bundeskartellamt. The German competition policy agency
RMC	Ready Mix Concrete
FOB	Free on Board
IBJ	International Bulk Journal
ICR	International Cement Review. International journal
JFTC	Japanese Fair Trade Commission
LTFV	Less Than Fair Value, dumping price
PCA	Portland Cement Association
P&Q	Pit and Quarry. US journal
RP	Rock Products. US journal
RTP Court	Restrictive Trade Practices Court (UK)
USFTC	US Federal Trade Commission
USITC	US International Trade Commission
WC	World Cement. International journal

DEFINITION

The units "tons", when used in official US data, refers to "metric tons" from 1993 and to "short tons" in earlier years. One short ton equals 0.907 metric tons, and 5.139 barrels.

FOREWORD

Suzanne Berger
Dorman-Starbuck Professor of Political Science, M.I.T.

The impact of globalization on the economies and societies of advanced industrial countries has raised a storm of controversy in research communities and in the public at large. Virtually every major claim about how changes in the international economy translate into changes in the well-being, autonomy, and future trajectory of advanced industrial nations can be challenged. Indeed, many of the claims advanced rest on little more than chains of deductive reasoning, illustrated by anecdotes. It is the great merit of the research by Hervé Dumez and Alain Jeunemaître in to have developed their arguments on the basis of a in-depth empirical analysis of a particular industry and to have examined evidence about changes in the structures of the cement industry under globalization over time and across a number of major producing countries.

First, even the starting point of most analyses of globalization -namely, the notion that it marks a radical innovation in the nature of the international economy- can hardly be taken for granted. If we step back from the changes in the world economy of the past two decades and consider the longer historical sweep of the period from before the First World War to the present, the vista we see is quite different. Researchers who have studied the international economy at the turn of the 20th century have raised a number of serious challenges to the now-conventional wisdom about the globalized economy by pointing to significant internationalization in the past. By 1913, in the most advanced countries, there were levels of capital and labor mobility across national boundaries quite comparable to today's levels.[1] Only in the 1970s and 1980s did the share of trade in GDP for OECD countries return to levels that had already been reached in 1913. As for foreign direct investment, it has been estimated in 1913 at 9 per cent of global GDP; subsequently it declined to less than half that amount; and by 1990 it had not yet returned to the 1913 level.[2] A recent *Economist* survey on states and the international economy notes that capital flows were as mobile before World War I as today and that net capital transfers were significantly greater.[3]

Even the idea that globalization undermines the autonomy and leverage of the national state is not a new one, but found strong proponents in this earlier period of internationalization. Indeed Norman Angell writing in 1913 had already focussed on the very same phenomena that today are imagined to be the motors of globalization:

> *'This vital interdependence...cutting athwart frontiers is largely the work of the last forty years...[It is] the result of daily use of those contrivances of civilization which date from yesterday--the rapid post, the instantaneous dissemination of financial and commercial information by means of telegraphy, and generally the incredible increase in the rapidity of communication which has put the half-dozen chief capitals of Christendom in closer contact financially, and has rendered them more dependent the one upon the other than were the chief cities of Great Britain less than a hundred years ago.'[4]*

---

1. See Carl Strikwerda, 'The Troubled Origins of European Economic Integration: International Iron and Steel and Labor Migration in the Era of World War I,' in *American Historical Review*, 98:4 (1993) 1106-1142; Robert Zevin, 'Are World Financial Markets More Open, If So, Why, and with What Effects?' in Tariq Banuri and Juliet Schor, eds., *Financial Openness and National Autonomy* (NY: Oxford, 1992); Robert Wade, 'Globalization and Its Limits: Reports of the Death of the National Economy are Greatly Exaggerated,' in Suzanne Berger and Ronald Dore, eds., *National Diversity and Global Capitalism* (Ithaca: Cornell, 1996).
2. Vincent Cable, 'The Diminished Nation-State,' *Daedalus*, vol. 124, n° 2 (Spring 1995), p. 24, p. 29.
3. 'Who's in the Driving Seat?' Special Survey of *Economist*, October 7, 1995, pp. 5, 9.
4. Norman Angell, *The Great Illusion* (New York: Putnam, 4th revised ed, 1913), p. 54.

From this financial interdependence, Angell deduced the irrationality, indeed the unlikelihood, of war, for it had become too costly to the fabric of international economic exchange to be a calculated option.

It would be a mistake, of course, to look too closely for lessons in the parallels between the situation obtaining in the international economic and political system linking the advanced countries of 1913 and today's international system. There have been real changes in global capital markets, relative even to the degree of integration achieved before the collapse during the two world wars and the Depression. The velocity and gross volume of capital movements today are on a scale that dwarfs that of the turn of the century. New financial instruments, new technologies of communication, and a greater concentration of assetholders with the entry of institutional investors have created quite a different environment. There are, arguably, constraints on the resort to war as a means of settling conflicts among the major powers that rule out a scenario like that of 1914. Still, seen from the longer perspective, the view is one not of an irreversible progression towards ever greater and unprecedented levels of internationalization. Rather the picture is one of high levels at the onset of the World War One, then a devastating shattering of the links of interdependence among the advanced countries, then, a gradual reweaving of the networks of the international economy, and a return by the turn of the 21st century to an international world with national constraints and opportunities that our grandfathers had already glimpsed. If the levels of flow of resources across frontiers do have historical precedents, we need to consider more fully than we have what we can learn from the past about the welfare of societies engaged in such exchanges and about the ability of national states to regulate these economic transfers.

The Dumez-Jeunemaître study of the cement industry starts from a such a historical analysis. The authors distinguish very usefully between internationalization and globalization (pp. 2-3). Internationalization refers to company strategies of implanting activities in multiple domestic and foreign markets and using the profits gained from first-mover or other advantages in local markets to support their overall operations. Like the strategy of Asea Brown Boveri (ABB) today, such organization across borders is "multi-domestic" rather than truly global, for it respects the basic conditions of each local market and does not attempt to integrate them. Particularly in the cement industry, where proximity of access to quarries and very high transportation costs for this heavy material were strong constraints on decisions about where to locate production facilities, internationalization was until recently the only way in which companies could move across borders.

Starting in the 1970s, however, a "technological breakthrough" in transporting cement in bulk for the first time made it technically feasible to conceive strategies that linked local markets to international trade. Dumez and Jeunemaître explain that the real measure of globalization is the actual competitive linkage of local to global markets, not simply the existence of trade. In the extreme, they argue, there can be extensive trade without globalization, so long as *'incumbent producers control the flow of imports ad exports in their local markets... Conversely, globalisation may occur without significant international trade. The likelihood of such trade, as a threat to the incumbent producers, weighs on the local market price equilibrium and produces de facto the interconnection of markets.'* In the 1970s and 1980s, a new actor, the trader, appeared on the scene, to control cement import facilities and ships, hence to control the flows of cement around the world. thus wiping out the walls that had once segmented local markets. From the 1980s, the world cement industry became a globalized industry in which the reality and possibility of obtaining supplies abroad began to affect local prices. As Dumez and Jeunemaître write, *'globalisation has more of an economic impact than simply the interconnection of distant local markets. There is also an economic impact relating to the potential threat that hangs over local markets...'* In this sense, the shift from internationalization to globalization is irreversible, for even when imports are not massively present in local markets, the fact that they could be brought in at a later point conditions local prices. Thus, for this industry at least, globalization has fundamentally reshaped local markets in ways that have no historical precedent.

Dumez and Jeunemaître's research also illuminates the second of the major debates over globalization: over whether it destroys the policymaking space for national governments. On this point they demonstrate the considerable weapons in government arsenals to regulate the terms of entry of foreign goods, in sum, to regulate the process of globalization. They analyze the use of anti-dumping measures and countervailing duty petitions by the United States, the major investigations of competition in the cement industry by the European Commission, and the deliberations of the Japanese Fair Trade Commission to demonstrate the "tremendous" impact that institutions and policies have on the evolution of this industry. In effect, in the US, they conclude, the effect has been to consolidate power over imports in the hands of the local producers, thus reasserting local market competition and preserving internationalization of the industry against globalization. These institutional mechanisms place governments in the role of regulating globalization--blocking or delaying it today, but potentially introducing it tomorrow, as for example they have in a limited fashion in the US to support more competition in local markets.

Through a detailed and concrete analysis of changes in one industry, Dumez and Jeunemaître enable us to understand how changes in technology, cost structures, and markets in the international economy become resources available to government for affecting change in their own domestic economies. In contrast to William Greider's frightening vision of a world economy out of control of impotent national governments,[5] (or Kenichi Omae's enthusiastic embrace of the same),[6] Dumez and Jeunemaître show how considerable the need, possibility, and precedents are for regulating globalization. In this admirable study, theory and empirical comparative research, work together to lay illuminate the space for public decision.

---

5. William Greider, *One World, Ready or Not* (New York: Simon and Schuster, 1997)
6. Kenichi Omae, *The Borderless World* (New York: Harper Collins, 1990).

INTRODUCTION

Markets have become global, with the world economy now operating on a planetary scale.

Yet markets are inherently local: consumer tastes are diverse; business strategies of firms result in the fragmentation of markets according to product lines and location; trade and competition policies vary from country to country.

What, then, is the meaning and importance of economic globalisation?

The best answer to an abstract question of this kind probably lies in the lessons that can be drawn from empirical analyses. However limited a case study may be, its empirical approach has several advantages, in that it provides a historical account of the question at issue, and highlights its multi-dimensional nature.

In line with this, our book is based on a particular case study, that of the cement industry. A more general perspective on market globalisation is developed from this study.

The choice of market is less strange than it might seem at first glance.

The cement industry is one that is often discussed in industrial economics textbooks. Cement is a homogenous product, and the processes involved in its production have been known for a long time. The acquisition of the technology to produce cement is not a barrier to entry. Any country can decide to set up cement plants where limestone quarries are available. In these terms, then, it is a mature and simple industry to deal with.

The competitive process is also well documented and part of common economic knowledge. As transportation costs are high compared to production costs, competition in the industry occurs at a local level. A cement plant located inland rarely sells outside of a 200 mile radius, and would normally sell the bulk of its production within 100 to 150 mile.

Given these conditions, the globalisation of cement markets may be thought very unlikely and of little significance. But globalisation has been taking place, and changes the approach to business within the industry. Thus, the cement industry can be understood as an extreme case of industry globalisation in an elementary economic context. It casts light on some of the essential dimensions of the globalisation process, showing its development in slow motion. It is to the study of market globalisation what the white mouse is to the analysis of the metabolism in animal and human biology.

The cement industry has had (and continues to have) a particularly rich history in terms of antitrust and competition policy decisions in Europe, Japan and the United States. From the mid 1980s to the mid 1990s, competition within the industry has also raised a number of important issues in international trade, mostly relating to anti-dumping and countervailing duty procedures, and to the negotiation of import quotas.

In addition to the points of interest mentioned so far, this study of the cement industry provides an opportunity to articulate some conceptual distinctions that are necessary for a good understanding of the globalisation process. In particular, we introduce and emphasise two important distinctions.

The first relates to the demarcation between competition and rivalry.

Competition, here, refers to head to head market confrontation focused on price rebates and sales volume, generally involving a fight for additional market share.

Rivalry refers to the search for competitive advantage primarily in the context of non-price competition, for instance from improved product quality, reduced production costs, or from the pre-emption of prime locations.

In many cases, competitors have a long experience of each other in local markets. As competition is a risky and costly game, efforts are made to move the competitive process towards one of rivalry. Such attempts are, however, regulated by antitrust authorities.

Our second key distinction is between internationalisation and globalisation.

Internationalisation often occurs in the context of stable local competition, where the competitive process is one of rivalry (at least this has been the case for the cement industry). Companies are able to use the economic surplus they extract from local markets to further their international development. But internationalisation, here, is viewed in terms of local competition, with firms considering each local market as governed by its own specific characteristics, and as a result, not truly linked to others. The process of internationalisation, then, upholds the geographic segmentation of local markets.

By contrast, here, globalisation is defined as the connection and coupling of distant local markets within a greater market ensemble, normally through a brutal process. The term globalisation implies that a new type of economic agent has emerged in local markets who is alien to the traditional ways of thinking about competition, and the search for market stabilisation. These new economic agents position themselves in order to take advantage of economic differences between local markets, with the end result being their unification. This process of globalisation is regulated by authorities that deal with international trade issues in antidumping and countervailing duty.

The first part of this book presents the basics of the cement industry. Chapter 1 clearly outlines of how competition operates within the industry. Chapter 2 identifies the various strategies used to stabilise local competition and move towards a rivalry game. Antitrust responses to these strategies are then examined in Chapter 3.

The second part of the book focuses on globalisation. Chapters 6 and 7 detail the prerequisites of globalisation, and how the process is set into motion. Chapter 8 then investigates the various strategic responses at the disposal of local firms to counteract the globalisation process.

Part 3 primarily concerns the recent and ongoing European antitrust case in the cement industry. This is of particular relevance to our discussion as it concerned both competition and market globalisation issues. In dealing with the case, the European Commission had to make a competitive assessment of, and decide on a course of action for, the industry at a time of globalisation.

The conclusion brings together the general lessons that can be drawn from our study of the cement industry.

CHAPTER 1

The cement industry as a model case

The cement industry is often used as a model case in industrial economics textbooks, as it has some key features that make it particularly easy to understand in terms of competition. It is a heavily capital intensive industry which produces a homogenous product, with transportation costs high relative to production costs.

Whilst reaffirming these basic characteristics, this introductory chapter makes two further points. Firstly, while the industry may appear to be a simple one, it shares in common with any industry key features of the competitive process and has experienced similar business developments. Secondly, that the study of market globalisation is helped by the characteristics of the cement industry. In particular, they enable us to visit the globalisation process at a slow pace. Before embarking on the economic presentation, however, a historical and technical overview will be useful.

Historical overview[1]

Cement has been used in antiquity. Basically, it is a material which when mixed with water takes on the property of hardness and becomes water-resistant. As a result, it can be used as a binding material, for example between the stones of a wall. Modern-day cement is called Portland

---

1. For a more detailed presentation, see B. Collomb (1993).

5

Cement, and was invented in 1824 by an Englishman, Joseph Aspdin. Portland cement is a chemical combination of calcium (normally limestone), silica, alumina, iron ore and small amounts of other materials. It is made by quarrying, crushing and grinding the raw materials, burning them in huge rotary kilns at high temperatures, and finely grinding the resulting marble-sized pellets (clinker) with gypsum into an extremely fine, usually grey, powder. Cement clinker manufacturing processes are classified as either wet or dry. The dry process is more popular as it is more energy efficient (US Department of Commerce, 1987). Joseph Aspdin called the hydraulic lime that he patented "Portland Cement", because it resembled a natural limestone quarried on the Isle of Portland, in England. Industrial production levels were reached around 1880, and since then, cement has been used to perfect pre-fabricated products (poles fencings, cement blocks. etc.) and to make concrete. Concrete is a mixture of cement, gravels, sand and water which hardens more or less quickly depending on the ambient temperature. Concrete is easily moulded, cheap, and becomes as solid as stone. These characteristics explain its popularity as a building material throughout the 20th century.

All countries use cement, although demand obviously varies with climate and construction habits. For instance, in the United States, the northern part of the country traditionally uses more steel and wood, and thus less cement, in its constructions, than the south. Given its seaside climate, Florida uses cement as a basic construction element (US Department of Commerce).

The production process for cement has evolved in major technological leaps (Tushman and Anderson, 1986), the first involving a movement from woodfired vertical kilns to rotary kilns. The introduction of powdered coal as fuel (at the beginning of the 20th century), allowed for a more regular flow of constituents into the kiln, and a more homogenous firing/heating process. Then came the introduction of the wet process (1925),[2] computerised production that allowed the use of huge kilns (1960s), and finally the generalised use of the more energy efficient dry process (1970s).

---

2. A major industrial difficulty lies in adding correct and regular amounts of the constituents on a large scale. One of the ways of doing this is to wet the constituents (the wet process); another is to mix them, and send them over a very hot gas heater (the dry process).

Economic characteristics

The product

Cement is a homogeneous material, with its quality defined by technical norms that vary only slightly between countries (for instance, for climatic reasons: cement used in cold and humid countries is not the same as that used in hot and dry climates).[3] Given the nature of cement, there is very little of a brand effect, particularly as it is generally sold in bulk.

When a buyer chooses between two cement producers, then, the decision is primarily based on price, with innovation counting for little in the competitive process. There have been improvements over time, with the technical characteristics of cement evolving. In particular, the hardening time has been reduced. But these technical changes require time and are often quickly adopted by the entire profession. At first glance, then, there seems to be little room for competition on aspects other than price.

However, differentiation between producers does exist in a number of areas: the producer of cement can make a difference in terms of the homogeneity of its quality, and on a major building site, it is important that the quality and colour of the cement remain constant throughout the entire construction time; cement buyers are concerned about delivery delays, as construction sites are always under intense deadline pressure; a producer can provide a buyer with technical assistance, allowing them to choose the cement best suited to their construction site, and to use it in optimal conditions; producers can plan deliveries in order to provide buyers with greater flexibility; buyers have different requirements depending on whether they buy cement to produce concrete for roads, or for construction. As in all industries, then, there is some differentiation among producers. But in terms of the quality/price combination, price is the main competitive variable. Differences in service quality are only likely to sway buyers if price differences are minimal.

---

3. In 1900, the United States established five normalised cement qualities. Standards in the United States were defined by the American Society for Testing Materials (ASTM). Quality norms defined by the Japan Cement Engineers Association were recognised by the Japanese government in 1905. In Europe, the standardisation of cement norms has required a longer period of time. Since 1992, a European cement pre-standard has been established.

Demand

Cement is a construction material, and demand is therefore determined by the business cycles of the construction industry. In construction, cement is used, to a greater or lesser extent, depending on climate and local habits. Overall, cement is reported to represent 2 to 5 per cent of construction costs. If construction slows, then a drop in cement prices will not help boost construction. On the other hand, if cement prices rise, even strongly, there is no real impact on demand, as there is no real substitute available to cement in the short run. So in the cement industry, price has no significant impact on demand. That is, in economic terms, demand is inelastic to price. Rather, demand turns on the level of activity in the construction and public works sectors. But these levels of activity fluctuate between booms and busts that are more or less pronounced. Broadly speaking, up until the first oil crisis in 1974, cement demand followed a general upward trend, with swings around this trend determined by the business cycles of the United States, Europe and Japan. Since then, growth in Europe, Japan and the US has slowed, and the swings have been more pronounced and erratic. Contrastingly, in other parts of the world, particularly in Asia and South America in the 1990s, countries with high economic growth have had booming cement markets. In 1995, in Japan, the per head average cement consumption was 634 kg per year, nearly equal to that of Italy and Spain, but well below countries such as Korea (1059 kgpy) or Taiwan (1329 kgpy).

Supply

On passing by a cement plant, an onlooker could instantly recognise the main characteristics of cement production and the massive investment required for the huge kilns and grinding facilities. The investment is only written off after several decades. For instance, in December 1995, the Lafarge group announced that it was to rebuild its Richmond cement plant in British Columbia, which supplied regional Vancouver markets. The cement plant dated back to 1958, and had, therefore, been in operation for thirty years. The cost of the new plant was, at the time, estimated to be more than $100 million.

New capacity investment goes along with important economies of scale that are achieved by increasing the size of the plant, with unit costs lower for larger plants. Each period of production in the past has been marked by technical constraints determining optimal plant size, such that economies of scale in production seem only limited by the technical constraints of the day (Norman, 1979; McBride, 1981). At present, the world's largest cement plant is the Donghae plant in Korea which produces almost 10 million tons of cement each year (*RP*, Tak Jeong-Bu. August 1984).

However, multi-plant economies of scale are non-existent. The acquisition of an additional cement plant does not provide a producer with an economic advantage with regard to unit production costs. Therefore, economies of scale in the industry relate to individual plants.

Anti-pollution regulations have increased the cost of investment in the industry, with dust collecting facilities currently representing 10 to 15 per cent of the construction cost of a cement plant (Collomb, 1993).

The burning of wastes in cement plants as a substitute for traditional energy sources such as coal and other fuels, is another environmental issue. The use of waste in heaters (calciners) can significantly dimish the energy costs of the plant. Where this is subsidised by other industries or local authorities, energy costs are not only minimised, but it might also prove to be a revenue source for the plant.

Given the large investment costs required to set up a plant, fixed costs in the industry are particularly high and significant relative to variable costs. Fixed costs are said to generally account for more than 50 per cent of overall production costs (US Department of Commerce, 1987). With the automation of the production process in the 1960's, labour costs have decreased, and most of the variable costs of production are now from energy consumption in the heating of kilns, even if subsidisation of waste burning in cement kilns pushes energy costs down. Finally, fixed costs are usually "sunk costs". Once built, a cement plant can serve no other purpose. If a producer shuts down a plant, or exits the market because a plant is not profitable, he will not recover a substantial part of his initial investment.

Since fixed costs are high in relation to variable costs, the break-even point is high. Thus, profits in the industry are very sensitive to the level of utilisation of production capacity. Important cash flow is generated when production increases beyond the break-even point. Conversely, when activity is low, losses are felt both quickly and severely.

Another economic feature of the industry that strongly influences competition is the importance of transportation costs relative to production costs. In the United States, average transportation and distribution costs account for almost 25 per cent of the cement price (Liba, 1987: 128). As a result, most cement plants sell their production close by, within a radius of 200 km.[4]

The costs of transportation vary depending on whether it is by road, rail or sea. Road transportation is the most expensive, followed by rail, with transportation by sea the cheapest.[5] If a cement plant is located on a railway line or close to a harbour, it can deliver its production to distant markets.

The importance of geography and history

Given the economic characteristics of the industry, the key decision when setting up a cement plant concerns location. The best location will combine three advantages. The plant will be set up in a quarry with a large quantity of high quality and easily workable limestone. It will be close to large urban areas that will become its main markets. It will be on a railway line or a river network allowing cement to be delivered as far as possible from the plant. However, there are often considerable difficulties in satisfying each of these characteristics. This can be illustrated by considering the particularly striking contrast between the cement industry of Japan and that of the US.

In 1948, nearly all Japanese cement plants were in the South-Western part of the archipelago (*P&Q*. Mitsuzo, July 1948). In the 1990's, the location of cement plants is very similar (*RP*. Pullman, April 1991). Fourteen cement plants are concentrated in a fairly small area, never more than 100 mile away from each other. Between 1948 and 1991, the number of cement plants hardly changed (moving from 36 to 41). Average capacity, however, given economies of scale, surged from approximately 0.5 to 2.75 million tons.

In Japan, two geographical characteristics have determined the location of plants. The main sources of raw materials are close to the sea, as are the

---

4. In 1988, Florida cement companies sold 70 per cent of their production within a radius of under 100 mile. In Arizona, New Mexico and Texas, where population density is low, 80 per cent of production was sold within a 200 mile radius (US International Trade Commission, 1991).

5. Per ton of cement, transportation by truck (trucking) was $7 for 50 mile, $14 for 150 mile, and $23 for 400 mile. By rail the price was $6.50 for 50 mile, $8.50 for 150 mile, and $17 for 400 mile. By ship, the price was $6 for 50 mile, and $7 for 400 mile. A highway transport truck carries about 26 short tons of cement, whereas rail wagons haul about 100 short tons. A standard barge carries approximately 1.500 short tons of dry material (USITC, 1991).

main cities. A typical example of a major Japanese cement firm (with a production of more than 5 million tons) is that belonging to the Chichibu group. It is located in the town of Kumagaya-Shi (40 mile north-west of Tokyo), in the Kanta district, one of the major Japanese cement markets (*RP*, Huhta, October 1984). The geography of Japan, then, is such that cement plant owners can benefit from economies of scale, without bearing too much of an economic handicap in terms of transportation and distribution costs. Half of domestic Japanese deliveries are shipped by sea.

The situation in the US is completely different. Raw material sites are scattered throughout the immense US territory. The population density is 12 times less than in Japan. The population of Japan is half that of the US, but the Japanese live in a geographical area smaller than the state of California. The US is made up of populated cities separated by vast deserted zones. It is hardly surprising, then, that Japanese production is scattered between 41 cement plants as against 110 in the US. Indeed, a Japanese cement plant is generally 2.5 times larger than its US counterpart (*RP*, Ullman, April 1991). But, the US river system plays a key role, covering nearly 25000 mile of navigable waterways. The Great Lakes region is akin to an enclaved sea, and cement plants in this region have historically outsized others, with ships being used to transport cement to the cities around the lakes. The most famous instance of this is the Alpena cement plant created by Huron Cement in 1907. The idea was to take advantage of economies of scale, and to distribute output throughout a network of inland terminals set up around the Great Lakes (*P&Q*, Avery, July 1949; *RP*, Bell May 1962).[6] In a similar way, in the Mississippi basin, it is possible to build cement plants along the banks of the river and to ship cement by barges. Were the US cement industry to be reconstructed from scratch, the optimal structure would be a network of cement plant units, with production capacity ranging from 0.8 to 1 million tons, scattered throughout the US (*RP*, Roy, October 1988).

By contrast, Europe is made up of fifteen independent states which have only recently coordinated their economic policy and pushed towards a single integrated market (Treaty of Rome, 1957, Single European market, 1993). As the investments required to adapt to the new environment are long term, it is not surprising that the unification of cement markets is taking a long time to materialise. Geographical features have also hampered the process. In comparison with the US, the European

---

6. When Alpena was sold by National Gypsum to Lafarge in 1986, the company owned a network of 13 terminals around the Great Lakes.

population is more evenly scaterred. Limestone quarries are abundant and spread throughout the national territories and the river network system is mostly less developed. Consequently, European cement markets are more regionally oriented and frequently landlocked. Thus cement is primarily delivered by road around cement plants with an average capacity of 750000 tpy (excluding Greece). However, there are exceptions. The Netherlands benefits from deep water harbours at the mouth of the River Rhine, itself linked to a network of canals, enabling inland delivery. The Netherlands' imports are primarily sea shipments channelled through Amsterdam and Rotterdam. They total half national cement consumption. Most of the cement, whether inland produced or imported, is shipped by barges to buyers.

The competitive process in the cement industry, then, has been heavily influenced, probably to a greater extent than in most other industries, by historical and geographical factors.

The simplified economics of the cement industry

The previous sections have detailed the main features of the cement industry. From these basic features, it is now possible to characterise the competitive process that is at work in the industry.

Each plant can be seen as at the centre of a "natural" market, the boundaries of which are determined by the relationship between production costs (which fall strongly as the size of plant and its rate of utilisation increase), and transportation costs (which rise with distance). A cement producer is secure from competition within his natural market as the price he will normally quote, given the combination of production and transportation costs, is lower than that which can be quoted by distant competitors. Thus, a producer is a price leader in the natural market of their cement plant, and distant competitors are price takers. If they want a share of the market, they have to align their price.

If a cement plant is not located alongside a railway line, a river or a harbour, and if demand is uniformly distributed around the cement plant, its natural market has a circular shape. If a plant is located on a railway line or river, the shape of its natural market is more complex. Cement is either delivered by truck to the area around a cement plant, or transported in wagons or barges, and then delivered by truck to buyers in the neighbourhood of the river or rail terminals. (see appendix 1 at the end of the chapter).

The natural markets of cement plants intersect. In the zones where they intersect, the combination of production and transportation costs is approximately equal for all plants (see appendices 2 and 3 at the end of the chapter).

Nevertheless, the expression "natural market" should not be misinterpreted. Whilst the boundaries of a natural market can be deduced from a calculation based on the production capacity of plants, average local demands for cement, and transportation costs, several points should be remembered.

Firstly, the boundaries of a natural market change depending on economic circumstances. When demand surges, the natural market of a cement plant tends to shrink. In such a situation, both demand, and the rate of capacity utilisation, are high. Producers sell to sites that are in close proximity to their plant, and do not need to search for buyers in more distant areas. The natural markets of their cement plants have a smaller radius. Conversely, when demand and the rate of capacity utilisation are low, producers have an incentive to find new buyers in more distant markets if they are to produce beyond their break-even points, and make profits. In this case, then, the natural markets of cement plants tend to expand.

In general, in order to ensure the full use of their production capacity, each cement producer is ready to supply distant buyers if demand from buyers that are geographically close to their plant falls. They will do so providing they consider themselves to have a cost advantage relative to their competitors. As a result, the natural market of a cement plant depends on the strategic options taken by cement producers regarding pricing policy. As a matter of fact, cement buyers that are situated in the vicinity of a producing plant are captive. If they have to buy from a distant producer, they will pay higher transportation costs, and therefore a higher delivered price. In this regard, cement producers are driven to price discriminate. In relative terms, they can charge higher prices to their nearest buyers (the highest possible price being the price that a distant producer would charge them). By doing this, a producer would more easily reach, and exceed, his break-even point. In addition to this, a producer could lower his delivered price to distant buyers in order to gain additional market share, improve his rate of capacity utilisation, and increase profits. Thus price discrimination works in the following way: a producer charges "phantom freight" to the nearest buyers (a higher price than if the real transportation cost had been charged), and he practices "freight absorption"[7] when selling to distant buyers (a lower price is charged than if the real transportation cost had been charged). A price discrimination strategy, therefore, enables a producer to modify the boundaries of the natural market of his plant.[8]

Freight absorption takes place each time a producer sells to distant buyers that are in the natural market of a competitor. The producer is bound to lower his delivered price, and align it with that of his competitor, who is better positioned with regard to transportation costs. Cement is mainly used for construction purposes, and insofar as construction sites open and close in many different locations, freight absorption is a flexible tool that cement producers can use to stabilise sales in the short term (Stigler, 1949: 1154). The use of freight absorption clearly blurs the boundaries between the natural markets of cement plants. As Loescher points out, this means that *'Regional cement markets are difficult to define since their geographic extensiveness varies with the allowance made for potential freight absorption.'* (Loescher, 1959: 41).

Our final point, here, relates to business routines. Each cement producer is used to selling in the geographical area of his natural market. When economic circumstances change, producers rarely switch to new business practices that would significantly alter the boundaries of their natural market, as their competitors would be likely to react in a similar manner. As a result, each producer stays in his own market.[9]

The strategy of price discrimination (phantom and freight absorption) is only workable if cement plants charge delivered prices to buyers. In this situation, buyers cannot isolate the price paid for transportation from that paid for the cement.

An alternative approach is to invoice for free on board (fob) prices. In this case, buyers come to the cement plant to pick up their order. Producers set the fob price in order that they can supply a natural market

---

7. In so far as additional market share reduces unit production costs, freight absorption does not necessarily mean selling below marginal delivered cost (McBride, 1983).

8. For further developments, see Phlips, 1983.

9. An internal Kaiser Cement memo dating from 1968, and seized by the US antitrust authorities in the Arizona case, reads: *'as you are aware, though Oregon Portland and Idaho Portland could have sold in the same area, they have refrained from doing so by creating an imaginary boundary line...'* (Welles, 1984). The "natural" market, as defined by objective economic criteria, is also a social construction resulting from deliberate strategies and business routines.

which allows them to pass their break-even point, and to operate at their maximum level of capacity utilisation, given the economic circumstances. No geographical price discrimination occurs under such a pricing mechanism, other than through secret rebates to particular buyers.

A third approach cement producers can adopt is to operate a uniform price system. In this case, there is a single cement price that is valid throughout a particular geographical area, which is more or less extended. Such a business approach is frequently used in urban areas where cement plants set a single price for deliveries.

Generalities and specificities of the cement industry

At first glance, the cement industry seems highly specific. But differences between it and other industries are less salient than one might think, and, in fact, make cement a more interesting case with regard to the globalisation of markets. There are also several general features that cement shares with other industries.

The generalities

Business strategies of cement producers do not differ from those of producers in other markets. Despite their product being homogenous and changing very little, cement producers can price discriminate between buyers. Within narrow margins, they can improve the quality of service in order to increase customer loyalty. As in many industries, independent purchasing power has developed *vis-à-vis* the industry. Large Ready Mix Concrete companies appeared in the 1960's and have continued to grow since then. They operate at the local level and are the largest buyers of cement.

As with other sectors, the cement industry has witnessed economic diversification. In the early 1970s, producers began to consider investing in cement plants in other geographical areas, or becoming conglomerates, and investing in alternative activities in order to protect themselves from the economic impacts of business cycles.

In short, cement producers have made use of diverse strategic tools and the cement industry has experienced the various features of competition, such as diversification, joint ventures, mergers and vertical integration, and in relation to pricing and product, they have had to face buyer bargaining power, to deal with secrete rebates, price cutting, price discrimination, and competition on service and quality.

Specifications

Features that are specific to the cement industry are also of particular interest when examining issues of globalisation. One key feature is the localised nature of cement markets, given the high level of transportation costs. Two points deserve attention here.

Firstly, markets that are local are invariably oligopolistic. As S. Scotchmer and J. Thisse (1993: 658) comment, *'the spatial competition process is de facto oligopolistic.'* This dual characteristic of being local and oligopolistic is particularly pronounced in the cement industry, but is often also present in other industries. Despite the international, and even global, nature of competition, markets remain local, both with regard to the distribution of goods, and to the maintenance of loyalty to local brands. From an economic perspective, the potential for producers to discriminate between customers given high transportation costs, has similarities to the situation in markets where producers have the ability to discriminate between customers by means of product differentiation and branding. In the cement industry, a distant producer, who is at a geographical handicap, can absorb freight in order to reduce his competitive disadvantage. In the case of an industry with differentiated products, branding can be seen as a substitute for freight absorption. An unknown producer will compensate for his competitive handicap *vis-à-vis* a well known one, by lowering their price, and backing their product with sales promotions. These business strategies occur in an oligopolistic context where there are a small number of producers who know that no-one will exit the market in the short run.

The cement market is inherently unstable, as there is a high risk of competitive disruption. Indeed, if local demand collapses, even on only a temporary basis, each producer risks severe losses. The immediate response is to lower prices to gain customers from competitors, and restore profits due to the increased rate of capacity utilisation. But as demand is inelastic to price, and depends rather on the construction cycle, if a particular producer increases sales in such a situation, it is to the detriment of their direct competitors who will see their sales drop, and even greater losses result. In such a situation, then, producers are in a zero sum game. What it gained by one is lost by another. At this point the competitor faces the choice of either exiting the market, or of drastically cutting their price in order to compete. Retaliatory price cut can lead to retaliatory price cut, disrupting the whole market, with the general fall in prices that results not leading to an increase in local demand. Rather, it simply aggravates economic conditions for competing producers. Losses rise as turnovers plunge, pushing the industry towards bankruptcy.

Such a scenario, however, is very unlikely to occur. In an oligopoly such as the cement industry, local producers know each other. As the product is undifferentiated, price cuts are quickly spotted. In particular, cement producers publish price lists which are readily available. Therefore, as has been frequently stressed, immediate detection of price cuts prevent the disruption of oligopolistic markets.

However, in practice, price cutting strategies are more sophisticated than simply granting a general price rebate to buyers. The process is a very different one. As Gus. J. Chavalas explained to the board of the US cement company Kaiser Cement, on December 3, 1973, *'Generally, falling prices follow an insidious path. They often start with an oral price cut by one company to a few accounts, and then they spread. Usually, when the new, low level of price is met by all the manufacturers, the downward spiral starts again by a company hoping to secure more volume through pricing.'* (US District Court for the District of Arizona, 1983: A57).

In fact, producers adopt a diverse range of strategies in order to remain undetected. They can offer secret and selective rebates to a few buyers, special terms of payment, or provide interest-free loans[10]. J.M. Clark referred to such market developments as part of a *'nibbling process'* that initiated movement towards a *'chaotic market'* (Clark, 1940: 252).[11] Disguised rebates of the kind that cement producers offer to buyers also

---

10. The Federal Trade Commission noted: *'In situations of oligopolies involving the marketing of a standardised undifferentiated product such as cement list prices or quoted mill prices plus delivery costs tend to be less reliable indicators of transaction prices in the context of surplus capacity than otherwise. During periods of high demand, when price increases are most frequently encountered, price adjustments are usually accomplished by changing the quoted mill list price. When faced with excess capacity, however, supplier pricing patterns become more complex; and though mill list prices may be adjusted downward such steps are usually taken only as final public disclosure of less obvious, but generally available, price concessions.'* (US Federal Trade Commission, 1966: 58-59). The FTC observed that rebates for "prompt payment" reached 10 per cent of the sales price, before taking into account the terms of payment schedules.

11. It is worth noting that J.M. Clark was a consultant for the Cement Institute in their antitrust case against the Federal Trade Commission. (see chapter 4)

occur, but in a different way, in differentiated product markets, for instance, when price cuts are initiated subsequent to an acceleration of the innovation process. In the 1980's, the micro-computer industry was close to a chaotic market situation. In such economic circumstances, *'the immediate short-run pressures are out of harmony with the conditions of long-run equilibrium.'* (Clark, 940: 249; Aranoff, 1991). The opposition between short-term and long-term business interests occurs among competitors but also in the management of companies. Salesmen seek to maintain sales volume by agreeing to rebates for buyers, but these rebates are both too widespread, and too high, compared with what general managers are prepared to accept. In particular, general managers are concerned about the resulting fall in profitability, the reactions of competitors, and the lack of coherence of the pricing policy as prices move away from reflecting production and transportation costs.

This process is common to many other markets, but in the case of cement, the occurrence of a chaotic market is particularly dramatic. A producer absorbs freight and delivers to a distant buyer who is situated in the proximity of a competitor's plant. The aggressed competitor will sooner or later retaliate, and will act in a symmetric way, offering a rebate to supply a distant buyer situated close to the plant of the aggressor. The result is that cement shipments pass each other on the road or railway line that runs between the two producers. This particularly absurd situation is known as cross-hauling. A good that is difficult and costly to transport is hauled in all different directions, far removed from any apparent economic rationale, with price cuts increasing alongside rising transportation costs. More significantly, a point is reached when there no longer seems to be any price structure or pricing rationale. Each transaction is dealt with in isolation based on multiple and uncertain criteria (day to day capacity utilisation, estimates of transportation costs, buyer bluffs about the price quoted by a competitor). The US cement market has had some experience of chaotic markets over time, particularly in the 1930's. This went so far, that an aggressive cement producer would sometimes quote a price so low to buyers situated in the vicinity of his competitor's plant, that he would have to buy the cement from the competitor, and ask him to deal with delivery in order to avoid making a severe loss from shipping the cement himself over such a long distance (Loescher, 1959). The chaotic markets that developed in the cement industry in the US and the UK during the Great Depression in the 1930s are particularly notable for the amount of cross hauling that occured seemingly without any economic foundation.

In the long run, if chaotic market conditions persist, either producers charge the additional costs of cross hauling to buyers, or the industry collapses, with producers unable to extract sufficient profit to modernise or invest in new plants.

A key factor bringing about the collapse of the market is the existence of disparate producers. They are a potential source of disruption when they have different demand forecasts, production costs, financial structures and views about managing plants. This is frequently the case where there is a mix of small and large producers. The small producers may have no possibility of increasing their output (they may have exhausted their quarry or be unable to adapt to required environmental programmes) and their production assets may be fully written off. If demand plummets, they will have an interest to produce at full capacity, even if this will result in a fall in price. Their competitors with large, modern plants would have difficulty retaliating. To force the small producers to exit the market, modern plants will have to price their cement below average cost, at the variable cost of production. The older plants of small producers benefit from fully written off capital investment. The losses incurred by the owners of modern plants will soon become unbearable. In particular, they will have to pay off high fixed instalments related to their investment in plant capacity. Also, even if continued retaliation against the small producers proves successful and the smaller producers go bust, they may face the situation where the old cement plant is taken over by an even more threatening new entrant. So, an obstinate small producer may be able to destabilise a local market on their own.[12]

The model case

From many standpoints, then, the cement industry is a particularly useful case from which to approach issues of market globalisation. It is

---

12. This fact has been emphasised by the deputy chairman of Holderbank, Thomas Schmidheiny: *'you cannot squeeze a cement plant out of the market. It is practically impossible because one company goes broke and the debt is eliminated, someone else will pick it up. They will then run the plant -even at high costs- because it will be competitive to a new plant with high debt. If you don't really scrap the plant, take the kiln out, somebody will restart it. I Know of some cases where the scrap metal people have started plants because they thought the cash flow was greater than what they would have got for it in scrap. They bought the plant for nothing. This is a danger, I think.'* (*RP*, Huhta, April 1982: 40).

oligopolistic, and shares many of the economic characteristics that prevail in other markets. But it also has some more particular features that are of advantage here.

Although innovation in the industry has occured in major waves, separated by periods of stability, the experience of the cement industry can be seen as similar to that of other industries, but in slow motion. This slower pace of change makes the influence of technological progress on the globalisation of markets easier to study.

Since cement is homogenous and undifferentiated, and its production process is the same in all markets, again, the analysis is simplified.

As the cement industry is capital intensive, when demand falls there is an immediate conflict between short and long term economic rationale, a conflict that exists in all industries. The interest, here, comes from the acute nature of the conflict in the cement industry, the analysis of which helps us to understand the relationship between short and long term perspectives on the globalisation process more generally.

As cement markets are regional, due to the high costs of transportation, competition has traditionally been local, with globalisation seeming very unlikely. The contrast between local and global is therefore at its maximum.

Thus, the cement industry as a case study is particularly well suited for an examination of the key dimensions of the competitive process and its regulation, in the context of globalisation. Economic characteristics that would blur the analysis and make it more difficult, such as frequent changes in technology, brand competition, or the management of conglomerates, are, in the first instance, avoided.

Appendix 1

"NATURAL" MARKET OF A CEMENT PLANT WITH ACCESS TO RAIL AND RIVER NETWORKS

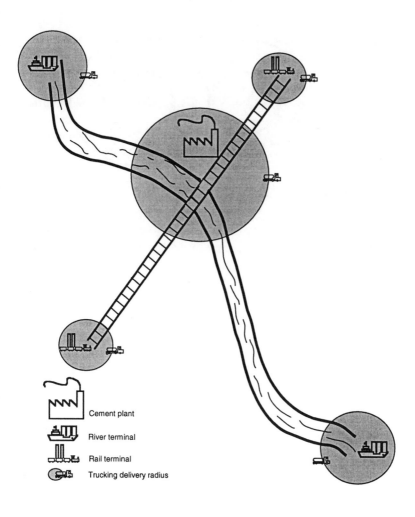

Cement plant

River terminal

Rail terminal

Trucking delivery radius

appendix 2

SPATIAL DUOPOLY

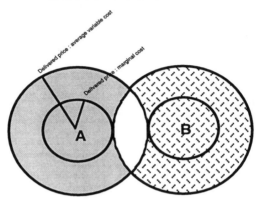

- "Natural" market of cement plant A
- "Natural" market of cement plant B
- region of maximum competition

Source : Gerard Adams and Wechster, 1990.

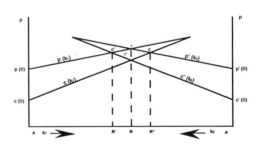

Source : McBride (1983) p. 1015.

K delivery distance
p(k) delivered price at point distance k
c(k1) transport cost at point distance k

PART 1

LOCAL COMPETITION

Because of the likelihood of a chaotic market in economic slumps, producers strive to stabilise the local market price of cement. They do so by shifting the competitive process to a rivalry game focused on economic factors other than price. These factors include the search for cost advantages in production, mergers or acquisitions in order to gain market share, and the pre-emption of key production sites (quarries) to prevent new entry into the market.

However, these attempts to stabilise and reduce price competition are carefully watched over by the antitrust authorities, and significant changes in industry structure or behaviour are scrutinised by them. In particular, they closely examine increases in concentration in local and regional markets, as higher concentration makes the exercise of market power over price more likely.

This first part of this book addresses the competitive process in terms of:

1. attempts by cement producers to stabilise the market price and avoid a chaotic market;
2. the rivalry process which ensues from stabilising price competition;
3. the counteracting role of antitrust authorities.

CHAPTER 2

Stabilising local competition

Cement producers are bound to have a long term view of their business. But prior to entering the market, they are also aware that they will have to deal with the short term business cycles of the construction sector.

In economic booms, they face a dilemma: should they expect a sustained growth in demand, invest in a very large plant, and benefit from economies of scale in production that will provide them with a competitive advantage over their competitors; or should they be more cautious with their expectations, and plan for either a slowing of growth or a fall?

In addition to anticipating future demand movements, cement producer's must also take account of the effects their decisions have on competitors. At the industry level, the aggregate outcome of individual producer's investment decisions is rarely optimal. Cement producers may correctly anticipate the direction of economic movements, but they cannot predict the magnitude of these movements with precision.

As a result, even if all industry members take a cautious view of future demand movements in their investment decisions, the aggregated outcome of their decisions can still lead to overcapacity.

There is, therefore, an inherent imbalance in the industry between capacity investment decisions and demand and the emergence of a chaotic market is a continually looming threat. In response to this, cement producers try to work out schemes that enable them to avoid the situation of excessive price competition. These attempts to ensure market discipline are now examined.

Cartellisation

Cartellisation provides market participants with certainty regarding price stabilisation.[1] Two particularly instructive cases are that of the cement cartel uncovered in Southern Länder in 1988 by the *Bundeskartellamt* (the German Cartel Office)[2] and the national Swiss Cartel investigated by the Swiss antitrust authorities (Kartellkommission, 1993).

We have already noted that even though cement is a homogeneous product, it is still difficult for cement producers to know the real price charged by their competitors with accuracy. Any producer can negotiate with buyers and move away from the official price list (Clark, 1940: 253). Bargain prices of this kind usually go undetected in the short run, but discounts will eventually work their way into the market place, with prices finally falling.

Freezing the market shares of competing plants renders opaque price discounting a useless strategy. Price competition is avoided by fixing production quotas rather than by means of an overt price control system. This type of cartellisation was observed in the southern part of Germany in the 1980s.

Each producer had a market share that was fixed in advance and in agreement with the other producers, the size of which was calculated to three decimal places.

Cement Maker	Market share in per cent
Heidelberger	48.724
Schwenk	17.774
Dyckerhoff	10.588
Buderus	0.181
Dotterhausen	9.274
Marker	0.274
Breisgauer Kleinkems	6.845
Zeag Lauffen	6.344

1. Cartels are scarce and secret in the US market. Senior managers of firms engaged in cartellisation are prosecuted and incur jail sentences.
2. See BKA, Judgement B1-2531100-A-30/88-4, 12 September 1988; a former cartel, involving the same group of cement makers had been sentenced in 1972; for a general view on competition policy and cartel laws in Germany, see H. Dumez and A. Jeunemaître (1993).

However not all of the regional cement producers were affiliated. In particular, Wössingen, a significant local producer, had for some time decided not to join the cartel, and only did so finally at the beginning of 1986.

Members of the cartel had to agree on the market share to be granted to Wössingen by common consent, and the production quota was eventually set at 12 per cent of the total regional market, including the natural geographical market covered by Wössingen. This changed the break down of the market shares between cartel participants to the following:

Heidelberger	42.835
Scwenk	15.626
Dyckerhoff	9.308
Buderus	0.159
Dotterhausen	8.153
Breisgauer	0.237
KleinkemsMarker	6.018
Zeag Lauffen	5.577
Wössingen	12.089

The day to day functioning of the cartel required sophisticated organisation. Once market shares were fixed, the cement price had to be used as the adjustment variable in order to comply with the quota agreement.

For example, during 1986 and 1987, one particular cement producer had a market share in excess of their allowed level, and was asked, by the other cement producers, to give up a 25000 tons order by offering the buyer a price that was higher than that of their closest competitor, Heidelberger Zement.

Thus, the cement price offered by the producer was changed, relative to that of its competitors, in order to match actual market shares as closely as possible to the agreed ones. The new price took account of the difference between the demand for cement as anticipated in the agreement, and that actually observed.

The lessons to be drawn from the running of this cartel are twofold.

Firstly, since, due to high transportation costs, cement plants have a natural regional market in the vicinity of their production site, cartels are primarily suitable at a regional level. It is notable that the boundaries of regional markets are usually stable over time, and, broadly speaking, the same cement producers face each other over long periods. In the example discussed above, it is not simply coincidental that the same companies were involved in a cartel agreement in 1972 as in 1988, and in both cases it was run by Heidelberger Zement. Over time the cartel grew to include markets and cement plants that were located in the neighbourhood of the main cartel participants.

Secondly, the cartel proved costly to operate. The managerial organisation that was set up by Heidelberg Zement is evidence of this. The scheme consisted of several steps. Cartel participants had, firstly, to agree on the allocation of market shares. A regional demand forecast had then to be estimated and ratified. Subsequently the agreed market shares were applied to this demand forecast in order to determine the yearly production quota for each cement producer. Finally, each cement producer had to allocate his production quota among his cement plants in terms of a monthly production schedule.

An authorised representative of Heidelberger Zement, operating from its company headquarters, phoned the cartel participants each month to find out their level of total sales for that month. Aggregating the data enabled them to ascertain how far actual demand was diverging from the forecast. In addition, the representative would calculate whether or not the sales made by each cement producer conformed with their allowed production quota, and adjust prices accordingly for the current month. In cases where there was a difference between scheduled and observed production levels, adjustments were made by manipulating the market price charged by cement producers.

Overall, then, coordination problems among producers mean that cartels will primarily be effective when on a limited scale, i.e. in a local or regional market that is dominated by a few cement plants.

The Swiss cartel gives another illustration of the lessons drawn above. Even though the cartel coordinated the sale policies of cement producers in Switzerland, a small, mountainous geographical territory (41290 km^2), the cartel management mechanisms were nevertheless cumbersome. Plant deliveries were fixed according to quotas. Cement prices were fixed and plants were only allowed to sell to wholesalers and not to final customers. Transport was controlled and an agreement had been reached with railway companies and road carriers, the latter having agreed not to compete with the railway companies. With regard to major work (orders in excess of 10000 tons), two consortia shared out the sales between the cartel members. Aside from this, several cement producers had joint sales offices and all of them had agreed not to individually advertise their product. The range of cements, according to its quality, was set by the cartel and no other cement type was authorised. Exclusive purchasing contracts were agreed with Swiss sack and packaging companies and with companies supplying the explosives used in quarries.

Thus, the details of these agreements and their management illustrate how cumbersome running a cartel can be, and therefore why cartels are essentially only conceivable in a small geographical area.

Operating a cartel on a large scale would quickly prove too costly, since it would involve a complex system that is hard to both initiate and operate. Moreover, it would probably be unstable in the long run as cheating would go undetected.[3]

In general, the cost, and difficulty, of managing large cartels, and the fact that they are usually forbidden by antitrust authorities, particularly if secret, has prompted cement producers to adopt more flexible approaches to coordination.

The basing point system

Facilitating practices are manifold (Salop, 1986). They can be achieved via contractual arrangements that bind sellers and buyers, such as a clause that a seller will meet a more favourable price if it is offered by a competitor. This provides a buyer with insurance protection against the lost opportunity of buying at a lower price from another seller. At first glance, such a clause would seem to ensure that price competition will prevail. In practice, however, it has a deterring and opposite effect.

No producers or service providers have an incentive to lower their price, as if one firm does so, their competitors will automatically align their price and retain their customers. The price cut will be revealed instantly in the market place, and as a result, the firm will not benefit from the surprise effect of the discount.

---

3. *'A cartel arises if it is able to cover the cost of organizing, and then survives if it establishes a sufficiently strong monitoring and enforcement (policing) system that is capable of limiting competition (for exemple, price competition, entry) to an acceptable level. Cartel costs vary with the characteristics of an industry (number of firms, geographic distribution of firms and consumers, etc.). When firms and consumers are geographically dispersed, organizational and policing costs tend to be high and the ability of the cartel to limit competition is lessened.'* (Benson, Greenhut, and Norman, september 1990: 963).

This is particularly the case in an oligopolistic competitive game, where there are only a few players, and where the lapse of time before an aggressive price change becomes known to all market participants is crucial. The earlier that price cuts are detected, the quicker the response from competitors will be, and the sturdier the price stabilisation mechanism.

In the cement industry, as in some other industries such as steel, where transportation costs are high, one facilitating practice that is used is known as the basing point system. The system was used in US cement markets from the beginning of this century up until the end of World War Two. It prevailed from the 1930s until 1987 in the UK, and has also been a dominant feature of competition in Italy.

The system itself rested on a simple idea. Consider an industry where, for historical reasons, production is highly concentrated in a particular area. Moreover, suppose that the industry is oligopolistic, with only a few players in the market, and that one firm dominates in the main production location.

It would be natural to expect that the leading firm would announce and set a price at their base mill. Prices to buyers would be calculated on the basis of the mill price of the leading firm, increased by cost of transportation from the base mill to the delivery point. Therefore, small competitors of the leading firm would be price takers. They would set their price in any particular location, based on the price that would be charged by the dominant firm in that location, taking into account the transportation cost element.

This simple competitive situation is similar to that which prevailed in the French steel industry at the turn of the 20th century. In that case, the market price was set according to the base mill price of the dominant steel maker's main production site in Thionville.

At about the same time, a similar situation existed in the US cement industry. The main cement producers had settled close to the most easily exploitable quarries, which were concentrated in the Lehigh Valley in Pennsylvania. They were also close to highly populated East Coast cities, which were large cement consumption markets. The cement price for any particular location in the US was calculated by combining the base mill price in the Lehigh Valley, and the cost of transportation from there to the delivery point.

The usefulness of such a pricing mechanism came from the fact that it offered a transparent price structure. Buyers and sellers had a common transportation cost schedule from which to calculate prices. From this, they could quickly work out the price that should be charged at any particular location by following a very simple calculation. This would involve adding the price at the base mill (known as the base point) and the cost of transportation from the base mill to the delivery point (given in a cost schedule). All competitors had agreed that there would be no hidden price discounts.

The single basing point system can easily be transformed into a more complex multiple basing point system. That is, in a particular area, several cement producers could declare themselves base points by publishing their base mill price. Then, the market price at any particular location will be the lowest price calculated from the different base mills. If a producer decides not to publish a base mill price, this simply means that he is willing to operate under the umbrella of existing base point plants, limiting himself to being a price taker in their natural markets.

Base points need not being set at particular plant locations, as producers can agree upon a base point at any location within a given area. In this case, an imaginary base mill price is calculated by equalising the different cement mill prices, and the cost of transportation to the agreed location.

However, while a basing point system has a price stabilising effect, it can also produce counter-intuitive outcomes.

Such is the case when new plants are built a long distance away from the historical production site location. Usually, at first, the new plants do not have the production capacity to satisfy all the demand from their surrounding regional markets. As a result, some deliveries are still made by the distant base mills. Consequently, it is sensible enough for the new producers to carry on pricing according to the distant mill's base price plus the transportation cost from that base mill.

In the early 1970s during the world oil crisis, the US started importing petrol from Arabic countries to preserve their national oil reserves. The petrol price at the US pump station was calculated on the basis of the free-on-board (f.o.b.) Arabic refinery price increased by the shipping cost from Arabic countries to the US, even if the petrol that was delivered at the pump was from US production sources. US producers were, therefore, charging customers a "phantom freight" cost. US customers were paying for petrol that came from US refineries as though it had come from Arabic countries. Whilst this made sense from a business perspective, given the imbalances between production and consumption, US customers protested vehemently (Haddock, 1982).

The US cement industry in the 1930s was in a similar position involving a cement plant that was located between the Lehigh Valley (the main production centre) and Philadelphia (a large cement consumption area). The plant was not big enough to force Lehigh producers to exit from the Philadelphia market, so the new producer chose not to declare himself a base point. Rather, he aligned his cement prices with those of distant Lehigh Valley producers when delivering in Philadelphia.

The business interest of the new cement producer was to charge the higher competitive price, that is, the price offered by his distant competitors, as he knew that he had an advantage over them with regard to flexibility and speed of delivery. However, deciding not to be a base point, and not to publish a base mill price, also meant that his delivered price would decrease on the way to the Lehigh Valley. Therefore, in the direction of the Lehigh Valley, price was higher in the vicinity of the new plant than it was in more distant locations. So, in this direction, the cement price decreased with distance, and the new producer charged phantom freight to buyers close to his plant.

Thus, the basing point system enables the biggest players to sell throughout the entire market, and smaller producers to prosper in a local or regional market around their plant. These smaller producers thrive under the umbrella of the bigger producers' natural markets. In this respect, the phantom freight charged by a smaller producer can be seen as compensation for the fact that they agree to remain a local competitor (Phlips 1993). The basing point mechanism provides them with an incentive to stay *'happy and small'* (Phlips, 1995: 120).

In dynamic terms, two important results are associated with the mechanism of the basing point system. The first point is that either supply and demand conditions in local and regional markets do not deviate, and the basing point system is likely to stabilise over time, or demand in the market of a local producer expands, such that it is in his interest to increase his production capacity and declare himself base point by making public his base mill price. New base points appear in the proximity of highly dense areas of cement consumption in order to make these markets as unattractive as possible to distant cement producers (Loescher, 1959, ch. 4). This is precisely what happened in the US cement markets. New cement plants were built in Southern and Western regions following the urbanisation of new States, and the Lehigh Valley progressively lost its dominance. In 1902, there was only one base point, the Lehigh Valley. In 1908 two more appeared, in Hannibal (Missouri), and in Iola (Kansas). By 1940, base points were scattered all over the US territory.

The second point relates to transportation costs. Means of transport, such as trucking and shipping, have variable costs according to the rate of capacity utilisation of the fleet of trucks, or ships. Fluctuations in transportation costs put the implementation of a basing point system at risk (Owen, 1991).

One solution is to charge buyers according to short term transportation cost fluctuations. However, this would require continuous computation and would undermine the simplicity and transparency of the basing point system. If prices are to be adjusted frequently and arbitrarily, then cheating by using price discounts would go undetected.[4]

The alternative is to price according to a fixed transportation cost schedule. In this case, prices include a fictional transportation cost element that is charged to the buyer. However, in order to make this system work, the cement producers must control transportation. If not, then when the fictional transportation cost exceeds the real transportation cost, buyers will choose to load their cement order at the plant, and transport it, either themselves, or through a contracted carrier.

The way in which American cement producers implemented the basing point system in the 1930s illustrates this latter point. In order that the cement price charged by competitors at any location could be easily calculated, producers had to refer to, and use, a unique transportation cost schedule, published by the freight railway companies. Cement, at that time, was primarily transported by wagons. The transportation cost schedule of the railway companies, unlike that of other forms of transport, had the advantage that it was published regularly, and that selective discounts from it were not on offer.

However, there were many railway companies, and as a result, schedule price changes were frequent and caused repeated disruption to the basing point system. Not only it was difficult to keep up with changes, but a producer could decide not to immediately pass on a cost increase following a price schedule change in order to take customers from competitors. For example, they could pretend to have been uninformed of a railway price change. Little by little, this would disrupt, and jeopardise the working of the basing point mechanism.

---

4. As one of the senior managers of Lehigh Portland Cement explained in an answer to a questionnaire forwarded by Arthur R. Burns and John M. Clark: *'The manufacturer, striving to figure his prices on indeterminate and fluctuating trucking rates and to meet the equally fluctuating and independent rates from his competitor's plants, quickly found himself engaged in blind, reckless and destructive competition....'* (Loescher, 1959: 111).

The cement producers tried to adapt to the situation by setting up their own uniform railway price list. For instance, in the North-Eastern region between 1911 and 1916, all competitors were required to use the Alpha Portland Cement company price list to calculate their transportation costs. Later, in 1930, the Cement Institute, a joint organisation to which all producers were affiliated, published a schedule of freight prices. As a memorandum taken from the archives of a cement company, and dated November 1929, stated: *'One of the principal features of this service is that our principal competitors will be using the same books as we are, resulting in uniformity.'* (Loescher, 1959: 99). In 1936, in Norfolk, Virginia, a sales manager of a cement producer was blamed by the managing director for having used a railway freight rate with a discount. In the correspondence that has occured between cement producers, one sometimes finds the use of the awkward expression "price books" to talk about freight schedules.

But getting rid of the possibility of buyer arbitrage with regard to transportation costs, required more than producers simply making use of the same railway schedule of freight prices. Buyers also need to be prevented from loading cement at the plant. Moreover, in adverse economic circumstances, producers would find it difficult to resist offering rebates to buyers who would pick-up their order at the plant if allowed. This issue was all the more worrying for producers who had decided not to be a base point. Their delivered price of cement to areas close to their plant was higher than that to distant areas. As a result, customer pick-up would prove even more financially attractive to nearby buyers and become a general feature. It would de facto transform the plant into a base point. Thus, the existence of non-base point producers requires a total control over cement transportation. The first attempt to prevent customer pick-up took place in Texas, in 1926. Cement producers refused to load trucks at the mill, except those of an authorised carrier on the basis of an agreed freight price list. At the end of 1929, a toll of 15 cents per barrel was imposed for loading at the mill, in the Lehigh valley. However, the deterrent effect of this was insufficient. Producers agreed, at the level of the Cement Institute, to encourage buyers to use railway transportation. By the end of 1932, most cement trucking East of the Rocky Mountains had disappeared, except in the Great Lakes district.[5] But, in this area,

---

5. Most plants were located on the banks of the lakes, and cement was firstly shipped to harbour terminals via the river network, and then delivered, by trucks, to customers.

producer pressure on buyers, particularly from Huron Cement, meant that trucking was at least partially controlled by imposing, as in Texas, the reference to schedule prices. Some producers went on to demolish the facilities that enabled them to load trucks at the plant, keeping only the installations assigned to the loading of railway wagons.

The basing point system has one particularly advantageous feature. It has been emphasised that coordination among oligopolists works best when cheating is swiftly detected, and when retaliation from competitors can be proportionate, and limited. Clearly, if retaliation can only be severe, and not well circumscribed, there is a greater risk of a chaotic market developing. But this is precisely what the basing point system allows producers to avoid, by enabling gradual and orderly retaliation.

The prices that a producer should charge are known by all market participants, and the process of calculation provides transparency.[6] If a cement producer takes a customer from a competitor by offering a secret rebate, he is very likely to be detected quickly given the information circulating in the market and contacts between buyers and producers. The competitors have a simple and brutal retaliatory tool available. They price as though the cheating cement producer had offered the discount, not simply to the particular customer that was lost, but to all of his customers. By making use of the freight price lists, the competitors can calculate the base price that would correspond to the discounted price which had been offered, and adjust their delivered prices in terms of this new base price. The secret rebate is generalised throughout the whole of the aggressor's market, such that he becomes subject to price discount competition throughout all of his natural market. His profits fall significantly, but in an orderly manner. The cement producer deviated from the basing point price calculation, and in retaliation, his competitors use it against him. So, there is justice in the retaliation, which is clearly defined and known in advance. Instead of putting the price structure in jeopardy, and leading to the development of a chaotic market, the price cut reinforces the basing point system. Even aggressors cannot question the appropriateness of the punishment. For instance, in 1935, the chairman of a cement company

6. It should be stressed that the buyers benefit from the market transparency. They do not have to shop around in order to know the cement prices of different producers, and the freight costs that they would incur for different carriers and delivery locations. Also, they do not have to calculate, and choose among, different price combinations (cement price plus transportation cost). These search and transaction costs can be significant, according to the classic study of Stigler (1961).

wrote to the magistrates of the US Supreme Court, acknowledging the fact that he approved of the retaliation his company had to endure when the basing point system was applied against it. On that particular occasion, he stressed that the process of retaliation was necessary in order to prevent the price structure from crumbling. However, he did call for the setting up of regional committees to examine the extent to which aggressive behaviour was intentional or mistaken.

Once a recalcitrant producer had been disciplined, and once he again applied the basing point system, competitors would increase their prices back to normal levels.

Loescher (1959: 141-142) has emphasised the properties that give the basing point system its *'beauty.'*

Firstly, once the calculation mechanism is approved, transportation costs harmonised, and carriage controlled, the basing point system works on its own, without the need for explicit collusion. It works even more effectively if the market is dominated by a small number of producers who control a significant number of plants that are spread throughout the market, as, in this case, systematic retaliation is facilitated.

Secondly, the system has limited objectives. It does not aim to partition the market, but simply to stabilise prices. Competition is shifted from price to customer service. The costs of organising and managing a cartel are avoided, and, unlike a cartel, the system is enforceable beyond the boundaries of a regional market. It also enables the avoidance of severe drops in prices during economic slumps: in the 1930s, cement producers managed to remain profitable even when their rate of capacity utilisation was below 50 per cent.[7]

Finally, with the effective threat of retaliation acting as a deterrent, the cohesiveness of the system is reinforced, and there is little risk of an escalation in price under-cutting.

While it is difficult to assess the economic consequences of the basing point system, four points seem indisputable.

Firstly, the system does not eradicate competition between producers, even where cement prices are known for all locations. Producers compete

---

7. *'Defensive monopoly being the objective of the cement industry, the kind of imperfect but effective, collusion inherent in rigid adherence to a formula price fulfilled the limited objectives of price stabilisation. Greater perfection collusion through agreements on inter-area base mill prices was never contemplated. The ultimate in collusion through the establishment of a formal authority to divide market territories was out of the question, both administratively and legally.'* (Loescher, 1959: 141)

on customer service elements, such as delivery time and technical assistance. The fact that crosshauling occurs under basing point systems is probably good evidence of such competition. When the boundaries of cement producers' natural markets are crossed by their competitors, (McGee, 1954; Scherer, 1970; Haddock, 1982), the basing point system is characterised as "imperfect collusion".

Secondly, the basing point system enables cement producers to limit their losses when demand falls. The stabilising effect on prices can be dramatic. For instance, in the US cement market of the 1930s, despite the fact that the rate of capacity utilisation was 51 per cent in 1931, 31 per cent in 1932, 26 per cent in 1933, and about 33 per cent in 1934-35, the financial results of cement producers were not that disastrous. In 1931, losses were limited to 3 per cent of average annual turnover (Loescher, 1959).

Thirdly, it is very likely that the maintenance of healthy financial results during economic slumps has delayed the adjustment of output capacity, including modernisation and restructuring. This has been observed both in the US in the 1930s and in the UK, where the system broke down in 1987.

Finally, the basing point system does not aim at maximising short term profits. The key point in capital intensive industries is the financial risk associated with business cycles. A market price stabilisation mechanism directed toward short term profit maximisation, is unlikely to reduce long run risk due to demand fluctuations, and would probably increase it by attracting new entrants. So the true objective of price stabilisation, is not short term joint profit maximisation, but rather the stabilisation of relatively second rate, but regular, cash flows in the long run. Therefore, the fact that flexible collusion practices have not historically lead to profits, is not evidence of their failure in terms of coordination. The main issue is the stabilisation of a minimal profit margin over the long run, and particularly through economic slumps (Waldman, 1988). Also, of course, a low profitability helps to deter new market entry (Harrington, 1984).

The attempt to foreclose the local market (vertical integration)

Rather than making use of flexible coordination practices, producers can attempt to stabilise their local markets through vertical integration.

It has already been noted that, from the 1960s, customers of cement producers were essentially concrete firms. As the cement and concrete markets are clearly distinct, and there are no economies of scale to be expected from merging the two activities. Vertical integration, for an upstream firm, is primarily aimed at gaining or securing market share.

At the end of the 1950s in the US, the fight for market share led to a flow of acquistions in the concrete market. From 1956 to 1969, 55 vertical integration deals occurred (Allen, 1971).

The foreclosure impact of this vertical integration activity was, a priori, difficult to assess, but some points emerged from the experience.

On the one hand, a market is never totally foreclosed. Firstly, concrete companies were the main buyers of cement, but not the only ones. Secondly, the acquired concrete companies carried on buying cement from other suppliers after having been taken over, although they did reduce the amount they purchased on the market.

On the other hand, a cement producer was unlikely to succeed in monopolizing a local cement market by acquiring concrete firms. The concrete market is highly contestable. Entry and exit can occur with few sunk costs. If having acquired a concrete firm, a cement producer engages in price competition with severe price cuts in the concrete market, a percentage of incumbent concrete companies will decide to temporarily stop doing business (mothballing). Having gained a significant market share, the producer will then put his price up, back to its normal level, at which point the mothballed concrete companies will restart doing business. All sand and gravel companies can also be viewed as potential entrants into the concrete market, as the assets they require in order to start selling concrete (mainly trucks and grinding installations) do not require large investments, and can be transfered easily to other local markets. Finally, it is possible for incumbent concrete companies to set up in adjacent regional markets insofar as the production unit are mobile. Therefore, the impact of vertical integration in terms of market foreclosure is unlikely to be significant (Kamerschen, 1974).

Building up a shared vision of the market

The basing point system makes price competition a transparent process. More flexible practices enable oligopolists to construct a common vision of their market, and, as a result, to stabilise competition. In an oligopolitic market, key strategic decisions over investment and price impact on all market participants. If decisions are made independently, and are incompatible, market de-stabilisation may follow. Therefore, it is in producers' interests to share information on market conditions and likely future intentions, in order to try and ensure a minimum level of consistency and cohesion within the industry.

Thus, the amount of information that is shared among competitors is surprising, and its extent often only surfaces at the time of antitrust investigations. A particularly stimulating case involving the cement industry is one that used to be referred to as the Arizona case, and which ended up in legal confusion of the kind that only the US courts seem able to produce from time to time. The case began in 1976, and went on for over ten years.[8]

The main channel used for information exchange is through industry magazines. In the US cement industry, the two main journals are *Rock Products* and *Pit and Quarry*. They disclose information on investment programmes that are in progress, available technological processes, and more generally, the economic situation of the market. Well known consultants commit themselves to contribute papers. They often worked for a cement company before setting up as consultants, and specialise in forecasting. A typical career profile is that of Roy Grancher. He was Market Research and Planning Director for Martin Marietta's Cement and Lime Division in the 1960s and 1970s. Later he was appointed Vice Chairman at Dyckeroff Inc., the American subsidiary of Dyckeroff Germany, in charge of the marketing department. Finally, in 1982, he became Vice Chairman of the Eurocon Corporation. In 1989, he was pictured in *Rock Products* as *'a veteran cement industry consultant.'* Another influential consultant has been Robert Roy, who was an economist for the cement trade association, PCA, before setting up his own consultancy unit, R.O.I. Economic Consultants. Another independent consultant, regarded most highly by firms, is Douglas Queen. The advice, diagnostics, and analysis of these consultants is examined by cement companies, and impacts on their decision making. This contributes to the harmonisation of opinions within the industry.

The direct exchange of information between companies is also widespread.

Firstly, there are informal contacts that are made between senior managers in the industry. At the Arizona case judicial hearings, the Kaiser

---

8. 250 testimonies were recorded during the investigation. The file was made up of 4.5 million pages of documents, with an enormous number of internal letters and notes, meeting reports, and memoranda that had been seized from the offices of cement producers. For a synthesis, see US District Court for the District of Arizona (1983) and Welles (*Newspapers*, 1984a).

Cement Chairman explained that he had kept records of all his discussions with competitors until the beginning of the 1970's. After that he stopped taking notes: *'I stopped writing very many of them, because they were so many. Didn't have time,'* he declared to the judge. The defendant's lawyers recorded no less than 7000 contacts made between managers, mainly positioned in local divisions, between 1968 and 1976. Issues discussed included research, technology, marketing, finance and recruitment policy. But there were also other unofficial meetings. The investigators got hold of an invitation to dinner, sent from the Chairman of the Whitehall Cement Co. to the Chairmen of the Lehigh Valley cement companies, to discuss sales promotion policy. Prices were also discussed. At the hearing, the following question was addressed to Peter Hass: *'You could discuss price trends in front of competitors?'* - *'trends, yes'* he replied, *'Trends were discussed everywhere.'*

But, dissemination of information did not only take place at random meetings, it was carefully planned. Reciprocal visits to cement plants were very popular in the industry. A Lone Star internal memorandum, dating back to 1970, indicates that a regional appointed executive had *'to gather and sort competitive intelligence information on cement companies and plants operating in our market area.'* The memorandum quotes the name of the cement plants to be visited, and requests that the information should be *'in sufficient detail to develop estimated production and shipping costs on short notice.'*

A 1971 correspondence between managers at Marquette and Lehigh established an exchange of confidential data on costs. Since the results of the comparison were unexpected, they went on to communicate their methods of calculation.

Cement producers also exchanged lists covering the names of managers that could be contacted at any time of the day, and included their addresses and work and home phone numbers.

Marquette's three-year business plan (1974-1976), including deliveries, prices and expected profits, were found in the files of Kaiser Cement. Also, Medusa's business plan (1974-1976), with scheduled price increases and a freight price list, were found archived in the Marquette offices.

The exchange of information on current prices occurred mostly via the Portland Cement Association. A 1975 note from Flinknote comments that: *'Without the leadership and efforts of PCA, the cement industry would be like "cannibals" constantly fighting each other at the expense of all. PCA serves as a catalyst for cement companies working to improve their common goal.'*

If the trade association (PCA) played a key role in gathering and disseminating information throughout the industry, Lone Star, the leading company, also assumed some responsibility. In an internal memorandum held at its headquarters, and probably dating back to 1967, the marketing director declared: *'we shall commence an educational campaign to encourage the cement industry to react more intelligently to supply/demand relationships. We shall contend that price cutting is not the answer to rival theories of industry organisation.'* Lone Star argued that prices should reflect a reasonable profit level, rather than supply/demand conditions (they should not lower in an economic slump, but rather, should increase given the inelasticity of demand with respect to price). This contention was put forward in numerous speeches, and copies of the speeches were sent to all industry executives.

The star attraction of this information campaign was an enterprise game, organised by PCA, the trade association, under the initiative of the Lone Star chairman, John C. Mundt: *'One notable example was a 1969 meeting of the association's subcommittee on market research during which the 48 industry executives attending were introduced by association representatives to a computerised game called SMASHED (Stimulated Management Action System to Help Executives Decide).*

Participants were divided into teams to run between four and eight hypothetical cement companies. The game was designed to help them evaluate the effects of "such things as building a new plant, closing an old one, or entering a new territory" and required them to make quarterly and annual "decisions on how to allocate their resources and to price their product." The philosophy behind SMASHED, which apparently was the idea of Mundt, of Lone Star, was that pricing cement to obtain a high profit and return on investment was preferable to pricing simply to garner a higher sales volume.' It was the apex of a training course that Lone Star, which considered itself a the leader in the industry, had launched a few years before.

Thus, exchanges of information in a relatively concentrated industry can be both frequent, and well organised. They can be channelled through trade associations, industry magazines, specialist consultants, direct contacts between executives (meetings, plant visits, etc.), or through the circulation of business documents.

Moreover, it appears that the intensive circulation of valuable information can, in itself, lead to coordinated investment policies, and that "fair" competition, that is to say, competition which allows a sufficient return on capital assets, and a satisfactory degree of rivalry, can emerge from it. This has been illustrated by Porter and Spence (1982) in the corn wet milling industry. However, as S. Winter has rightly emphasised, the case is hardly a representative one, making it of little relevance in terms of generalisations. The effect of constructing a common vision of the industry is difficult to assess in practice. Exchanges of information can lead to mimetism in the behaviour of competitors and as a result to damaging outcomes for the industry (Dumez and Jeunemaître, 1996).

Multipoint competition

Multi-market or multipoint competition refers to '*a situation where firms compete with each other simultaneously in several markets. A common example of multipoint competition is firms competing against each other in different geographical markets for the same product.*' (Karnani and Wernerfelt, 1985: 87). Although it is common to most industries, it has been studied a relatively small amount from both a theoretical and an empirical perspective. Worth noting are the seminal works of Karnani and Wernerfelt (1985) and Bernheim and Whinston (1990).

Historically, cement firms entered different local markets as a business expansion strategy, with the view of taking advantage of rapidly growing markets, and also to hedge against local economic fluctuations. At the regional and national level, this has generally resulted in greater concentration and head to head confrontation between a reduced number of large multiplant firms competing in many different markets.

Multi-point confrontation can help stabilise markets, but it requires a particular set-up.

Firstly, there is the simple case where two competitors face each other in two different markets, with each of them having an important difference in market share, and a symmetrical position with regard to the multi-market situation. Let us consider two markets, A and B. The first competitor dominates market A, and the second market B. The first competitor has a small market share in market B, and, symmetrically, the second has a small market share in market A. If by cutting his price in market B, the first competitor can seriously damage the situation of the dominating second competitor in that market, and reciprocally, if by cutting his price in market A the second competitor can seriously damage the situation of the first competitor in that market, then a reciprocal and potential threat hangs over the two competitors in both markets, and neither of them has an incentive to initiate a price war. Of course, in practice, the multi-market situation is normally more complex and intricate than a head to head confrontation between two competitors. However, concentration in the cement industry has frequently resulted in a small number of cement groups dominating their home market, and then entering distant marmets and competing with local firms there. These competitors, being in an identical situation acted similarly. The market of competitors themselves leader in their home markets. Thus, although multi-market competition is complex, the simple case developed above has relevance in many cement markets situations. Moreover, cement groups enter markets dominated by their competitors with a view to creating potential retaliatory threats. Once reciprocal multi-market competitive threats have been created, each competitor is generally left with a "sphere of influence" (Bernheim and Whinston, 1990). The building up of spheres of influence increases the chance of competitive stabilisation. Under a multipoint competitive regime, each producer has possession of "hostage" local plants owned by their competitors. They have strengths and weaknesses in various locations. They can retaliate against a competitive attack that occurs in one market, by attacking in a different market where their competitor is weak. This interplay gives credibility to non-aggressive agreement, as well as to the threat of retaliation for transgressing rules (O. Williamson, 1985).

However, a second point is that the chance of stabilisation is lessened by the fact that there are monomarket competitors in the sphere of influence of each of the large competitors. As they are only locally based, in adverse economic circumstances, they can destabilise the market, nullifying the stabilising effect of multi-market competition. Larger producers buying smaller independent ones can help reinforce the multi-market competition game. Competitive aggression becomes less likely, or at least less widespread if it does occur, leaving a "limited war equilibrium": *'In such an equilibrium, attacks are defended locally and fighting is 'contained' within small isolated regions. Formally, we define such a situation as one in which the firms compete actively in only some of the markets in which both participate. A limited war equilibrium permits each firm to signal its determination to fight while avoiding both the costs of a total war and the risk of misunderstood friendliness.'* (Karnari and Wernerfelt, 1985: 89).

It can be understood from above that, as a general rule, the effect of multi-market presence on competition stabilisation is complex, and at any rate not easy to isolate from other economic factors. However, the recent changes that have occurred at the beginning of the 1990s in the Venezuelan cement market seem to illustrate the stabilising effect of multi-market competition.

In 1989, the Venezuelan economy was in an economic slump. The banking system, on which the cement companies were dependent, collapsed. The International Monetary Fund imposed a harsh monetary and public spending policy. In contrast to previous economic slumps, the Venezuelan government was deprived of the possibility of launching construction and infrastructure plans to boost the economy. Consequently, the cement markets were depressed. The three Venezuelan cement producers engaged in price competition. Price discounts generalised into price warfare. The price of a 42.5 kg sack of cement went down from US $3.70 to $3.10. But in addition, producers also absorbed part of the freight delivery cost and provided customers with payment facilities, blurring real pricing strategies and intensifying the price warfare. Soon, the behaviour of competitors seemed irrational with regard to the losses they experienced. At the end of 1994, Vencemos, the market leader, had a loss of $117 million.[9]

As it is frequently the case, the outcome of the price warfare proved disappointing for the producers, who incurred massive losses while their market shares were left unchanged. They were to be taken over. Holderbank, the Swiss cement group, acquired the first a small independent producer, Cementos Caribe. Then, at the beginning of 1994, Cemex the largest Mexican producer, acquired the Venezuelan market leader, Vencemos. A few months later, Lafarge, the French number one, took over Fabrica Nacional de Cemento (FNC). Lafarge also had a minority stake in Cementos Catatumbo. Finally, in 1995, Holderbank took over Consolidada de Cementos (Conceca). The Venezuelan financial crisis was at that time still going on but from the moment the Venezuelan cement industry was acquired by the largest foreign cement groups, the competition game changed drastically. *'Once the new shareholders were managing the industry, starting in 1994, new sets of rules developed relating to market shares, competition and, in general, the status of the industry.'* (*WC*, Duarte, December 1995: 23).

---

9. As Lösch has emphasised (1954: 157): *'Dumping in the market area of a competitor is often a sign of disintegration or panic, or a result of megalomania, and to this extent concerns more the psychiatrist than the economist.'*

How can the sudden market competition stabilisation be explained? Firstly, before and after the taking over of the Venezuelan cement industry, the political and economic situation of the country was not healthy, particularly in 1994 and 1995. Secondly, the market structure remained unchanged after the episode. Therefore, there are no economic explanations to be found either from the demand or the supply sides of the activity. Also, one cannot relate the change in the behaviour of the cement producers to the fact that they had been taken over by more experienced firms. The Venezuelan producers were experienced producers. They had invested in the activity at the beginning of the 20th century, and at the time of the price warfare, a reduced oligopoly had been in operation: three producers had dominated the national market for several decades. But, in spite of this long established oligopolistic situation, each producer had attempted to survive the economic slump by engaging in price discounting.

Therefore, the movement from a local perspective to a multi-market one appears a convincing explanation of the sudden change in pricing policy, particularly when considering the interconnectedness of the potential threats of retaliation of the foreign firms involved in the Venezuelan takeover wave. Cemex is the number one producer in Mexico (68 per cent market share), but the second Mexican producer, Apasco (13 per cent market share), is a subsidiary of Holderbank. In Spain, Cemex became the leading producer on acquiring Valenciana and Sanson in 1992. Lafarge is the second Spanish producer via its subsidiary Asland. Holderbank also has cement interests in Spain, Horns Ibericos Albas. The three cement groups, Cemex, Lafarge and Holderbank have important cement holdings in the US. Cemex which had only owned cement terminals before 1994, had bought the ultra-modern plant of Balcones, in Texas, from Lafarge. Overall, the three cement groups shared multi-market interests with multiple geographical means of retaliation.

Deterring market entry

Entry into the industry is easy insofar as the production process is known, available, and well understood, but it does require heavy investment. Once, entry has occurred, exiting the market is too costly to be thought of. A stable local or regional market equilibrium can therefore be easily disturbed for a long period of time, simply because of entry. Strategic moves aimed at deterring entry are therefore essential in order to stabilise the market.

Incumbent firms have three means of deterring entry. Firstly they can engage in a capacity race, each firm building up excess capacity that will create a credible price threat over potential outside competitors. Because of excess capacity, competitors who contemplate entering the market anticipate a severe drop in price if they decide to do so (Lieberman, 1987). However, once again, it has to be stressed that markets are inherently local. Therefore general excess capacity at a national level is of little relevance where there is no excess capacity in regional growth markets, and it is very unlikely that excess capacity can be built up so that no point of entry can be profitable, particularly when taking into account transportation costs.

The second means consists of developing a geographic space packing strategy. Comparative empirical studies seem to reach the conclusion that, in the 1970s, US cement producers had recourse to this strategy (Scherer, 1980: 257). But its effectiveness is doubtful. The Colorado case provides a good example of both these points. In the early 1950s, there were two cement plants operating in the state, both owned by Ideal. Ideal seemed, at that time, to have saturated the Colorado market. Yet by 1959, Monolith built a distribution terminal in Denver, served by its Laramie plant in Wyoming. Then, in 1969, Martin Marietta built a new plant at Lyons, which was approximately the same distance away from the two Ideal plants (Johnson and Parkman, 1983: 437 -footnote 25). The saturation of a regional market is therefore difficult to achieve for incumbent firms. Also, in the 1960s, US cement producers added numerous terrestrial distribution terminals. This move turned out to be extremely costly, and precipitated the collapse of the US cement industry in the 1970s (*RP,* Bell, May, 1962).

The third means of entry deterrence is linked to the effect of pricing systems making use of freight absorbtion. Freight absorption is acknowledged to delay the setting up of plants that could have been built to serve distant local markets.

State intervention and market stabilisation

State Intervention can indirectly or directly help incumbent firms stabilise the market.

For instance, the price control policy which was in use in France until 1986, very likely dampened price competition, and facilitated coordination amongst competitors (Dumez and Jeunemaître, 1989). In theory, this should not have happened. Price controls were implemented to curb inflation (the increase in the general price index), not to set prices. Companies did not have to automatically incorporate the inflation forecast into their price list. They could, and had to, compete on price whatever the government price control policy. However, in practice, price competition was undoubtedly distorted by the price controls. The price control mechanism required negotiations which were led by trade associations rather than firms. Discussions focused primarily on the increases in production and distribution costs that firms were facing, and the extent to which they had an alternative to passing increases on in full into their price lists. Usually, the administration would challenge increased costs alleged by firms, and would stress the potential for productivity gains. Prior to the discussions, firms would meet at the trade association headquarters and exchange data on their level of activity, production costs, productivity gains, output levels, etc. Thus, price controls necessitated a centralising of information, involving exchanges of data and points of view within a semi-official framework.

Assessing the impact of price controls on competition is not straightforward. Producers used to refer to the price control period as the black years for the industry (Collomb, 1993: 104). However, this view is somewhat inconsistent with the economic success of the French industry, Lafarge becoming the world's second largest producer, and Ciments Français one of the world's leading cement groups, even before their buy-out by Italcementi. Two factors played a key role. Firstly, the exchange of information within the trade association, and the announcement of a maximum price increase (that producers would automatically align on), facilitated the stabilisation of competition. Secondly, the price increase that was negotiated applied to both small and large producers, and was set such that the weakest would survive, but at a level that would result in high returns for the fittest, following effective performance.

In short, price controls led to the exit of some marginal firms from the market, whilst allowing more efficient firms to earn significant rents. In the absence of effective mergers and acquisitions regulations, price controls indirectly pushed the cement industry towards a more stable competitive environment, and led to increased market concentration. The combined market share of the five leading cement producers rose from 50 per cent in the 1940s, to 70 per cent in the 1970s. By the beginning of the 1990s, the two cement producers, Lafarge and Ciments Français, accounted for 77 per cent of the total French market.

Another mode of intervention is when the government directly encourages the stabilisation of the market. The decision to exit, or partially divest assets, is a costly one in the cement industry. During periods of overcapacity, competitors are unwilling to make either of these decisions, given the knowledge that if they do so, the market conditions for their competitors will significantly improve. Therefore, overcapacity may remain for long periods of time. In such situations, the government may decide to try and help reduce output capacity through direct intervention. The cement market in Japan in the 1980s, provides an example of such direct intervention (Mutoh, 1990; Tilton, 1996).

In the early 1980s, Japanese cement consumption slowed down. After 1983, the export market collapsed. National production reached a peak of 87.4 million tons in 1980, before falling each year until 1986.

In an attempt to deal with the issue of production overcapacity, the Japanese cement producers tried to introduce a recession cartel, which was to be effective from 1 July 1983 to 31 December 1983. Output and sales quotas were agreed on the basis of average production levels over the past three years (national production was not meant to exceed 36.65 million tons). Market shares were to be frozen, and a target cement price was set at 15500 yens per ton.

Nevertheless, the recession cartel failed, and the cement price did not rise above 14500 yens per ton.

Then, the Japanese cement producers began contemplating the possibility of the "Law on Temporary Measures for the Structural Improvement of Specified Industries", the so called "Structural Improvement law", being implemented. A study group was set up, in October 1982, at the *Cement Manufacturers Association*. One year later, it recommended the restructuring of the industry under the improvement law.

MITI set up a subcommittee attached to the *Industrial Structure Council*. It was to examine how the restructuring should be organised. In its final report, in line with an 80 per cent rate of capacity utilisation target which, in principle, would ensure satisfactory returns on investment, the Council proposed:

1. a 30 per cent reduction of industry production capacity. This implied getting rid of 25 million tons of obsolete production capactiy. The target was to reduce output capacity to below 99 million tons to match a domestic cement consumption forecast of 77-79 million tons.
2. the setting up of common regional sales counters organised around the five leading producers: Onoda group (19.3 per cent market

share): Onoda Cement, Nippon Steel Chemical, Toso Corporation, Hitachi Cement, Mitsui Mining;

3. Nihon Group (21.4 per cent): Nihon Cement, Osaka Cement, Daiichi Cement, Myojo Cement;

4. Mitsubishi Group (16.7 per cent): Mitsubishi Mining and Cement, Tokyuamasoda;

5. Sumitomo Group (20.3 per cent): Sumitomo Cement, Aso Cement, Tsugura Cement, Denki Kagaku Kogyo, Nittestsu Cement, Hachinohe Cement, Toyo Cement, Kanda Cement;

6. Ube Group (20.3 per cent): Ube Industries, Chichibu Cement, Tsugura Cement, Ryukyu Cement.

Each sales counter would have to allocate the capacity reductions among producers, and rationalise the network of cement terminals in its region. The aim was to create common sales offices that would be used by all cement producers.

On 27 April 1984, the private office of the Ministry agreed to apply the Structural Improvement Law regulations to the cement industry. On 3 August 1984, MITI made public the rationalisation scheme. In February 1985, the *Cement Manufacturers Association* approved the scheduled capacity reductions. One cement producer, Toyo, ceased production. The others agreed to implement the plan, which translated into a 5 million tons capacity reduction per leading cement producer: Onoda (5.178 million tons, 12 kilns to be shut down, which equated to 33.7 per cent of its total production capacity); Chichibu (5.020 million tons; 12 kilns; 46.5 per cent); Nihon Cement (4.936 million tons, 17 kilns, 27.5 per cent).

The plan was carried out swiftly, and by the end of March, 76 kilns, and 24.65 million tons of production capacity had been shut. In March 1986, 13 additional kilns (6.35 million tons of capacity) were also closed down. At first sight, the restructuring effort seemed tremendous. However, one must bear in mind that 25 million tons of production capacity were known to be obsolete, so that the reduction plan only applied to 6 million tons of effective production capacity.

The common sales policy came into force gradually. In August 1985, the Nihon cement group decided to use a common brand name for their sacks of cement. In April 1986, the other four leading producers did the same.

Following the implementation of the plan, cement prices recovered slightly - from 14.150 yens per ton in 1983, to 14.254 yens per ton in 1986. While the sales of cement producers only stabilised between 1983 and 1987, their financial situation clearly improved. There is no doubt that the plan had a beneficial effect on the industry, and partially restored the profitability of producers.

However, despite the drastic capacity reductions, the general outlook was bleak. The plan aimed for an 80 per cent rate of capacity utilisation, but, on average, it only reached 62.4 per cent in 1984, 71.7 per cent in 1985, and 65.5 per cent in 1987. In fact, the government and the producers had underestimated demand fluctuations. The *Industrial Structure Council* drew up the plan under the assumption that cement consumption would be 81 million tons in 1983, and would fall slightly to 77-79 million tons in 1987. However, demand proved much more sluggish. The economy was experiencing a slump, and cement demand fell to an all time low of 64 million tons in 1987. Moreover, cement imports from Korea significantly increased, given the strength of the yen from 1985 onwards.

Again, efforts to stabilise the market had been ill-defined. After 1986, the cement price fell slightly. As a result, in April 1987, the Japanese cement producers asked for the enforcement of the "structural adjustment law". The law is complementary to the "structural improvement law", and is aimed at helping individual companies, or regions, to adapt to a new environment. Under the law, the industry firstly proposed a plan that detailed a reduction in the number of plants and kilns. It outlined the characteristics of the capital stock and companies involved. The plan was submitted to the Ministry, which had to examine whether or not it contravened competition law. In the case of the plan getting approval, a series of measures would have been available: fiscal bonuses, financial aids, etc. In August 1987, MITI repealed the cement structural improvement agreement and, in October 1987, it applied the structural adjustment law to the industry, focusing on the disposal of unnecessary kilns. The plan was officially approved in September 1988.

Thus, the Japanese government directly intervened to help its national cement producers overcome an oversupply crisis which would have resulted in chaotic (ruinous) competition. MITI initiated and managed the policy in connection with the Japanese cement trade association (the trade association itself recruited Ono Masabumi, a retired civil servant of MITI, in 1984, at the time when the capacity rationalisation scheme was decided) (Tilton, 1996).

In conclusion, although cement is a homogeneous product and the competitive game is local with a reduced number of competitors, an array of more or less explicit coordination schemes to stabilise price and volume competition at times of significant falls in demand can be observed.

Perhaps tacit collusion does not emerge as easily or spontaneously from non-cooperative strategies as the results of game theorists, with respect to concentrated industries, suggest.

But even in the case of explicit and organised collusion, the stabilisation process remains imperfect. In the German cartel case, Wössingen used to be a maverick competitor destabilising the regional market. By the same token, competition in volume remained by means of cross-hauling in the case of the US basing point.

Appendix

THE BASIC POINT SYSTEM

Lehigh Valley is the base point. Prices are delivered prices. In any delivery location, the delivered price is equal to the base mill price in the Lehigh Valley plus the transportation cost from the Lehigh Valley to the delivery location. Therefore, the delivered price in location B is less than the delivered price in location A, given the difference in transportation costs.

Suppose the demand for cement moves West, and a cement plant settles in Chicago. Assume that the plant does not have the production capacity to supply all of the Chicago regional market area. The plant faces two alternatives:

1. it can decide not to be a base mill. It will not publish a cement price at the mill, and will be a price-taker. It aligns its price with the delivered price, as calculated from the base mill price in the Lehigh Valley. Consequently, the cement plant in Chicago sells its cement at a higher price at A than at B, although it is less costly for it to transport the cement to A than to B. Therefore, the plant makes higher profits in A, and has an interest in selling as much of its production in the locations close to its plant.

2. it can decide to be a base point. It will publish a cement price at the mill. Then the plant will quote a delivered price that increases in

proportion to the distance from Chicago. It quotes a delivered price at B that is higher than the delivered price at A. To make profits, the cement plant in Chicago, has an interest in increasing its production, and, over time, its production capacity. The Chicago cement plant constrains the business behaviour of the Lehigh cement plants, forcing them to absorb part or all of their transportation costs (freight absorption) if they wish to sell in the Chicago area.

CHAPTER 3

Local market stabilisation and rivalry

The fact that producers seek to stabilise price and volume competition in local markets does not entail that all means of competition have been removed. Rather, competition focuses on other activities. In such cases, we will refer to the competitive process as one of rivalry rather than competition. Therefore, in what follows, the word competition will primarily refer to situations where producers focus on price and volume in order to gain or defend market share. Rivalry will refer to competition based on other factors, such as customer service, product quality, the pre-emption of the best production sites, the search for cost advantages over competitors, and improvements in distribution networks.

The balance between competition and rivalry will hinge on the industry's current state of adjustment to the business cycle. It is reasonable to expect that in periods of recession, competition, as previously defined, will be less likely to be important: cement producers will do their best to avoid price wars that put their market share at risk, and offer no real advantage in terms of their final outcome. They will use these periods to focus on gaining advantage in terms of efficiency gains and cost conditions, in order to have an edge over their competitors during the upturn of the business cycle. As a result, prices and market shares will deviate little compared with what one would expect given the impact of economic slumps on capacity utilisation. However, when the economy is booming, competition at the fringes of natural markets is more pronounced, with pre-emptive moves, and the gradual erosion of market shares, changing the balance of power between producers.

Cost rivalry during times of recession

Suppose that demand either falls or levels off in a local market, but that none of the producers in the market attempts to gain volume or additional market share by engaging in significant price cutting. This situation could only take place if there was some form of implicit or explicit co-ordination between producers in order to stabilise price competition. In such a case, rivalry substitutes for competition, and producers devote their efforts to improving production processes and distribution channels, and reducing plant running costs. This is precisely the situation observed in the cement industry. As technological change is controlled by a few production device designers, producers can secure an advantage over competitors by more speedily acquiring, and mastering, innovations in production - past innovations in the production process include the use of rotary kilns, and the shift to the dry production process. Changes in technology lead to a competitive race. When a technological breakthrough occurs that allows for economies of scale in production, and enables current production levels to be exceeded, a rationalisation of the distribution network follows. For example, the position of "traffic manager" was developed in the cement industry in the 1960s, and given the role of optimising the costs of distributing cement to more distant locations. Traffic managers seek to make better use of the network of terminal distribution points, and to contract out the delivery of cement from these terminals to the customer. The optimising of distribution and transportation is a key factor relating to profitability in the cement industry, and, as a result, an essential element of cost competition.

Producers have also continually developed new tools to diagnose and control unnecessary costs. This is another feature of the rivalry process. In 1992, Ciments Français decided to implement an "expert software system" in order to improve the management of their plants. The system itself required the setting up of a huge data base of equipment suppliers, forecasts and plant efficiency measurements (*Newspapers,* Bommel, 1992). Specialists from Technodes SA, the Ciments Français subsidiary, were able to access the expert system from a simple micro-computer, and to gauge the performance of any cement plant in the world. The expert system was also designed to formulate the appropriate conduct for the running of the plant according to circumstances. Chemists, mechanics, and managers in the plant had to comply with the directives of the expert system. The expert system dealt with the day to day running of the plant, the maintenance of equipment, the level of stocks, and the management of the organisation. It calculated the gain in production efficiency brought about by the introduction of new pieces of equipment, and the expected return on investment from them.

Thus, the simple observation of weak price competition does not do justice to the underlying and potentially competitive influence of the rivalry process which is at work in recessionary periods. The focus on price competition misses the less visible but constantly renewed efforts to create productivity surpluses in production and trade. In this game, some producers perform better than others. On the one hand, securing cost advantages does not entail short term shifts in market shares. The search for cost and productivity advantages builds up, but advantages gained are not revealed in the market place, as, by common consent, because of the economic slump, producers do not translate them into price competition. On the other hand, the building up of cost and productivity asymmetries among producers paves the way for more price aggressiveness when cement demand starts growing again. They prepare for a new market equilibrium consistent with their changes in costs and productivity. However, as has already been noted, efforts to stabilise price competition are imperfect. Besides, the rivalry game may lead to sporadic and limited price aggressions at the very end of economic slumps as producers may have different expectations about the strength of the growth in demand to come. Therefore, price aggressions are not irreconcilable with the search for market price stabilisation. Econometric modelling has shown that under particular circumstances, price wars are compatible with collusion among producers notably because of unusual demand shocks and uncertainty about pricing, discounts and output production (Green and Porter, 1984).

Limited price warfare at time of economic recovery

It is rather at times of economic recovery, when the rate of capacity utilisation has been low for several months, that price aggression occurs. In the cement industry, economic recovery frequently coincides with the emergence of new markets (for example, investments in new infrastructure or the rise of new cities). While competition remains more or less stable in long existing markets, aggressive pricing occurs in newly emerging or rapidly growing markets. Each producer fights to secure the largest market share in the new area in the hope that this aggressiveness will go undetected because of the recovery of local markets (Rotemberg and Saloner, 1986; Rosenbaum, 1986). According to an industry representative, the European cement industry has developed and been structured primarily under the influence of rivalry, and not competition, with the constitution of a few large cement producers between 1930 and 1950:[1] *'If the key players of the industry fiercely compete to increase their national market share [...], they do so primarily in trying to get the lion share of the expansion surplus more than in putting into question the existing natural markets.'* (Collomb, 1993: 104; see also Tanguy, 1987: 123 ff.). Rivalry intensifies due to the fact that the boundaries of local markets are in constant change. Economic recovery is sluggish in some markets, while others experience rapid economic growth. Krugman (1991) has illustrated, with the backing of economic modelling, how such economic regional discrepancies have a small initial impact, but then quickly start to have an important cumulative effect.

The economics of pre-emption at times of economic recovery

The profits secured from market stabilisation, together with the accumulation of financial surpluses from rivalry and the profits achieved in growing markets, allow for the economic expansion of producers. They are all the more necessary, as the level of investment required in order to increase in size is extremely high.

Thus, to simplify, there are two stages of the competitive process: firstly, the starting position of firms, their combination of plants, quarries and the natural markets they control; secondly, there is the competition which follows in the market place. The attempt to stabilise price competition provides the producer with the means to expand in other markets. The two stages are interdependent, and the process is circular. The way in which producers position themselves in the various local markets (the first stage of the competitive process), impacts on the type of competition that is likely to prevail (the second stage). For instance,

---

1. Such a phenomenon has been analysed in the Brazilian cement market by Lima (1990: 2-3): *'Rivalry is greater in times of expansion, and co-operation is tighter during stagnation'* [...] *'Competition could be observed in periods of rising demand when producers could compete between themselves, each one trying to capture the largest market share of the market rise.'*

depending on the control of existing production sites, the local markets of the producers may overlap or be distinct. In the former case, price competition is more likely to emerge. The difficulty for producers is that once the map of local markets, and the overlaps between them, is drawn, it is quite irreversible, and extremely difficult to reshape, particularly in the short run. Building a new plant or increasing production capacity requires important investments over time. These investments are sunk, and running a plant has high fixed costs. So, according to the configuration in existence, cement producers have to cope with more or less potential price competition.

Suppose now that, in the first place, a few producers have taken control of the most profitable production sites. The first stage of the game results in a competitive configuration where new independent entry is likely to be unsuccessful or, at least, not easily profitable. In such circumstances it is in the interest of the restricted oligopoly to attempt to stabilise competition (the second stage). If the producers are successful, they will extract financial surpluses. They will, then, use these to shape the competitive configuration to their own advantage, buying and selling assets between themselves, divesting or investing in local markets, acquiring new positions (new first stages). This two stage process, with feedback, was modelled for the first time by Hotelling (1929). His model consists of a spatial duopoly game, where two firms have in the first place to position themselves at one location in the high street of a town. Consumers are uniformly distributed along the high street. Each consumer buys according to the best price he can get from the two firms. The price is equal to the price at the factory gate plus the transportation cost. In this duopoly game, first, the firms choose a location along the high street, then they set their factory prices. In other words, in the first move they have to anticipate the kind of price competition they will face in the second stage of the game. This basic model has had numerous extensions (Scotchmer and Thisse, 1993; Ponssard, 1995; d'Apremont, Encaoua, Ponssard, 1999).

The rivalry process that develops, in order to get a better market position, applies to the setting up of new plants, and probably with more relevance, to the pre-emption of the best locations. Insofar as the market is dominated by a restricted oligopoly with high investment costs, and as the starting positions are of paramount importance (a few production and location sites are better than the others), none of the producers can allow themselves to lag behind their competitors. A premium will reward the first mover, but it will decrease as new entrants settle in the market place. This result is encompassed in the economic conceptualisation of the "first mover advantage" (Patterson, 1993). Hence, rivalry in terms of pre-emption results in long waves of strategic movements and restructuring.

One of the most significant waves occurred in the cement industry at the end of the 1970s, and continued into the 1980s. First European, and then also from 1988, Japanese, cement producers took over the American cement industry (PCA, 1992).

At the end of the 1970s, the American cement industry was in bad shape. It had undergone successive economic crises without having been able to stabilise price competition. The Clean Air Act imposed massive investment costs on producers for anti-pollution devices. Many kilns had to be shut down and a good deal of plants stayed in business with large amounts of debt on their balance sheet. The collapse was such that shortages of cement had arisen in a few US States.

The 1970s had also been marked by price controls. The Nixon administration froze prices in the fourth quarter of 1973. This was an additional blow to the industry. Financial conglomerates progressively decided to withdraw from their cement activities and to use the cash to diversify. Emphasising the need for massive investment in modernisation in order to put the industry back on its feet, even before the oil crisis, Roy Grancher (*RP*, December 1972-69) questioned: '*Where will the money come from? The obvious conclusion is that if those within the cement industry are not going to be allowed to be attracted towards building that necessary capacity, others will! Be they users; be they "outsiders"; be they overseas interests-cement sources will be found somewhere. The need is too great and too important to be neglected.*' As US producers had benefited from low oil prices, given important national oil reserves, many kilns were not cost effective with regard to energy consumption. The oil crisis revealed that the industry was lagging behind its European and Asian counterparts in terms of production technology, making the need for finance to modernise the industry still more urgent. The weakness of the US dollar on the foreign exchanges also helped foreign investors.

The take-over wave started in the 1970s, and, at first, involved joint ventures. Lafarge signed up with Lone Star in order to build a plant to produce a specific type of cement, ("calcium aluminate cement"), in Norfolk, Virginia. In May 1976, Ciments Français announced its intention to provide technical support to Coplay Cement (Lehigh Valley) in its modernisation. Coplay had acquired Giant in 1972, and been in financial difficulties since. In December 1976, Ciments Français took control of Coplay. The take-over and restructuring wave reached its peak in 1986, when twenty four American cement producers changed ownership: CBR

(Belgium) acquired Genstar; Beazer (United Kingdom) acquired Gifford Hill; Holderbank, the world leader (Switzerland), acquired Ideal Basic; Lafarge, the world number two, acquired the cement subsidiary of National Gypsum, an American cement producer which owned one of the largest US plants, Alpena, situated in the Great Lakes area. Overall, within fifteen years, two thirds of US cement production capacity had come under foreign control.

The fall of the Berlin wall put a halt to the European wave of American acquisitions, with their pre-emption strategies moving towards Eastern Europe. Within a few years, the bulk of Eastern European production capacity had come under the control of the leading world producers. By 1991, they had taken over the whole of the then Czechoslovakia's production capacity. On buying Karsdorf, near Leipzig, Lafarge acquired a third of the ex-East German market. Holderbank also invested in Hungary, and in April 1992 acquired Kunda Tasement in Estonia. CBR and Heidelberger Zement acquired cement plants in Czechoslovakia. RMC bought Rudersdorf, a large cement plant on the outskirts of Berlin.

Another acquisition wave was concentrated on the Mediterranean coast, and seemed to supersede the Eastern European wave. In 1989, Lafarge took control of Asland in Spain. That same year, Ciments Français acquired five cement plants in Turkey, where Lafarge had already invested. In 1992, the Italian concrete producer Calcestruzzi, a subsidiary of the Ferruzzi group, bought Heraclès, the leading Greek producer (with a 44 per cent share of the Greek market), and the first European exporter (3.5 million tons in 1991). In August 1992, Cemex, the leading Mexican producer, bought two key Spanish producers, Valenciana dos Cementos and Sanson, giving them 28 per cent of the Spanish market. Lafarge and Ciments Français increased their holdings in Morocco.

Restructuring seems to have continued unabated in Europe and in other parts of the World. In September 1993, Heidelberger Zement bought CBR from the Société Générale de Belgique, and became the fifth largest world cement producer (second in the US, number one in several Eastern European countries). At the same time, Lafarge raised funds, by issuing new shares, with a view to reducing its debt exposure and investing in South East Asia, the part of the world experiencing the fastest economic growth. They now operate a cement plant close to Peking under a Franco-Chinese joint venture deal. Asia has become the focus of attention for foreign investors in the mid-1990s. The Japanese cement producers plan to set up 8 million tons of production capacity in Asia before the turn of the century. The biggest project is the joint Thanh Hoa project between Mitsubishi and Nihon in Vietnam, who plans to create a 2.3 million tons of plant capacity, including harbour facilities, for a total amount of $346 million. Second is the Onoda Cement project in Chinwang Tao (China), involving 1.4 million tons of capacity (*ICR*, August 1994: 14). Holderbank is also said to have development projects in China. Whilst Blue Circle has denied being interested in investing in China, it has stressed its interest in Malaysia, Singapore and Vietnam.

Entry in new markets, then, is cumulative. As location is essential in the competitive process, and insofar as the best locations are available only in limited numbers because of the quality of quarries and communication networks, where a market is expanding it is crucial for each producer to secure the most profitable sites early, and not to be the last to invest. While the size of the investment involved makes it a risky venture, the first mover advantage that is associated with the pre-emption of the best locations gives rise to mimetic behaviour among producers (Dumez and Jeunemaître, 1996). Hence, the building up of similar strategic moves produces the pattern of an acquisition and restructuring wave which indicates the intensity of the rivalry process. Thus, when Martin Marietta, a US financial conglomerate, decided to sell its cement assets, all of the European cement producers visited the headquarters of the firm to make them an offer. A similar situation occurred when the Greek government decided to sell the state owned producer Heracles. Calestruzzi struck the deal after all the key European cement producers had given up. As Roy Grancher, quoting an old adage, rightly put it: *'No opportunity is ever lost. The other fellow will surely take those you miss!'* (*WC*, Grancher, July/August 1984).

The economics of entry and exit

The economics of pre-emption focuses on the "first mover advantage" but it has a dual aspect: the economics of exit. As a matter of fact, mimetic behaviour in acquisitions and investments frequently creates production over-capacity in the market place. Suppose a cement producer settles in a new market. His competitors think that the strategic move is profitable, and imitate by also entering the market. If, when the newly built production capacities are set into motion, demand is less than had been expected, the profitability of all cement producers lowers. In such circumstances, the key issue is avoiding a fall in the market price in the short run. In the long run, the issue is which of the cement producers will exit the market to restore a proper balance between demand and supply. But if the first mover advantage is for entry, the last mover advantage is for exit. They are symmetrical strategic moves in terms of returns. Thus, the first to exit the market is likely to do so in disastrous financial condition,[2] and in doing so he will automatically improve the profitability of the remaining producers. Of course, the first to exit the market does so to spare the unprofitable capital tied up in the running of the plant, and to invest it in more promising business operations. He can expect to gain an advantage over his competitors who will be stuck in a disappointing market that will not provide them with high returns. But new profitable opportunities should arise, and in the meantime, by exiting the market, the producer is certain to improve the profitability of his competitors. So no producer is likely to exit the market quickly. Rather, all producers have an interest in a wait and see strategy, hoping for a U-turn in demand. This explains why production over-capacity can last for long periods of time in the cement industry. Therefore, the decision to exit a market is as important as that to enter one, with regard to the rivalry between producers. They are both strategic decisions, although exit decision are sometimes forced because of technical reasons (for example, old kilns that require massive financial investment).

An example of forced exit of this kind could be seen in Lehigh Valley in the mid-1970s. At the beginning of the 1970s, the US demand for cement was constantly increasing. In four consecutive years (1970 to 1973), the average rate of capacity utilisation exceeded 90 per cent. At the end of 1974, it declined to 89 per cent, with demand having fallen by 9 per cent. In the following year, 1975, demand continued to fall, this time by 15 per cent. Since capacity in the cement industry is not flexible, the rate of utilisation dropped to 61 per cent. But most of the Lehigh Valley cement plants were obsolete, with many of the kilns dating back to the 1950s. It was in this economic context that Coplay cement announced its joint venture with Ciments Français to modernise its plant. Roy Grancher noted that this announcement sent a "shudder" through the valley (*RP*, Grancher, October 1976). His paper was entitled: *'Into the Valley of Pennsylvania: an existing guessing game as to whose cement plant might close down.'* The planned modernisation forced the other producers to

---

2. Not only will the producer lose his initial investment in the plant, but he will incur significant direct costs related compliance with anti-pollution regulations in developed countries.

consider their alternatives, either to invest in order to meet the competition, or to exit the market.

Strategic alliances

Strategic alliances, as has been shown, are part of the rivalry game for at least two reasons. Firstly, in the short run, strategic alliances usually help to stabilise the market: producers that join forces exchange information and develop common interests. It is unlikely that they will fight against each other and fiercely compete on price in order to gain market share from each other, at least in the short-run. As a result, an alliance can mean the withdrawal of one competitor from the market. Secondly, strategic alliances make entry easier in newly emerging or growing markets. When trying to get a foothold in a potentially hostile environment, it is preferable to have allies that are knowledgeable about local market practices.

Strategic alliances are diverse.

As has been mentioned, Lafarge gained its foothold in the US from a joint venture with Lone Star (*RP*, Ironman, April and May 1978), although the joint venture, at first, was only concerned the production of aluminate cement. The plan was to import it in sacks from France, and to distribute it in the US. In 1973, a grinding unit was set up, with facilities for packing sacks. Lafarge signed a clinker supply contract with Lone Star for a total amount of 270000 tpy. Later, in October 1976, Lafarge and Lone Star jointly built a cement plant and decided to extend their agreement. However, in 1977, by common consent they ended their collaboration concerning the grey Portland cement and only continued the joint venture in relation to aluminate cement. In July 1977, Lafarge made an independent entry into the US cement market by taking over the Citadel Cement Corporation, which made it a significant US producer. However, this did not prevent Lafarge from signing another joint venture contract with Lone Star in 1981 concerning a cement plant in Brazil at Cantagalo.

So, the Lafarge entry did not disturb the equilibrium in the market. Entry occurred in a niche market, aluminate cement, that was not widely produced in the US. It had no significant impact in the short-run. In the long run, Lafarge became one of the leading US cement producers. At the beginning of the 1980s, Lone Star were the number one cement producer in the US, but they went bankrupt and placed under Chapter 11 in 1990/91. The collapse of Lone Star occurred after the sale of plant assets and numerous joint ventures: with RMC in the concrete industry, with Centex, with Adelaide Brighton (Australia) in 1985, and with Onoda

Cement in 1988 (providing the Japanese cement producer with their first opportunity to enter the US cement market).

It is somewhat difficult, then, to, a priori, assign a particular role to joint ventures. They are complex strategic moves in the rivalry process that governs the cement industry: *'Joint ventures can help a corporation achieve such specific objectives as market entry, reduced risk, decreased capital exposure, obtaining upgraded production, increasing capacity utilisation, or even may stand on their own as promising business activities.'* (*RP*, Grancher, April 89: 44).

The large cement producer Dyckerhoff chose a different means of entering the US cement market (*RP*, Ironman, October 1980). Taking advantage of the fact that US cement plants were not very cost effective given their lack of modernisation and high energy consumption, at the beginning of 1980s, Dyckerhoff set up a subsidiary, Dyckerhoff Engineering, with a headquarters located in Wiesbaden. It specialised in technological expertise and consultancy. The subsidiary was also to do business in Turkey and Egypt, but was primarily to deal in the US in Balcones (Texas) with General Portland. In September 1980, Dyckerhoff Engineering opened a US branch in Atlanta, Georgia, and Roy Grancher, was appointed vice president.

Strategic alliances can also consist of cross financial participation between producers, as has been the case in Europe. Once again, this type of alliance, combined with interlocking directorates, is likely to help stabilisation in the short run.[3] In the long run, the threat of a full take-over or the sudden withdrawal of one participant looms. The Coplay/Ciments Français joint venture was terminated only a few months after an agreement on plant modernisation was made, following the Ciments Français take-over of Coplay.

Rivalry and internationalisation

As Chandler (1990) has rightly noted, internationalisation is one dimension of the rivalry process, and it does not call into question, or put in jeopardy, attempts to stabilise competition in local markets. On the contrary, the stabilisation process in local markets assists the

---

3. Even though it seems possible to contend that such alliances could have competitive effects in particular circumstances: *'Increasing cross ownership can reduce the likelihood of collusion. Moreover, high levels of cross ownership can be less conductive to collusion than no cross ownership at all.'* (Malueg, 1992).

internationalisation process, without the latter calling into question the former. Here, a clear and careful distinction has to be made, from a conceptual perspective, between companies going international and the globalisation of markets.

Internationalisation does not mean the interlocking of local markets, that is to say, market globalisation. Each market has its own context and rules, and is managed independently. There can be a flow of imports and exports between local markets, but the trade is under the control of local producers who on facing shortages of cement import from distant markets. Thus, the flow of imports and exports occurs with the agreement, and under the management of local producers. It does not disrupt the market stabilisation process. Cross-border trade between local markets is helped by the internationalisation of the largest producers.

The history of the world's leading cement producer, Holderbank (*RP*, Ironman, April 1979 and June 1979), illustrates the distinction between internationalisation and globalisation from both a foreign investment and managerial perspective.

Holderbank is a village in Aargau, located forty kilometers West of Zurich. Its first cement plant began operation in 1913, and its first international involvement came eleven years later in 1924. That year, a team of Holderbank engineers designed and set up a cement plant in Beaumont, near Paris, in France. In 1925, Holderbank acquired an interest in Ciments d'Obourg, a Belgium producer. From the early days, the company was thought of as a loose structure consisting of independently run subsidiaries. The holding company, Holderbank Glaris SA was created in 1930. From then onwards, Holderbank has continued to invest abroad, in Europe, the USA, Africa and Asia. Entry into the foreign markets has regularly occured in line with the prevailing local competitive rationale. Evidence of this is given by the strategy of entry, and the management principles of the company.

Holderbank's investment strategy in foreign markets has primarily focused on the technical suitability of entry into the local competitive environment. The only centralised element has been the core technical competence which assisted subsidiaries abroad. In 1942, a technical branch was attached to the holding. In 1963, the technical team of the St Lawrence Co., in Canada, became an independent subsidiary (Holderbank Consulting Ltd, the headquarters of which are situated not far from Toronto). At the end of 1969, they were grouped, with four other departments of the holding company, into one entity, Holderbank Management and Consulting Ltd (HMC).

The consulting activity starts at the level of prospecting for the best sites. They assess the geological quality of the available quarries and propose appropriate extraction and production processes. Upstream of this, HMC carries out market and competition analyses. Also, on the request of clients, HMC negotiates the financing of operations with banks and lenders, and deals with the paperwork involved. They assist at the beginning of production, and also finalise specific accountancy methods to help with the management of the plant.

Even when Holderbank do not own all of the cement plants that they help to set up, they frequently contract technical assistance agreements with external clients that de facto tie them to the group.

The holding company has developed links with its foreign clients and subisidiairies, and the importance they give to locality is illustrated by their internal management principles:

1. *Local partnership.* Management and investment decisions should be made in relation to local partners. Although it would be easier to centrally control management and investment decisions, the local partnership gives value to local experience, and lowers business risks.

2. *Federal and decentralised management.* The subsidiaries and associated partners have a separate and independent management. Only functions that can benefit from the holding (engineering, R&D, finance) are centralised, and these are managed in concert with local partners.

3. *Local management representatives and training.* The managing directors of a subsidiary should be natives of the particular country. This is aimed at facilitating the integration of the company within the socio-economic local context. They are, however, given extensive training at the international level.

4. *Continuous assistance and systematic exchange of experience.* Efficiency can only be achieved if what is learned at the holding level is passed on to the local subsidiaries and vice versa. The communication of knowledge within the group should work in continuity, and information should constantly be updated. There are "general assistance agreements" signed between the subsidiaries and the holding company that bind subsidiaries to take part in the payment of the holding company's overheads. These costs are assumed to be largely compensated by the efficiency gains that come from the agreements.

5. *Socio-economic integration in the environment.* As well as respecting local regulations and practices, each subsidiary should be integrated into local political and public life, and actively partake in promoting key principles of a free society, such as free enterprise, and advanced social and environmental policies.

These different elements are helpful in describing how the internationalisation process has developed within the framework of the preservation of local markets, without interlocking or globalising markets. Thus, internationalisation is part of the rivalry game, but is not directly related to competition, in terms of price and volume competition as defined earlier. The economic surpluses stemming from stabilised local markets made internationalisation possible. Reciprocally, internationalisation does not profoundly alter the functioning of local markets.

Internationalisation and multi-market rivalry

Rivalry has fostered internationalisation. In return, internationalisation has weighed on the rivalry game. By investing in foreign markets, the leading producers have finally met each other in a plurality of markets, creating a multi-market rivalry game. The table below shows the head to head confrontation of the five leading cement multinational producers in the mid 1990s.

	HOLDERBANK	LAFARGE	CF/ ITALCEMENTI	CEMEX	HEIDELBERGER
HOLDERBANK		Brazil Bulgaria Canada France Germany Hungary (Duopoly) Romania (Duopoly) Spain U.S.A. Venezuela	Belgium Canada France Spain U.S.A.	Malaisie Mexico (duopoly) Spain U.S.A. Venezuela	Belgium Canada France Germany U.S.A.
LAFARGE	Brazil Bulgaria Canada France Germany Hungary (Duopoly) Romania (Duopoly) Spain U.S.A. Venezuela		Canada France Spain U.S.A.	Spain U.S.A. Venezuela	Canada Czechia France Germany Turkey U.S.A.
CF/ ITALCEMENTI	Belgium Canada France Spain U.S.A.	Canada France Spain U.S.A.		Spain U.S.A.	Belgium Canada Czechia France Turkey US.A.
CEMEX	Mexico (duopoly) Spain U.S.A. Venezuela	Spain U.S.A. Venezuela	Spain U.S.A.		
HEIDELBERGER	Belgium Canada France Germany U.S.A.	Canada Czechia France Germany Turkey U.S.A.	Belgium Canada Czechia France Turkey US.A.		

Firstly, the table pieces together information gathered from specialised magazines such as *International Cement review, Pit and Quarry, Rock Products,* and *World Cement,* and cannot be considered exhaustive.

Secondly, it is an oversimplification of multi-market rivalry, as cement markets are regionally focused. For instance, all cement groups have footholds in the US, but this does not mean that they confront each other in one or more of the US regional markets. Cemex has essentially set up and developed their trade in the Southern States of the US. They face Holderbank in Texas, but not the cement groups set up in the North of America. In Canada, only Lafarge operates in all the regional markets, the East Cost (Ontario) and the West Coast. Accuracy about the structure of multi-market rivalry would require going into the details of regional markets. Besides, if such study was to be carried out, the end result would only be a snapshot of multi-market rivalry. The map of the head to head confrontations between international cement groups constantly changes as new entries and acquisitions occur, and growth in cement markets shifts from one region to another.

Thirdly, the table gives no indication about the presence of independent cement producers in the national markets considered. It has been emphasised in a previous chapter, that market stabilisation is more difficult to sustain when, in a regional market, multi-market firms are confronted with independent mono-market local producers. For example, the table indicates that Holderbank and Lafarge have both holdings in Brasil. However, the leading cement producer in Brasil is a family run company (Votorantim, owned by the Ermirio de Moraes family) which has a nearly 50 per cent national market share. Besides, there are five other family cement groups (Joao Santos, Brennand, Soeicon, Caue, Ciplan). If market stabilisation is at work in the Brasilian cement markets, it is very unlikely that the multi-market situation between Lafarge and Holderbank plays a key role in it.

Fourthly, a multi-market game multiplies the possibility of retaliation from one local market to another. The table shows that the fifth largest cement producers met each other in many markets. This allows the retaliation process of price aggressions to be more organised and constrainted, contributing to the stabilisation of national markets.

In addition, the multi-market situation adds another feature to the rivalry game which is not included in the table. Meeting each other in many different local markets, cement groups get used to thinking of the rationalisation of the industry at a different scale than independent local producers. They negotiate market positions from one local market to anoher, buying and selling assets and shareholderships. For example, as mentioned earlier, in 1994, Cemex bought out to Lafarge its minority share in Vencemos (Venezuela) and simultaneously its Blacones cement plant in Texas. Moreover, the largest cement groups are key players in the international trade of cement, and may find themselves engaged in a joint strategy. For example, in Port Klang (Malaysia), the Holderbank siloship, Aqaba Falcon, sells and distributes Cemex cement. The increase in interactions, and the longterm perspectives of the largest cement groups suggest that cooperation mechanisms can emerge in the industry (Axelrod, 1984).

Before studying how antitrust policies have dealt with market stabilisation, a brief point should be addressed. The outcomes of market stabilisation can be diverse. It is very likely that these different outcomes lead to different degrees of rivalry. Looking back, the recourse to the basing point system in the US, as in the UK, seems to have resulted in a certain amount of drowsiness in the market place, with a lack of modernisation and frequent periods of over-capacity. Conversely, the French market, which has been subject to massive concentration, vertical integration and successive price controls, appears to have performed better, with more dynamic producers. Thus, if it is assumed that the local market stabilisation process moves competition towards rivalry, stabilisation efforts can result in more or less intense rivalry. What might determine the intensity of this rivalry?[4]

---

4. This issue is particularly puzzling. It opens up a new field of research that goes beyond the main purpose of this book, but deserves attention: what is the link between the intensity of the stabilisation process and the vigour of rivalry? How should it be measured?

CHAPTER 4

Local market stabilisation and competition policy

Antitrust agencies have responsibility for vetting attempts to stabilise competition in markets, as well as the various forms of the rivalry process.[1]

Few industries have had such a notable history with regard to antitrust.[2]

Firstly, the industry has always had a bad reputation. To many, the cement industry is equated with cartels, as are the oil industry, the chemical industry, and the glass industry. As there have been successive major antitrust cases this reputation has been maintained over time, although it is frequently not based on an in-depth analysis.

The economic characteristics of the industry have been influential. An economist who is looking for an elementary industry, where the basics are easy to capture and model, but at the same time where subtle variations exist, would think of an industry like cement. And it will be seen that in effect economists have had a key role in the antitrust debates about the cement industry.

Political factors have also been important in the development of the industry. At first, the cement industry had little political significance. In 1972, Robert R. Salyard, the then chairman of the cement branch of

1. Antitrust policy (US), competition policy (Europe), antimonopoly policy (Japan).
2. See the appendix to the chapter.

American Cement, noted: '*Total annual sales volume of the cement industry ($1.45 billion) is the same as that of the retail sales of the greeting card or the carpet industry. This is not a huge industry, and it cannot realistically be thought of as if it were in the same size category as oil, steel, or autos. In 1970, there were 84 US industrial corporations with individual annual sales greater than the total cement industry.*' (*RP*, Anonymous, 1972: 107). In terms of both annual turnover and employment, then, the cement industry was not a major industry. In addition to this, the industry had a low concentration ratio. Cement plants were scattered throughout the national territory, and the collapse of a few of them would not put the wealth of a town or a region into jeopardy. The cement industry certainly cannot be ranked among "strategic" industries, such as high technology. Worse, it is associated with environmental issues. There are local pollution problems, and it is difficult to integrate ugly cement plants into surrounding scenery. Also, today, cement plants are supposed to have their lot in the global warming effect. So if antitrust or competition policy needs to make an example, the cement industry is a particularly appropriate target. No lobbies or political pressure groups will oppose. There will be no preferential treatment as in strategic sectors, where industrial policy has a say against competition policy.

The industry had dug its own grave from the beginning. It should have known in advance that the views expressed by industry representatives would shock antitrust authorities. In an often cited letter of 17 March 1934, that was sent to the chairman of the NRA Code Authority (Loescher, 1959: 85-86), John Treanor, the Chairman of Riverside Cement, and Trustee of the Cement Institute, made the following memorable, but unfortunate, declaration: '*The truth is of course -and there can be no serious, respectable discussion of our case unless this is acknowledged- that ours is an industry that cannot stand free competition, that must systematically restrain competition or be ruined. We sell in a buyer's market all the time. The capital cost, as distinguished from the out-of-pocket cost, of producing cement is extraordinarily large. In free competition this capital cost is whittled away and this means loss and ruins.*'

These points cast some light on the disputes that the industry has had with the antitrust authorities. These disputes will now be discussed in greater detail by examining the diverse attempts the industry has made to stabilise competition, and the reaction of the antitrust authorities in the US, Japan and EC members states.[3]

Cartels

Secret cartels have not been the primary focus of the antitrust disputes. When uncovered, they have been declared unlawful and heavily fined. In 1988, Heidelberger Zement was given the heaviest fine ever levied by the Bundeskartellamt in Germany for having initiated and taken part in a cartel agreement.

In Japan, the Japanese Fair Trade Commission first interfered when the industry was implementing the MITI restructuring scheme under the "structural adjustment law" in October 1987. It opposed the joint construction of a distribution terminal on Ishikari Island that was to be shared between five cement producers. As a result, MITI and the cement producers had to change the shareholdership of the distribution terminal. This delayed the approval and implementation of the scheme until September 1988 (and, in fact, the scheme was only implemented in December of that year). Under the MITI policy, the cement groups formed five joint sales companies. The JFTC demanded that no joint sales company had a national market share exceeding 20 per cent and 25 per cent in the metropolitan Tokyo market.

Barely a year and a half later, on the 8 June 1990, the JFTC opened an investigation against two of the leading cement producers, Nihon Cement and Onoda Cement, on the suspicion that they had set up a cartel in the Hokkaido and Chugoku regional markets. In January 1991, the JFTC imposed an $90 million fine on the cartel participants, the largest fine ever levied for anti-competitive practices in an OECD country. However, the Japanese cement producers could argue that they had been lucky, since, at that time, fines for cartellisation had a fixed ceiling of 1.5 per cent of the turnover achieved during the functioning of the cartel. Within six months, in July 1991, this threshold was raised from 1.5 per cent to 6 per cent.

While secret cartels are usually heavily fined, antitrust authorities may in some cases reach a decision on grounds other than a purely competitive assessment. The Swiss Cartel Commission has given its clearance for past

---

3. The fight against the cartellisation of the cement industry dates back to the thirteenth century, when there were several well known cases in Venice. The "Serenissima", on unveiling a cartel, sequested kilns and put them up for auction. It was forbidden to own more than one kiln, and cement prices were subject to price controls (Lane, 1973: Ch. 11).

Swiss cement producers' agreements which guaranteed that half of cement deliveries would be shipped by rail. The Commission did so as it took into consideration that limiting road transportation would have a positive impact on the environment. However, price, volume, sales and packaging agreements were forbidden. Thus, the Commission considered that a limitation of competition was desirable in regard of the public interest.

The basing point system

The basing point system has been, and still is, the focus of intense economic debates, that, particularly in the US, have involved the most talented economists. Proceedings have lasted for over fifteen years, have seen numerous developments, and have resulted in fairly contrasting decisions. In the UK, the basing point system was examined under a different procedure to that of a purely competitive assessment, but involved decisions of a similar importance to those made in the US. It is particularly interesting to follow the circumstances that led to the different decisions that have been made, and to draw lessons from their comparison.

Antitrust policy and the basing point system in the US

The aim is not to go too deeply into the details of the US case. For further information, the reader can refer to the remarkable and masterful book of Samuel Loescher (1959). Here, we simply outline the main elements of the antitrust debate.

The emergence of the basing point system in the US cement industry at the turn of the century has already been discussed. The main cement producers were concentrated in in a particular region, the Lehigh Valley. They set their price at any delivery location point on the basis of their mill price and the costs of transportation calculated on the basis of the rail freight price list. The first cement plants that settled outside the natural regional markets of the Lehigh Valley, near the Mississippi river, found it easier to align their price with the price for delivered cement quoted by the Lehigh Valley producers. As a result, they charged phantom freight to the buyers (see chapter 2).

This was probably the first issue that attracted the attention of the Federal Trade Commission.[4] From the outset, it was clear that the

---

4. It is common knowledge that the Federal Trade Commission and the Department of Justice are in competition with regard to antitrust cases. They divide their workload on agreement, but can sometimes act independently. In

Commission did not view this business practice favourably. Besides, complaints were mounting from customers located in the neighbourhood of the Mississippi river plants. The buyers were not prepared to pay the high prices charged by the remote Lehigh Valley cement plants when they were asking for delivery in close proximity to the plants.

In addition, a cement plant might accidentally cease to be a base point, adding confusion to fair pricing. For instance, assume that a plant is in competition with two other plants. It increases its base mill price while the other two plants, independently from each other, lower their prices when negotiating with their customers. The new base mill price of the first plant could be so high that it will be disregarded. Customers might think that the price quoted by the first plant includes a large amount of phantom freight, while in fact the cement plant is simply not in line with the market price.

Moreover, the decision to become a base point, and to make public a base mill price, is strategic with regard to competing beyond a market umbrella. Over time, many cement plants have shifted from being price takers to being base points. So, at one particular time, a cement plant may be a base point, while at another time it is not, according to the competitive pressure (Clark, 1938). In fact, many changes have occurred with regard to opportunities of getting an important order. If a large volume of cement was to be ordered close to a plant, the latter would temporarily declare itself a base point. Once the order had been secured, and the cement delivered, the plant would return to its previous status as price taker.

Whatever the situation, it was known that the FTC felt strongly about the phantom freight practice. This may explain why between 1937 and 1940, most US cement plants decided to be base points.

Other serious issues worried the Commission. They surfaced between 1929 and 1933. In the 20s, the US economy had been booming. Growth in demand was so high that bottlenecks formed in the delivery of cement by rail. Trucking came into general use as a transportation substitute. Plants invested huge amounts of money in production capacity. However, the 1929 crash brought this whole process to an end. The industry faced considerable production over capacity. The rate of capacity utilisation plummeted to a record low of 30 per cent between 1932 and 1935. The

---

the cement case the appropriate jurisdiction was the FTC. However the DoJ stayed behind the scenes, prepared to take action, if the FTC were over-ruled by the Supreme Court.

situation in trucking was similar, and carriers began offering increasing discounts. A chaotic market emerged.

In mid-1931, attempts to stabilise competition materialised. In July 1931, and then later in January 1932, representatives of the Cement industry and of the railways companies met at the Cement Institute. On the 17, 18, and 19 November 1931, the producers of the Chicago region gathered to analyse the market situation. They all agreed to eliminate uncontrolled trucking (trucking had been left uncontrolled since the 1st December). By August 1932, most trucking was controlled.

In addition to this, in 1931 and 1932, punitive action had been taken under the basing point system against recalcitrant producers. By August 1932, it seemed that the market had been normalised. Although demand was still at its lowest, and the market particularly depressed, Lehigh Cement, which was considered the leading producer in many parts of the territory, increased its base mill prices at all plants other than in Cleveland. Prices in Cleveland were increased six months later. By July 1933, the price increases had disseminated, and prices levelled off until the second world war.

However, at the same time, a further issue had arisen: the Roosevelt administration had launched the New Deal. The aim was to restore growth, and the plan relied on infrastructure investment to stimulate the economy. New roads were built, and the Federal government, State administrations, and local councils placed cement orders. This created temporary new cement markets that were frequently situated outside of the main urban centres, distant from the plant locations. In order to reduce costs, and to get large volume discounts, the administrations did not place orders with wholesalers, or negotiate directly with producers. Instead they used public procurement procedures. Tenders were submitted in sealed orders, and, strikingly, the prices put forward by producers were identical, as far as the decimal points, reflecting the use of the basing point system formula. For distant locations, where no market existed, producers used a more advanced formula. In 1933, the governor of Illinois tried a different approach. He publicly announced the need for 3.3 million barrels of cement in the coming year, and asked the cement producers to submit written offers specifying an f.o.b. mill price. It turned out that no submissions were sent to his office. Later, when the depression had worsened, and state orders of cement were at their highest (with, for example, the construction plan of the Tennessee Valley Authority), the same problem arose.

A priori, as prices were determined according to the basing point formula, there was no need for explicit collusion, although, as noted earlier, a few meetings had been arranged. Besides, it was common knowledge that there were phone calls between producers from time to time. To the antitrust authorities, it was unrealistic that all cement producers would have be able to quote equal prices under a sealed envelope procedure unless there had been dialogue.

By 1931, the Senate had already asked the Chairman of the FTC to examine the competitive situation in the cement industry. The FTC reported to the Senate in March 1932 (US FTC, 1932). His main finding was that the basing point system introduced stickiness into the price system and reduced competition. In the meantime, complaints had been flooding in from State administrations and the federal government. Governor Horner of Illinois played a key role in the dispute, opposing the basing point system. In July 1937, a formal inquiry was established. Four years later, in 1941, the FTC staff presented the results of the inquiry, and outlined the anti-competitive effects of the basing point system.

Systematic price and freight discrimination that had the effect of equalising the delivered price of all producers was under attack. On 17 July 1943, the FTC issued an order to "cease and desist". However, the order was equivocal. The use of a delivered price and freight absorption was not in itself condemned. In the appeal, the Circuit Court, reacted strongly. It considered that the Commission had not been decisive enough about what it wanted to prohibit. (*Aetna Portland Cement Co. v. FTC,* 157 F 2d 533, p. 561 (7th Cir. 1946)). As a result, the FTC had to clarify its position. It did so in a brief to the Supreme Court, which explained that it did not oppose the basing point system as such, including the delivered price and freight absorption, with the latter being the only means for a producer to compete in the natural market of one of his competitors. What was questionable was not the use of the basing point system by a single producer in order to compete with other producers, but rather the management of the system by the entire industry. It was the collective management of the basing point system that had enabled the firms to produce a perfect equalisation of prices under the sealed order procedure. In his testimony, Charles Weston added: *'It is curious that the market price at all destinations is exactly the price which the formula produces. What we rely on more than the identity in price in particular markets, is that it is made in the same way in all markets, with certain specified variations.'* (*FTC v. Cement Institute,* 333 US 683 (1948): 260). The Supreme Court finally endorsed this view by six votes to three.

Behind the scenes, and at the heart of the legal dispute, had been a spectacular battle between economists. In 1934, the board of the Cement Institute appointed J.M. Clark as its economic expert, and he remained in that position for four years. He first gave a synthesised account of his views in 1938 at the very start of the litigation process, and years later, in 1949, he issued a comment on the Court ruling, but his main contribution was to write a seminal article, one of the most prominent papers in economics, on the concept of "workable competition". Confronting him were FTC economists, who were heavily influenced by the work of Frank A. Fetter, a professor of economics at Princeton University, who also gave his own assessment of the Court decision.

J.M. Clark probably put the issues more clearly. Firstly, the cement industry has specific economic characteristics such that it cannot fit the perfect competition regime described and analysed in economics textbooks. Secondly, it is salient that the basing point system does not provide the industry with monopoly power. Were they competitive alternatives (not theoretical alternatives, but real business practices, i.e., systematic freight absorption versus non systematic freight absorption, uniform discount prices versus non uniform discount prices, f.o.b. prices versus delivered prices)? What would be the economic impact of the different alternatives on competition, given that under adverse economic circumstances the industry can topple over towards a chaotic market (with non-uniform discount generalising, prices go down with no certainty about where the fall in price will stop, or if it will stop at a satisfactory market equilibrium, that is to say an economically correct price)?

The economists studied the various pricing alternatives.

The first issue to arise concerned f.o.b. mill pricing, where the cement plant announces a base mill price, and customers manage their own transportation from the plant. As there is no freight absorption, each plant dominates its geographical market. The size of the natural market of a plant hinges on its competitive aggressiveness when setting its base mill price. If a plant seeks to extend or reduce its geographical market, it can simply modify its base mill price. A buyer in an urban market that is situated on the boundary of several cement plants markets will be indifferent between them, with the delivered cement price (i.e., f.o.b. mill price plus transportation costs) identical whichever plant is chosen. The interest in a f.o.b. pricing regime comes from the fact that price discrimination and cross-hauling[5] are removed,[6] as are all artificial sales outlays that have a social welfare cost. But long before more recent developments in game theory (notably the modelling of competition using repeated games with learning experience processes), it was understood that if a market was transparent (in other words, that secret rebates would be immediately known by all market participants), market stabilisation would occur under such a system, and be stronger than under a basing point system regime.[7] A few scholars of Fetter, from the FTC staff, argued in favour of the f.o.b. mill price regime. Fetter himself argued that the Court ruling was promoting it.

J.M. Clark argued that a multi-basing point system based on the use of railways transportation price schedules, but allowing the customer to pick-up cement from the plant was the optimal solution.

The resulting Court ruling prohibited all collective arrangements that would support a rigid implementation of the basing point system: attempts to get rid of customer pick-up and trucking; the refusal to sell directly to contractors (a way of maintaining the dominance of traditional sales distribution channels consisting of dealers and wholesalers, and a way of avoiding direct price competition); systematic freight absorption from the automatic use of the basing point formula; the exchange of information between producers. But, the Court authorised the basing point system when managed on an individual basis and required the producers to agree to sell at the mill. It allowed the producer to charge non-systematic and significant freight absorption if aimed at competing with other producers.

---

5. Paradoxically, the FTC has an aversion to cross-hauling, although this can indicate competition among producers. The explanation of such an attitude is probably to be found in the fact that the collective management of the basing point system, which the FTC opposed, resulted in both price rigidity and cross-hauling. Consumers did not benefit from the advantages of price competition, but a drawback of price competition, the waste of transportation due to cross hauling, was still present.

6. It has to be pointed out that the basing point system has been referred to the Courts under the FTC Act as "unfair method of competition" and in addition at that time, under section 2 of the Robinson Patman Act which prohibited discriminatory practices. The issue of price discrimination raised by the basing point system was therefore the main focus of the investigation. The uniform f.o.b pricing is the only pricing method that excludes discrimination.

7. Using game theory tools, Thisse and Vives (1988), reach a similar conclusion. Uniform f.o.b. pricing can be less competitive than systematic price discrimination. This is because uniform f.o.b. pricing provides the producer with fewer possibilities of retaliation than does a price discrimination situation.

Indeed too small or too important freight absorption would have meant little competition.[8]

Years later, in the 1970s, the antitrust case referred to as the Oklahoma case confirmed the FTC and Supreme Court analyses. In a period of low demand, three cement producers controlled three quarters of the regional market and competed on a similar basis to their predecessors in the 30s:

'(a) *exchanging, collecting and compiling information concerning prices, and terms of conditions of sale of Portland cement;*

(b) *establishing and maintaining a system of pricing for Portland cement resulting in respondents quoting and charging identical delivered prices to each destination point;*

(c) *refusing to allow customers to pick up Portland cement at the site of manufacture or at a terminal site;*

(d) *refusing to allow customers to arrange for the transportation of Portland cement from the site of manufacture or a terminal site by a licensed hauler of a customer's choice;*

(e) *refusing to permit the use of any hauler, other than their designated hauler, to transport Portland cement manufactured by respondents from manufacture or terminal site; and*

(f) *controlling and attempting to control the point of use of Portland cement sold to customers.'* (USFTC,1976: 991-992).

These business practices had various economic impacts, among them to:

'(a) *stabilise prices and provide certainty in the pricing of Portland cement;*

(b) *stabilise prices and provide certainty in the bidding for sale of Portland cement for use on public projects;*

(c) *reduce and hinder actual and potential competition among respondents in the sale and distribution of Portland cement;*

(d) *prevent use of the cheapest and most efficient mode of transportation of Portland cement; and*

---

8. The DoJ had, in the very early stages of the case, endorsed a similar view. In its opinion, the two key factors that would enable competition in the cement industry were: the authorisation of customer pick-up, which would prevent trucking from being controlled, and non-systematic price discrimination with freight absorption.

(e) artificially raise the price paid by consumers, public and governmental bodies, and other customers for Portland cement.' (idem, p. 992).

Consequently, they were condemned.

'*It is ordered that the respondents:*
Shall [...] where a delivered price is offered to a customer from a mill or distribution point, also allow that customer the option of obtaining a point of origin price at that mill or distribution point and arranging or furnishing transportation from that mill or distribution point for the purchase of Portland cement in quantities of at least a truckload in bulk cement vehicles [...] when the customer furnishes or arranges transportation physically compatible with respondent's facilities and complies with reasonable loading schedules and loading procedures of respondent.
(2) shall not exchange with its competitors information concerning prices, discount rates and other terms and conditions pertinent to the sale of Portland cement, except in connection with a bona fide sale to, or purchase from, any such competitor or in connection with negotiations related thereto.
(3) Shall not control or attempt to control the place of use of Portland cement which has been sold to a customer, provided that, nothing contained herein shall affect respondent's right to obtain contractual assurances necessary to comply with the Robinson-Patman Act.' (idem, p. 994).

However the FTC was cautious about how their order could be interpreted:

'*It is further ordered, That, consistent with the definitions contained in Part I of this order, nothing contained in this order shall be interpreted as prohibiting the respondent, when acting individually, (1) from exercising its right to establish the price at which and to select the customers to which it shall sell; (2) from selling at a point of origin or delivered price established in good faith to meet equally low price of a competitor; (3) from absorbing all of any part of actual freight charges on shipment to any geographic area; or (4) from charging the same price to all customers within an established geographic area. No pricing*

*practice engaged in by respondent shall be deemed immune or
exempt from the antitrust laws by reason of anything contained in
this paragraph.'* (idem, pp. 994-995).

In the FTC ruling, the extreme difficulty in reaching a clearcut conclusion
about what should be authorised and prohibited is blatant. It can be noted
that the position of the US antitrust authorities has not altered over time.
Since the Supreme Court decision, the basing point system as such has not
been prohibited, but the collective management of the market and
excessive price rigidity has. The DoJ has continued to promote customer
pick-up at the factory gate, or at a distribution terminal, either with their
own trucks, or contracted out to independent carriers.[9] Does this mean that
the antitrust authorities' ruling has been implemented in practice? J.M.
Clark has made the following thoughtful, but disenchanted, remark: *'So
the method remains a hybrid, of the baffling sort in which years are spent
arguing everything about the case except the effects (legal and economic)
of the order that will finally be issued.'* (Clark, 1949: 431).

The basing point system and the UK competition policy authorities

Concern over the basing point system arose in a very different context in
the UK. The UK competition policy authorities, in this case, the
Restrictive Trade Practices Court, based their ruling on the imprecise
public interest criterion (Dumez and Jeunemaître, 1991; 1993). In addition
to issues relating to competition, the public interest criterion also includes
issues of welfare, national sovereignty, unemployment, and regional and
environmental policy.

The UK cement producers implemented the basing point system, in an
overt manner, soon after the economic crisis of the 30s. Prices had fallen
severely, cross-hauling had become widespread, and several cement
producers had gone bust. The industry was weak and drained. The
producers had in mind the period when trucking and river shipments had

---

9.   To be fair, it must be said that customer pick-up is technically difficult to
     manage for cement plants, limiting its expansion. Economists also argue that in
     industries where spatial competition is of paramount importance, the risk of
     perfect or imperfect collusion is high. In that context, the means of
     transportation (road, railways, ships) and their independent management are
     key factors in the avoidance of collusion (Owen, 1991).

enabled them to sell cement in London that was produced in South Wales while at the same time cement produced in South Wales was sold in the London market. In 1934, the Cement Makers Association which was set up in 1918, secured a deal with the producers based upon the use of the basing point system. The "scheme" delineated sale conditions, and involved a written agreement referred to as "the white book". It was clearly stipulated that the agreement was not legally binding, and that no fine, or sanction of any kind, could be enforced in the case of a defection. A producer could withdraw from the scheme once it had informed the trade association.

The agreement included detailed price lists according to regional markets. '*There are eleven price schedules, nine for different districts in England and Wales, one for Scotland, and one for Northern Ireland. These schedules specify the delivered prices of Portland cement to current British standard specification at the different places in the district.*' (RTP Court, 1961: 249). In England and Wales, each cement plant, or group of plants close to each other, was declared a base point within a five mile radius territory around the plant. If a customer picked up cement at the plant gate, they would gets a rebate (of 2 shillings per ton if in sacks, 3 shillings per ton in bulk). When the cement plant made the delivery, they charged a delivered price that increased according to a system of circular lines that were drawn around the plant, or group of plants, at a five mile radius, and for each subsequent five mile: transport up to 30 mile from the plant was charged at 2 cents per ton per five mile; above 30 mile, the charge was 1 cent per ton per five mile. The circular lines stopped each time they crossed the line of a competitor. Thus the whole country was covered by circular price lines. In Cornwall and North Devon, where there were no cement plants in operation, the circular price lines were drawn based at harbours, and along roads going away from the harbours. However, for various reasons, the base mill prices of plants were not equal.[10]

This system came into operation in 1934. At that time, cement producers were mainly concentrated in the Thames Valley, and many harbours were base points. Over time, more inland cement plants were set, and harbours ceased to be base points (except, as already noted, in Cornwall and North Devon). In the first year of the system, prices were

---

10. In fact, and the Court did not mention this in its judgement, base mill prices did not vary significantly (more or less than 3 per cent) for 90 per cent of industry capacity. They were fixed independently from production costs.

fixed with reference to the level they had reached during the price wars. Between 1934 and 1947, the trade association decided to bring in several price increases. However, from 1939, they had to get ministerial approval for such increases. This price control ceased in 1951. In 1947, the Board of Trade set up the Forde Committee to investigate the scheme. The Committee found the scheme to be *'not unreasonable,'* but made proposals to improve its management. An "Independent Cost Committee", made up of a Chairman, and an accounting expert, was set up. This was to keep an eye on the cost and profit fluctuations in quarterly data submitted by the cement producers. *'The weighted average costs and results for the whole industry (but not those of any individual manufacturer) for the quarter and for the preceding twelve months are then circulated to all members.'* (idem, p. 252). If the Committee, which could only make recommendations, deemed a price change necessary (either an increase or a decrease) in order to keep profits at a reasonable level, they met with the trade association, which then voted on the recommendation.

In addition to these quarterly meetings where price levels were discussed, the Independent Cost Committee also reviewed the setting up of new cement plants, and their base mill prices. They applied the following simple, but key, principle: *'The "base" price of a new works must not exceed the current price, based on a "distance zone" from some existing works, at the place where the new works is erected.'* (idem, p. 253). Given this, producers had to consider the circumstances in which their initial investment would give them a decent rate of return. An examination of production costs (costs of raw materials and energy consumption), the depreciation of an initial investment, and the size of the geographical market of a new plant were part of this analysis.

A final responsibility of the Independent Cost Committee involved reviewing base mill prices, and the distance-based zone increments. There were price reviews in 1949, 1951 and 1957. The 1949 review had been carried out during the time when administrative approval was required before price increases could be introduced. The chairman of the Committee was poised to launch a new review in 1960, when the basing point system was referred to the RTP Court. None of the previous reviews had recommended radical changes to the scheme. However, changes had occurred in relation to the price differential between the increment for transportation to distant zones, basing point prices, and pick-up rebates. Distant customers benefited from these changes, with the scheme run such that the nearest customers subsidised more distant ones.

In 1956, the Restrictive Trade Practices Act became law, and the RTP Court was set up, with responsibility for vetting anti-competitive agreements referred to it by the Registrar. The Registrar soon dealt with the basing point system, that is to say the various agreements between the producers known as "the scheme".

The cement industry argued their case, emphasising that the scheme provided customers with lower prices than would be the case under a competitive regime. They reminded the Court that the cement industry is a capital intensive industry, with high transportation costs, and high investments risk. It was argued that the scheme allowed producers to maintain a low but certain profitability, and that the excessive profits that could be sustained under competition were avoided. The cost of capital was, therefore, lowered. In addition as the scheme organised competition it enabled the producers to coordinate their capacity investments and to adjust with more certainty to the demand prospects. So, inappropriate investment decisions were said to be less frequent, and not financially supported by customers. Moreover the scheme was said to discourage the distant deliveries, and did away with cross-hauling. Thus, transportation costs were also reduced. It was argued that these cost savings were not taken in higher profits, but were passed on to customers through the Independent Committee procedure. The economic facts supported this view. The UK cement price was among the lowest in industrialised countries, and industry profitability was only average. Whilst the scheme introduced cross-subsidisation to the advantage of buyers in more distant markets such as Scotland, competition would also result in higher prices being set for customers in the neighbourhood of cement plants. Other gains from the scheme were substantial. Customers avoided the cost and trouble of "shopping", and the market power of the largest producer was restricted. Trade association decisions required the agreement of at least four producers before being approved. The largest cement producer, APCM[11] had a 62 per cent market share, whilst the second largest, Tunnel, had a market share of only 12 per cent. However, APCM only had 36 per cent of the voting rights and therefore could not veto a decision on its own. The Cement Makers' Federation sent questionnaires to a sample of 4022 customers. The findings were impressive. 98 per cent replied that deliveries were efficient and quick, 99.5 per cent stressed high quality, 99.68 per cent good service, 97 per cent reasonable prices, and 87 per cent declared that they would like the scheme to continue.

---

11. Associated Portland Cement Manufacturers.

The Registrar was the prosecutor.

With regard to prices, the Registrar firstly noted that the scheme introduced artificial pricing. Cement prices were not directly related to cost at delivery locations. In general, the trade association argued that prices were lower than they would be if competition prevailed. But, no organisation was able to know in advance what the market price would be if the scheme were removed. What they did know, was that there was a distortion to competition. In particular, the nearest customers were subsidising distant ones. The consequence of this was that it deterred producers from setting up cement plants in locations where there was none at that time. The cement producers argued that profitability was only average, and that this was the result of reasonable pricing. But the picture was quite different from this. For one thing, there was no certainty about the figures. For example, profits were calculated after deducting depreciation charges that were particularly high given the replacement cost of any plant. However, even if the figures were taken for granted, it was noticeable that the smallest cement plants made high profits, as they primarily delivered to nearby customers, while the largest plant had lower profitability, as they delivered to distant customers.

In summary, the Registrar argued three points: 1. The scheme dissuaded customers from picking their cement up from the plant, and, as a result, there was market capture of the closest customers; 2. The scheme gave no incentives for cement plants to compete outside their local markets. There was no room for competition; 3. In subsidising distant customers, the scheme discouraged new investment and potentially more effective new entrants, while at the same time, it didn't encourage the removal of obsolete capacity; 4. Buyers had no bargaining power (rebates were moderate for large customers).

In its final assessment, the Court concluded that the scheme had had some positive effects. It had suppressed cross-hauling, which they considered to be uneconomic. It provided producers with an incentive to build plants close to the largest cement markets. They also held that the Registrar had not sufficiently demonstrated the negative economic impacts that had been identified. Profits were not that high in the industry, and supply seemed to have have conformed with demand. They argued that if new cement plants were to be set up in distant locations, production over-capacity could ensue, the rate of capacity utilisation would tumble, and a solution to the resulting problems would have to be worked out. Also, they argued that in a competitive regime, producers run a greater risk, and need a higher return on investment, than allowed by the scheme (the Court put forward a 10 per cent rate of return under the scheme against a 15 per cent to 20 per cent rate of return under a competitive regime).

As a result, the basing point system was found "not contrary to the public interest".

Various aspects of the court proceedings illustrate how the decision was reached. The Court was most impressed -remember that it is a British court- by the testimony of Sir Malcom Eve,[12] the Chairman of the Independent Cost Committee. The cement producers flooded the Court with documentation and economic studies at the beginning of the hearings rather than a month before, when they should have been submitted. While the case did not initiate an economic debate on a comparable scale to that in the US, the RTP Court ruling did interest British academics.

Their assessment focused on the notion of risk. It was considered that in a competitive market, producers would run substantially higher risks with regard to their return on investment. As a result, it was considered that producers would only invest if their return on investment could be substantial. Therefore, it was assumed that in a competitive market, prices would be higher. As this opinion had been argued in a very general way, it raised the fundamental question: does this vindicate any cartel? *'Since security and avoidance of the strains and stresses of a competitive life is an important motive in cartel formation,* noted A. Beecham[13] (1962: 342), *cartels may frequently be making only moderate profits.'* In the UK basing point system case, a specific claim had been made that strengthened this general belief: the scheme had been able to reduce costs in the industry, and particularly transportation costs.

J.B. Heath (1963) and J.R. Gould (1963) pinpointed the inconsistencies in the rationale of the Court. What would the additional risk be that a producer would face if competition was to prevail? At first, they would run the risk of price cutting to gain market shares. But then how did this relate to the Court's presumption that the price in a competitive market would be higher than under the scheme? Another risk that the producer would run, came from the imbalances between supply

---

12. In its inimitable British style, the Court declared: *'Having had the advantage of hearing the evidence not only of Sir Malcolm Eve and Mr Slimmings [the independent accountant] but also of responsible representatives of each of the makers we feel justified in thinking that they will continue to operate the price agreement with the same sense of responsibility and restraint as they have done up to now,'* (Beecham, 1962: 341).

13. A. Beacham, professor at the University College of Wales (Aberystwyth), testified with regard to the Registrar.

and demand. But there again, this contradicted the position of the Court, which argued that demand and supply would be in line in the years to come.

J.B. Heath rightly noted that some key questions had not been put forward at the hearings: what would the market conditions be under a competitive regime? What strategies would producers adopt if the scheme was brought to an end? How would they manage their investment risk? It was probably the elimination of cross-hauling, which seemed intolerable to many, that had been the key point in the decision of the Court.

Vertical integration

In 1959, the US economic situation started to deteriorate. Permanente Cement Company took over Pacific Building Materials Company of Portland, an Oregon concrete producer. It signalled the beginning of the 1960s wave of vertical integration which occurred in the cement industry. The FTC blocked this deal and others. But flooded by the number of cases, it requested the bureau of economics to report on vertical integration (USFTC, 1966a). Following the report, the Commission organised public hearings, and invited cement producers and concrete companies to give comments (*RP*, Stearn, August 1966). The outcome of this, based on recent antitrust investigations and the findings from the economic report and the hearings, was that, in January 1967, the FTC issued a "statement of general policy enforcement" prohibiting cement producers from taking over the concrete industry.

The economic report was based on a large amount of data and information, with the final part putting forward a set of arguments against vertical integration. In particular, the FTC economists argued that the vertical integration wave was aimed at foreclosing the market, and was detrimental to competition. There would no longer be independent buyers of cement in the concrete industry, and as a result there would be less competition. They also argued that vertical integration would raise barriers to entry. Before the development of vertical integration, entry could occur independently at the upstream (cement) or the downstream (concrete) level. Once vertical integration had been achieved, potential entrants would have to enter the market at both levels at the same time.

The data and information used in the report were not discussed. They simply fed the economic debate, and little in the way of additional facts or new evidence came to the fore. However, the findings of the FTC were severely criticised and challenged. To give a fair account of the debate, it is probably easier to begin with the points that were not the subject of discussion.

Firstly, there was no record providing economic evidence that vertical integration between cement and concrete companies produced economic gains. The only point that had been investigated by the FTC was its effect on the quality of concrete. Cement producers had qualified technical teams that concrete companies could not afford. As a result, the technical assistance of a cement producer could help a concrete producer gain greater control over the quality of his product. But one could question whether vertical integration was necessary for this. A cement producer could always provide his concrete buying customers with technical assistance of this kind, in order to keep them as regular customers.

Secondly, a priori, the concrete industry did not seem a particularly interesting industry to diversify into. There was little economic value to be added from merging the two activities, and their profitability was, on average, equal. Moreover, the interest of cement producers in diversifying is to reduce their financial exposure. In order to do this, they could invest in an economic activity where profitability does not depend upon construction business cycles, as it does for both cement and concrete producers. Economic crises in the construction industry reverberate in both the concrete and cement industries. Thus, conglomerates, such as Martin Marietta, that had important interests in cement, also had holdings in the aircraft and arms industries.

Thirdly, the motives for vertical integration are diverse and complex. Clearly, some cement producers integrate vertically to fend off attacks from competitors. When Atlantic Cement set up a new distribution terminal at Norfolk, Lone Star reacted by taking over the number one Ready Mix Concrete company in that market, South Materials. Later, Atlantic Cement had to shut down its Brooklyn distribution terminal in New York after Colonial Sand and Stone and Marquette had taken over the main RMC companies in New York. In the same way, cement producers that intended to enter new markets frequently did so by taking control of the local concrete producers (for example, between 1962 and 1965, Mississippi River bought RMC companies in Saint Louis, Memphis, Kansas City, and Cincinnati, before its Festus cement plant became operational in 1965). Thus vertical integration has been used as a weapon both to defend and to conquer a market. Another feature had been concrete companies setting up or taking over cement producers, vertical integration, in this case, going from the downstream to the upstream level.

Fourthly, and this point was underlined in chapter 2, market foreclosure is always imperfect and incomplete. Integrated concrete companies continued to buy from suppliers other than their parent company, even if this was only on a small scale. Also, concrete firms were disseminated and numerous. Even if the biggest ones were taken over, independent concrete producers would remain in the market place.

Given these general observations, it is not easy to give a clear-cut rationale for vertical integration in the cement industry, and it is particularly difficult to give a convincing and decisive assessment of its economic effects. The FTC emphasised that downstream vertical integration was aimed, above all, at creating captive and foreclosed markets, and stressed its potentially anti-competitive effects. Many economists were sceptical of this position. Peck[14] and McGowan[15] attempted to prove that market foreclosure was not anti-competitive. Liebeler (1968) went further than this, by seeking to demonstrate that it was actually pro-competitive. Years later, in a retrospective study, Allen (1971)[16] compared profitability in the cement industry before and after vertical integration. His main finding was that there was no significant difference. Vertical integration did not seem to lead to improved profitability compared with firms that stayed separated.

Ex post, the most likely explanation was given by McBride (1983),[17] following a similar line of thought to Liebeler's work. Profitability in the cement industry is directly related to the rate of capacity utilisation. It has been stated that when demand falls, producers are likely to lower their price in an attempt to increase sales and improve their capacity utilisation. As demand is inelastic to price, such a strategic move was said to be detrimental to competitors. As a result, competitors retaliate, and the market deteriorates. But vertical integration provides an alternative to this. The cement producer that is first to integrate vertically, can pass some of his production over-capacity on to other producers. Market production over-capacity does not change. It is simply that the first producer to be integrated has a captive share of the market, and can increase its rate of capacity utilisation to the detriment of other local producers. It is difficult for competitors to react instantly to such behaviour, as they need to find

---

14. Merton J. Peck, Professor at Yale University, testified at the FTC hearings in Summer 1966, as economic adviser for Lehigh Cement.
15. Criticised by Wilk..
16. The work of Allen has been reviewed and criticised by Meehan (1972). Allen replied in a comment to the review (1972).
17. McBride's paper has been criticised by Johnson and Parkman (1987).

other concrete firms that they can take over. *'The longer response lag and the possibly limited number of desirable candidates for acquisition mean that the first firm to integrate can prevent its rivals with a fait accompli.'* (McBride, 1983: 1018). In other words, vertical integration can be seen as a form of "non price" aggressive competition. It is all the more appealing because there is a first-mover advantage. However, the strategy can only provide a temporary respite for the market, as, sooner or later, price cutting cannot be avoided. Therefore, vertical integration can be viewed as an aggressive move, but one which can only provide a stopgap, given an imminent U-turn in the business cycle. The statistical analysis of McBride confirmed this interpretation.[18] For vertical integration, the first mover advantage consisted of gaining what John E.D. Grunow, the then Atlantic Cement chairman, refered to as "a plum", a large and well equipped concrete company, owning aggregates quarried close to the main urban markets (*RP*, Utley, December, 1965: 122). Competitors can, of course, sell to competing concrete companies, but they will usually be smaller, scattered and not as well situated. As a result, competing cement producers will face greater delivery costs.

The other important point about vertical integration is that the process is a cumulative one. When there is both potential for a significant first mover advantage, and market uncertainty about the strategic moves of the competitors, mimetic behaviour is observed among members of the industry (Dumez and Jeunemaître, 1996). Each producer is convinced that his competitors will adopt a similar strategy to that of the first mover, and, as a result, that they are under pressure to acquire the best companies before their competitors. Thus, the structure of the market changes over a short time. In the US in the 1960s, cement producers who had thought that vertical integration with concrete firms was not profitable, were caught up in this process, and left with no choice but to mimic their competitors. For instance, in its 1962 annual report, Marquette Cement Manufacturing Company announced that it saw no advantage in integrating vertically into the concrete businesses. One year later, it declared that it would vertically integrate into the concrete businesses in retaliation to competitive attacks. In 1964, under threat of cheap cement imports and new entry (Atlantic Cement), Marquette acquired three RMC companies in the New York regional market. Similarly, in 1965, Lehigh Cement bought an RMC

---

18. Part of Johnson and Parkman criticism included flaws in the statistical analysis, see Johnson and Parkman (1987)

company which was one of its regular customers after a competitor had made an offer for it (Allen, 1971: 267-268).

As a result, at the time of the FTC hearings in Summer 1966, a significant part of the industry urged the FTC to halt the vertical integration wave. Many cement producers were not interested in taking over concrete businesses, but claimed that they would be forced to do so if vertical integration was left unrestrained. The two leading figures at the time of the hearings were W.J. Conway, the executive Vice President of Ideal, and Raymond S. Chase, marketing Vice President of Dundee.

Conway declared that he was delighted to comply with the FTC order to desist and which forced him to divest his concrete subsidiary, Builders, in Houston. Builders had been a regular customer for twenty years, but had been on the verge of being taken over by one of Ideal's competitors, when they had decided to acquire it. When asked about what he was expecting from the FTC, he replied that it should: *'Deal with a heavy hand! Put cases to bed in a hurry!'* (*RP,* Stearn, August 1966: 68). For his part, Chase explained how the Memphis market had been foreclosed because of the vertical integration process that his competitors had engaged in.

However, in practice, it was actually established that a cement producer would be able to foreclose a market by buying customers, or by making use of predatory pricing before increasing prices after market power was achieved?

Surprisingly few empirical studies have been carried out on these issues.[19] One case study, based on a private antitrust litigation, relates to the concrete market in Memphis (Kamerschen, 1974). The legal proceedings, once again, enabled facts to come to light that otherwise would have remained unknown.

The findings are penetrating. The local market was relatively concentrated. In the Memphis area, three firms accounted for 85.3 per cent of the market in 1965, and 58.5 per cent in 1970. However, the main and best located firms did not control entry and exit into the market, both of which could occur at low cost. When prices went down, the smallest concrete firms practiced "mothballing", stopping production until prices went up again. This activity required only little investment, that mainly covered trucks. The owners of aggregate quarries would simply enter the

---

19. Listing previous papers, McBride notes: *'These authors present different views on the motivation for the vertical acquisitions. Statistical evidence in support of their views is minimal or non-existent.'* (McBride, 1983: 1012, footnote 2).

market when profitability was satisfactory. The market also included mobile producers, that had a market share of 10 per cent. These were small fleets that settled indifferently in one market or another. The accusation was that Mississippi River Cement, a cement producer that was active in the Memphis concrete market through its subsidiary, Denies, was practising predatory pricing. However, it appeared that during the alleged period of predatory pricing an independent entry had occurred in the market. The cement producers had soon circumvented the FTC prohibition on vertical integration. Instead of vertical integration, they made binding agreements with customers. For example, while the FTC ordered Texas Industries to divest its concrete subsidiary Fischer (January 1968), the cement producer Pen Dixie lent Cordova Sand and Gravel Co. Inc. $100000, free of interest, in order to buy a fleet of trucks (1967), and then a further $40000, again free of interest, to cover their cement purchases for the following two years. A competitor of Cordova, Allen Ready-Mix Concrete, received for its part interest free loans from Missouri Portland Cement Co and from Marquette Cement Co. (Kamerschen, 1974: 149- footnote 24 and 150 -footnote 28). The head of the FTC mergers task force, William J. Boyd, expressed his concern with regard to the surge of new vertical links in the industry at the annual conference of the *Sand and Gravel Association* and the *Ready Mix Association* held in Chicago on 28 January 1970. His speech was entitled: *'The decline of direct acquisition; the emergence of indirect leverage.'* The speech (as intended) produced a certain amount of agitation amongst the attendees (*RP*, Grancher, October 1971).

As a result, during the 60s, the FTC adopted a dynamic view of the industry. Their objective was to prevent the cement industry from absorbing the downstream market of concrete either by vertical integration or vertical ties, despite the fact that the economic argument for foreclosure assumption had not been convincingly proven.

But by a strange twist of fate, during the 1980s, when imports were flooding into the US market, the survival of a significant independent concrete industry was shown to be crucial in the regulation of competition in the cement industry. It was as if the FTC had been right, but for the wrong reasons.[20]

---

20. Although the FTC economists were right about the importance of the exercise of purchasing power by big concrete companies on cement producers

Exchange of information and "spontaneous" co-ordination

In an oligopolitic industry that produces a single homogeneous and undifferentiated product such as cement, the exchanges of information are frequent, intense and diverse. Can it be avoided? Does it have genuine anti-competitive effects?

Competition policy has been active in this area for a long time. In the 1920s, the US DoJ sued the cement producers for exchanging information, in particular transportation price lists, and confidential data from individual firms. Judge Knox endorsed the view of the DoJ before a District Court, and the case was taken before the Supreme Court. Three judges out of nine supported the DoJ, but were in minority. The Court upheld the testimony of the *'distinguished economists in support of the thesis that in the case of a standardised product sold wholesale to fully informed professional buyers as were the dealers in cement, uniformity of price will inevitably result from active, free and unrestrained competition.'* (*Cement Mfrs Protective Association v. US,* 268 US 588 (1925),[21] p. 605). The Court considered that, given the specific economic characteristics of the cement industry, the sharing of transportation price lists under the basing point system may well have lead to more rapid price quotations and promote competition. In other words, they argued that the fact that prices were perfectly equal at a given location could be due to either competition or collusion, and that it is up to the antitrust authorities to provide a clear demonstration that there is collusion and not simply exchanges of information.

However, it is probably the Arizona case that best illustrates the type of analysis that the antitrust authorities applied to the exchange of information.

On 15 August 1971, soon after having declared the floating exchange rate of the US dollar, the Nixon administration decided to freeze both prices and salaries (Dumez and Jeunemaître, 1988). The freeze occurred at a time when cement prices were at their lowest. As the price of a single homogeneous product in an oligopolistic industry is easier to control than those in more sophisticated industries, the cement industry had no escape, and the freeze was effective. On 27 November 1973, the price freeze ended. Unfortunately, the oil crisis had begun, prices were freed when the demand for cement was plummeting. At the beginning of 1974, cement

---

21. This is usually referred to as the "old cement decision".

prices increased slightly, probably because of the fear of a return to price controls. Between mid-1974 and 1975 prices increased sharply. But after a price freeze period, that they would usually make up for lost time (Dam and Schultz, 1977). In 1976, the local council of Phoenix invited tenders in sealed orders. The quoted prices were identical in all replies. As a result, the Arizona State administration decided to sue the cement producers. The investigation unveiled exchanges of information, contacts between competitors, and meetings that had enabled co-ordination (see chapter 2).

Lawyers for the defendants pleaded the harmlessness of such business practices. *'There's nothing wrong about a lot of guys making speeches about getting prices up. Of course, if everybody then gets together in the back room and agrees to charge higher prices, that's something else. But they can't prove that.'* However one lawyer for a defendant acknowledged the antitrust violation: *'There was a tacit understanding [...] we haven't found a smoke-filled room or a smoking gun [...]. These are very sophisticated businessmen. They didn't get out their cigars, put their feet on the table and say, "we're going to fix prices".'*

Thus, there had been exchanges of information that would have psychologically prepared producers (chapter 2 showed how a business game could serve a similar purpose) and enabled co-ordination, without explicit collusion or agreement, once the leading producer gave the signal. A dramatic example of this took place in Texas, and was outlined by Gus J. Chavalas, the President of Kaiser Cement, before the board of directors of the company on the 3rd December 1973:

'We found ourselves in this situation[22] in Texas where our mill nets started falling. We decided it was imperative to not only stop the downward trend, but more importantly, we wanted to turn it upward. The strategy we adopted was risky, but we felt strong action was necessary; otherwise, our prices would continue to slowly drop. Consequently, rather than just meet a $4.00 a ton price deviation that had been implemented in the market, we sent a letter to all customers stating three things:
First, we met the $4.00 a ton price cut.
Second, we further reduced our prices an additional $2.00 a ton for two months.

---

22. secret and unsystematic price cuts.

And Third, we announced a price increase of $10.00 a ton to be
effective in four months. Incidentally, we did not expect to get the
full $10.00, but we wanted to start high.
Our announcement went out in letter form to insure that our
position would be clear and not be eroded by any
misunderstandings by customers. After our announcement, price-
cutting activity began to slow down, and stabilised at our level. At
the end of the two month period our competition went up $2.00
and also announced subsequent $5.00 a ton increases consistent
with our date. We felt that we not only caused a bottoming-out of
price deterioration at that time in Texas, but more importantly, we
created an upward pricing atmosphere.' (US District Court of the
District of Arizona, 1983: A-57-58).

How did the antitrust authorities deal with the case?

The first important ruling came from Judge Manuel L. Real. As a
matter of fact, the Phoenix litigation case, initiated by the assistant general
attorney of the Arizona State, Kenneth R. Reed, led to other antitrust
cases. At the end of 1976, the State of California, the largest US State
cement consumer, sued the cement producers, and were soon followed by
Oregon, Nevada, Missouri and Florida. The judge decided that the
complaints had to be dealt with separately insofar as the relevant cement
markets were regional. The Phoenix trial was held on the 6 September
1984. The first general testimonies about the cement industry and
exchanges of information at the national level were video recorded, and
later used to lodge other antitrust complaints. However, each State
jurisdiction had to deal which the alleged antitrust infringements. It was
the first time that legal proceedings were video recorded, with Judge Real
getting authorisation from Chief Justice Warren, the President of the
Supreme Court. It remained to be proven that the exchanges of
information had anti-competitive local effects.

The prosecution did not succeed, and there were many settlements
made out of Court. However, those who decided not to compromise,
Kaiser Cement and the cement trade association, PCA, were able to get the
State of Arizona sentenced, forcing them to pay back the legal costs of ten
years proceedings (*RP*, Huhta, March 1986: 11).

Overall, the antitrust authorities have found it difficult to get the exchange of information sentenced.[23] This is mainly due to legal reasons. The exchange of information tends to have a general or individual content that is not clearly distinct from common knowledge in the public domain. Therefore, its is rarely direct evidence of anti-competitive behaviour, and the courts have adopted a cautious stance. Recent economic research supports this attitude. One of the most significant developments can be seen in the work of the economist Louis Phlips, the author of a major book on price discrimination (1983). Until recently he had argued very much in line with the German school thinking (Mestmäcker, 1952). That is, exchanges of information among the members of an oligopoly are reprehensible *per se*. More recently, however, he has considered that *'conscious parallelism - the matching of price changes announced in advance by competitors - can be modelled as a (perfect) non-co-operative behaviour that gives a precise meaning to the otherwise vague concept of tacit collusion.'* (Phlips, 1987: 96). In general, the passing of information can be compatible with non-collusive behaviour.

Horizontal mergers, multi-market rivalry and strategic alliances

In many countries even if they had not a developed antitrust policy, the authorities have traditionally attempted to limit market power and control concentration.

In their economic assessments, the US authorities have primarily focused on the effects of concentration in local markets. As far as possible, they have sought to maintain a number of independent competitors at the local level. For a long time, the FTC has applied a simple rule. In so far as a cement plant had a natural market within a radius of 150 mile, any acquisition by a competitor situated less than 300 mile from the plant was blocked. In line with this principle, the FTC forced Lehigh Cement, a US subsidiary of Heidelberger Zement, to sell its Hannibal cement plant (Missouri), and its three distribution terminals in Illinois, Iowa and Missouri, when acquiring Universal Atlas (a US Steel subsidiary) (*Lehigh Portland Cement Co. and al.*, 98 FTC 856, 30 October 1981).

---

23. See for example, the US Ethyl antitrust case (*E.I. Du Pont de Nemours and Co. v. FTC*, 729 F 2d 128 (1984)), and the recent nullification by the European Court of Justice of the EC decision concerning the sentencing of the woodpulp industry - Decision *A. Ahlström Osakeyhtio and others v. Commission*, on 31 March 1993.

However, the approach of the FTC shifted towards a more flexible approach with the 1982 guidelines of the DoJ. When Lafarge bought the Alpena cement plant from National Gypsum, an economic model was developed that reproduced the DoJ rationale. It showed that *'a small but significant and non-transitory increase in prices'* (this was the wording in the 14 June 1982 guidelines) would immediately attract competitors having access to the network of the Great Lakes, particularly as ship transportation was low cost. Consequently, the relevant geographical market was taken to be much larger than 150 mile and the acquisition was cleared.

As seen earlier, in Japan, in the 1980s, the Japanese Fair Trade Commission has also attempted to limit market power by opposing any merger that would have given a cement producer more than a 20 per cent share of the Japanese market and a 25 per cent of the Tokyo market.

But in the early 1990s, a number of important horizontal mergers occured: in 1991, Mitsubishi Materials acquired Tôhoku Kaihatsu; in 1993, Onoda merged with Chichibu; in 1994, Sumitomo merged with Osaka. It resulted in a significant increase in concentration at both national and local levels. For example, the Onoda-Chichibu group had a national market share in excess of 20 per cent, and, Sumitomo and Osaka a 30 per cent market share of the Kansai regional market (Osaka and Kyoto urban markets). Finally, at the end of 1997, Chichibu-Onoda and Nihon announced their intention to merge their activities in October 1998. The consolidated group would then have a 40 per cent domestic market share and be of comparable size to the world leader Holderbank. It remains to be seen if the Japanese FTC will give its go-ahead.

At any rate, antitrust authorities find themselves in a awkward situation. Their firm control on local concentration encourages the producers which seek expansion to invest and make acquisitions in multiple markets. This in turn, reinforces multi-market rivalry which may lead to an increase in market stabilisation. Therefore, competition policy may be an incentive to concentrate nationally with a multi-market rivalry dominance. The FTC has for long raised that issue:[24] '[...] *cement markets tend to be oligopolistically structured. In all regions for which data are available the patterns of concentration are sufficiently high so that each seller will tend to be acutely aware of the competitive strategies employ by*

---

24. In the court judgement, Beatrice Foods, on 26 April 1965, the FTC analysed the anti-competitive effects of a geographical market expansion: it made retaliation easier, and competition easier to stabilise.

competing sellers. In this context any action which shifts the allegiance of an important buyer or group of buyers is likely to influence noticeably the reaction of rivals. The cement industry is so structured that firms cannot establish policies without reference to the practices of specific competitors. Due to the multiplant, multi-market structure of leading firms in the cement industry, oligopolistic relations among firms may transcend individual markets and embrace many simultaneously' (USFTC, 1966a: 31).

However, although acknowledging the importance of the issue, the antitrust authorities of the different countries have not been able to put forward a proprer and suitable conceptual framework to deal with it. Undoubtedly, it is going to be an essential task in the years to come. It is probably one element of the EC competition policy which tends to promote the concept of joint oligopoly dominance (P. Williamson, 1994).

Finally, the strategic alliances between competitors are one of the headaches of the antitrust authorities. If the alliance is between a local competitor and a new entrant, it is generally cleared. The antitrust authorities gamble on the fact that this may be a first step before full independent entry into the market. Conversely, alliances between two competitors can provide a means of restricting competition and are generally treated with suspicion by the antitrust authorities.[25]

---

25. On antitrust issues raised by strategic alliances, see Kwoka and White (1989) on the General Motors/Toyota joint venture.

Appendix 1

CHRONOLOGY OF ANTITRUST CASES
IN THE CEMENT INDUSTRY

1932 (USA)	-	The FTC reported on the basing point system
1943 (USA)	-	The FTC released an order "to cease and desist" with regard to the basing point system
1948 (USA)	-	The Supreme Court confirmed the FTC ruling on the basing point system, *FTC v. Cement Institute,* 333 US 683 (1948)
1961 (UK)	-	The Retrictive Trade Practices Court legalised the basing point system which was found to be "not against the public interest"
1967 (USA)	-	The FTC issued a statement of general enforcement policy blocking vertical integration into the Ready Mix Concrete industry by the cement industry
1976 (USA)	-	The Arizona Case opened. The trial was held in Phoenix in September 1984
1981 (EC)	-	The Cement producers from Belgium and the Netherlands notified the European Commission of their plan to put a basing point system into place
1988 (Germany)	-	The Bundeskartellamt fined the German cement producers indicted for cartellisation
1991 (Japan)	-	The Japanese Fair Trade Commission fined Nihon Cement and Onoda Cement indicted for regional cartellisation (Hokkaido and Chugoku)
1993 (Switzerland)	-	Kartellkommission und Preisüberwacher decision on the Zement Swiss Kartel. Price agreements and market sharing are forbidden. Only transportation agreements are allowed in view of encouraging rail transportation which is deemed to be in the public interest
1994 (EC)	-	The European Commission fined 76 European cement producers for an infringement of Article 85 of the Treaty of Rome. The case is on appeal before the Court of First Instance

CHAPTER 5

Concluding comments

The local competitive regime is influenced by three key factors: the companies' strategies to stabilise the market; the vigour of rivalry in the market; the rulings of the antitrust authorities.

The US antitrust authorities have strongly opposed attempts to stabilise the market, in particular the basing point system and vertical integration. Horizontal mergers have also been under close scrutiny except where they were seen as a means of independent entry into local markets. Competition in the US market followed a dynamic path between firms' attempts to stabilise the market and antitrust decisions.

During the 1930s economic crisis, US cement producers used the basing point system to stabilise competition. They managed to remain profitable despite an all time low rate of capacity utilisation of 20 per cent.

The FTC banned the collective management of the basing point system. A final decision was made by the Supreme Court in 1948. This had little impact on the market at the time, as the economy was booming, and the industry faced shortages due to insufficient production capacity. Its economic impact came later, when the business cycle turned.

At the beginning of the 1960s, following a surge in investment in the late 1950s, the cement market entered a period of over-capacity. Following the prohibition of the basing point system, cement producers had to find new ways to stabilise local markets. A wave of vertical integration ensued.

The FTC blocked vertical acquisitions into the concrete industry and imposed divestment in 1967.

When the market recovered at the end of the 1960s, US cement producers were cautious when investing in production capacity. They chose to use their cash to diversify. Overall, this approach proved to be a failure.

Later, in the early the 1970s, the market returned to economic growth. However, industry production capacity was too low, and cement shortages appeared, opening the market to imports. High cement price increases coincided with high inflation in the economy, and the Nixon administration froze prices. When price controls were repealed, the cement market collapsed under the impact of the oil crisis.

The next move for the US cement producers was to try to recoup lost profits due to the price freeze. The leading representatives of the industry organised an information campaign to convince producers of the necessity of sustained price increases. This resulted in the Arizona Case. The legal proceedings did not result in a condemnation, but the trial left traces on the behaviour of the industry during the recessionary period of 1980-1982.

Because of the lapse of time in antitrust proceedings, the impact of rulings on the behaviour of producers takes time to materialise. It is usually visible in the way the industry manages the next recession period. Thus producers and the antitrust authorities race against each other. Producers develop strategies to stabilise the market. The antitrust authorities clear some of them, but ban others. Producers then develop new strategies, setting in motion the regulatory dynamics.

Three important points can be made with regard to the dynamics of regulation.

The first point relates to the use of the economist as expert in the field of antitrust. As R. Schmalensee has noted (1988), the economic analysis produced by the authorities has greatly improved since the end of the 1970s and the beginning of the 1980s. However, this improvement has probably been accompanied by the use of more general and normative principles when clearing company moves. Aside from elementary cartels, competition cases are progressively assessed on an individual basis. Referring to facilitating practices, and in particular to the basing point system, W. Comanor (1990: 52-53) has stressed: '*What these practices have in common is their promotion of interdependent price setting; which is the hallmark of tacit collusion. However, in each situation, the practice can sometimes be used to achieve more efficient outcomes, whether for the firm or the overall market. As a result, these practices are uniformly examined under the rule of reason.*' At present, economists are very cautious about the business practices of oligopolies and their economic impact on competition. To what extent would it be reasonable to allow an oligopoly to stabilise local competition, foreclose a market or prevent market entry? Between utopian perfect competition and cartels that should be banned, defining precisely what should be acceptable as workable competition is particularly difficult. J.M. Clark, from his experience of competition in the cement industry, was one of the first to acknowledge this difficulty. He even showed that in an oligopoly context, trying to impose the rules of perfect competition could be worse than do nothing. Not many economists shared his view at that time.

The second point has already been emphasised. It is not easy to grasp. Firms seek to define market rules that isolate markets from outside economic fluctuations and influence. In this context, they do not compete, they become rivals. The fundamental issue, then, that is not, as such, addressed in economics textbooks, is: how should one think about, assess, and, if required, regulate and manage the intensity of rivalry within the market? If it is considered that the stabilisation of markets through facilitating practices is not that harmful, how can firms be prevented from settling into a cosy rivalry environment? Do they not run the risk of sudden collapse after having gradually lost their technological know-how and business skills? The case of the cement industry strikingly illustrates the dynamism of companies that, in Europe and Japan, have developed in more or less stabilised markets that experience intense rivalry. This rivalry took the form of high investments in R&D and international expansion. In contrast, the US cement industry has been subject to heavy-handed antitrust policy, with competition imposed in local markets that did not provide a basis for rivalry. The industry went bankrupt within fifteen years between 1975 and 1990.[1] The issue of the intensity of rivalry, which is so difficult to encapsulate in existing economic data given its inherent qualitative nature, is a primary theme of this book.

However, there is a third item to be stressed: the immense role of competition policy in the opening of markets, which paves the way for de-localisation. Of course, if there is a consistency in competition policy, it is in the assistance it gives to the formation of economic powers countering dominant incumbent firms, such as independent new entries into a market. To curb oligopoly power, the antitrust or competition authorities will help maintain significant independent buyers (big wholesalers or distributors). They will see the take-over of a small independent producer by a large

---

1. Two thirds of the US cement industry was acquired by foreign companies, most of them European cement companies, during this period of time.

foreign company favourably, knowing that a significant new entry will intensify the competitive process. In seeking to shake up cosy business relationships, antitrust authorities not only assist the internationalisation of markets, but also their globalisation. In this regard, there is no difference between the USA, Japan[2] or Europe.

---

2. See for example, how the Japanese authorities supported the entry of the American distributor Toys "R" Us into the Japanese market (Upham, 1996).

PART 2

GLOBALISATION OF LOCAL MARKETS

The globalisation of markets does not eliminate local competition. The various components of the local competitive game remain: attempts to stabilise competition in the local market, the role of the antitrust authorities in promoting local competition, and rivalry, are still at work.

However, the globalisation of markets introduces new economic agents (in the cement industry, the traders) who are alien to the local competitive process, as well as new authorities that are specialised in international trade. Hence, the globalisation of markets will confuse, upset and modify the strategies of incumbent local competitors. The point is that new economic agents who promote and take part in the globalisation process do not have the same rationale as traditional local competitors. They do not see themselves as being involved in the building up, and management, of a long-term view of the industry. The decision making process is somewhat short-term oriented. Equally, international trade and anti-dumping authorities do not have the same economic rationale as antitrust authorities.

But what is the meaning of globalisation? Unlike the international process which has developed from rivalry with respect to local markets, the globalisation process is based on linking local markets that were previously unconnected, usually in a sudden and brutal way.

For globalisation to happen, key conditions have to be met (see Chapter 5). Local markets need to be integrated within larger trading areas, generally as a result of the strategies of local producers. Integration within larger trading areas is very often accompanied by the rise of buyer market power, and large independent consumers or wholesalers, which is at the heart of the success of globalisation.

The globalisation process will only succeed if there is a significant and sustained difference between the economics of local markets (for example, produced by changes in exchange rates, or rates of growth in the local markets, or by changes in producer cost functions) such that new economic agents (traders in the case of the cement industry) can place themselves in the position of arbitrageurs, able to make substantial short term profits from equalising the differences between local markets (see Chapter 6).

Traditional local competitors will adopt strategies to counteract this process, and to regain control of their local markets. They will strive to integrate the position of arbitrageurs into their businesses, engaging in competition on similar grounds (international trade) with the new economic agents. In addition they will make deliberate attempts to involve antitrust and the international trade authorities, in order to block the globalisation process (notably, imports), where detrimental to their local business interests (see Chapter 7).

However, even when independent arbitrageurs (traders) have been overcome by local producers, the globalisation process is still in progress. The arbitrageurs have been defeated, or taken over, but the arbitrage function remains. It has simply been internalised by local producers, either through external acquisition, or through the establishment of a subsidiary. They still have to cope with the antagonism between the short-term rationale of the arbitraging function, and the long-term view in the industry. If a local producer tries to leave the arbitrage function dormant, new independent arbitrageurs will immediately re-enter the market. This internal contradiction is one of the features of the globalisation process.

These different points on the globalisation process will now be illustrated with the case of the cement industry.

CHAPTER 6

The internal conditions of globalisation

The case-study of the cement industry demonstrates that the globalisation process is not a chance occurrence. National markets have already evolved and matured internally in a way that has prepared the route for globalisation.

Several developments have taken place. Changes in production process have led to a geographical market expansion. This has entailed massive investments in transportation and distribution. Cement companies are now producers and managers of network transportation and storage systems. In order to avoid being solely involved in cement-based activities, they have diversified. Producers now have to deal with the independent purchasing market power that has emerged.

The interconnection of local markets by local producers

In the mid 1950s, the Gordian knot of expansion in the cement industry - that transportation costs raise with distance but plant costs decrease with the scale of production, leaving a plant capacity equilibrium in the industry which is impossible to improve- was cut in particular markets, and especially in the US. The optimal size of a plant shifted for technical reasons. Computerisation of the production process enabled a better control of chemical reactions in the kilns. In distribution, new systems of loading and unloading barges were introduced. As a result, a new way of thinking about the business came to the fore in the industry. Where it was geographically feasible, it was possible to set up huge cement plants that would distribute cement by barges to distribution terminal depots in distant markets. By doing this, the cement plant would be able to compete with distant producers. This expansion strategy, which was initiated by local cement producers, was to begin linking local markets.

In the US, the Mississippi Valley was the first market to be revolutionised. The local markets of the East Cost became interconnected following strategic decisions made by Dundee Cement (Holderbank) and Atlantic Cement.

Holderbank was the first European producer to settle in Canada. The Saint Lawrence Co. (400000 tons), Quebec, started producing in 1954. A second cement plant started operation in 1957 at Clarkson in Ontario (800000 tons).

In 1958, Holderbank became the first European producer to invest in the US.[1] They opened the Dundee cement plant in Michigan (1 million tons). Later, in 1968, they opened the Clarksville cement plant in Missouri, which became operational with an annual production capacity of 1.235 million tons.

The Dundee cement plant was the first attempt to take full advantage of economies of scale in production, and was three times the average capacity of a US cement plant (2.7 million tons). At the same time along with this huge investment in production capacity, a distribution network had been organised. This included six distribution terminal depots (one of which was in Chicago, and one in Cincinnati), which were supplied by barge shipments from the plant. However, whilst Dundee represented a new way of marketing cement, its natural market remained a regional one, the Great Lakes region.

In fact, Clarksville was the first cement plant to make full use of this new business approach (*Press,* Anonymous, November 25, 1967). The success of Dundee had shown that it was a step in the right direction, as combining huge plant capacity with river transportation enabled a significant reduction in cement costs. As a result, Holderbank decided to repeat the operation but on a larger scale.

---

1. If one ignores the Broadhead cement plant (Pennsylvania), part of National Portland Cement, which had been set up with Danish financial support (*RP,* Grancher, May 1973: 100-145).

It has been reported that the construction of a cement plant had never previously been subject to such in depth analysis and careful attention as the new plant was.[2]

The site of Clarksville was chosen. It was 65 mile away from Saint Louis and had particular characteristics. The quarry was of good quality and the natural reserves were estimated to guarantee 400 years of production. The plant was located on the banks of the river, close to a railway line and a motorway.

The kiln, which, for a long time, was the largest in the world, began operation 21 months after the first works on the site.[3] After intense economic debate, the wet production process was finally chosen.

The production line was entirely computerised, after the technical team of Holderbank had worked with IBM engineers for a year. The computerisation of the kiln improved the quality control of the cement.

But the most innovative aspect of Clarksville, was its network distribution system. The economic and technical studies showed that it would be more efficient to use 1400 ton barges without embarked unloading cement systems (*P&Q,* Anonymous, July 1968). 34 barges were ordered, and it was announced that one hundred would be operational within a few years.

The barges could be loaded within two hours. A pusher ship, the "Hans Gygi" (the company chairman's name) took them out of the harbour. Then, in groups of fifteen, they travelled down the turns of the river from Clarksville to Saint Louis. From Saint Louis towards the lower part of the Mississippi, ship-trains could be made up of 40 barges. The Holderbank technical department had elaborate unloading and storage barges moored at the distribution terminal, each of which cost $250000. Their height adjusted to that of the cement barges as they were unloaded (the unloading operation took 8 to 10 hours).

The river distribution network included eight terminals which covered a market area from Minnesota to the Gulf of Mexico. They were set up in Minneapolis, Rock Island, Nashville, Saint Louis, Houston, New Orleans, Mobile and Chicago. Thus, the river network system enabled them to reach 24 out of the 48 continental states of the US. 41 days were required

---

2. The construction of the plant had been managed by the internal technical department of Holderbank. At that time, it had not been made a subsidiary, distinct from the other parts of the holding.

3. Until 1960, the largest cement plants used the same kilns as the smallest. They simply used a number of identical kilns to increase plant capacity. It was only after 1960, that bigger kilns, with important economies of scale, were built.

for the cement to be shipped from Clarksville to Houston. A computerised model was used to optimise the rotation of barges in the river network.

The terminals system proved particularly convenient to customers. It reduced delivery time, and made it unnecessary to stock cement, and run the risk of its deterioration.

The total cost of the operation was 70 million dollars, 40 million of which was for the cement plant, and the rest for the distribution network. The Holderbank Financière SA had invested 25 of the 70 million dollars.

At approximately the same time, two iron mining companies, Cerro Corporation and Newmont Mining Corporation decided to joint forces, and to enter the cement market. They set up the Atlantic Cement Co..[4] The basic concept was similar to that of Dundee. Dr Bernard Ulrich was placed in charge of the project. He had extensive experience of setting up cement plants in Europe, and had worked under the supervision of Saint Lawrence Cement (Holderbank). Ravena, near Albany, on the Hudson, was the chosen site, and the planned production capacity was 1.7 million tons. The plant started producing in November 1962. The total cost of the operation was 64 million dollars, 44 million of which was for the cement plant, and the rest for the distribution system.[5]

The company had three of the world's largest cement barges, the Angela, the Alexandra and the Adelaide, each holding 90000 barrels. Each had loading and unloading cement systems and could be towed.

The distribution network system included 11 terminals, situated in Ravena, Boston, Middletown, Bayonne (NY), Baltimore, Norfolk, Charlotte, Savannah, Jacksonville, Port Everglades and Tampa. Ravena, Middletown and Charlotte (which was connected to the railway network) were inland terminals. In the case of a sudden shortage, each terminal could be supplied by its nearest counterpart.

Thus, the strategy of combining economies of scale with a river/terminal distribution network was made operational in the 1960s by two new entrants to the US market, one a Swiss company, and the other from combined activities of two mining companies.

At this stage, it is useful to make a few points.

---

4. In 1965, Atlantic Cement was sold to the UK cement producer, Blue Circle. The production capacity of the cement plant was estimated at around 2 million tons.

5. To get an idea of investment costs, at that time, the cost of an average inland cement plant was between 8 and 14 million dollars, and the cost of a large cement plant was roughly $ 25 million (USFTC, 1966a).

Firstly, the new approach to the business did not aim at disrupting competition in local markets. The large capacity new plants gambled on the fact that by duplicating terminals they would be able to serve numerous local markets as an additional supplier at the fringe, without turning the competitive process upside down. They expected this to be the case, as they had forecast continuous economic growth which would enable their production to be absorbed (Scherer and Ross, 1990: 394-395). Thus, if the new plants were only to take about a 5 per cent market share of many distant and disseminated local markets, rivalry could continue to prevail over competition (i.e. price and quantity competition). Dundee and Atlantic Cement thought that they could only reasonably expect to compete with local producers in relation to demand surpluses.[6] The disruption of local competitive processes, then, was not the planned outcome. It occurred due to the rather unfortunate fact that the new cement plants, which were set up at the end of the 1950s, became operational as economic growth slowed down. Competition became fiercer than the new entrants had anticipated. The new plants had to increase their production in order to make their initial investments profitable. Suddenly, competition in price and volume superseded rivalry. Price cuts in the distant markets disseminated, interconnecting local markets.

A wave of vertical integration (that has already been examined in the context of antitrust policy) ensued. To avoid being forced to exit the market due to their higher operational costs, the oldest cement plants began to acquire their customers. For example, in 1964, Marquette bought three Ready Mix Concrete companies in the New York market to protect themselves against Atlantic Cement.

Secondly, the positioning of the American cement companies had changed. Before the linkage of local cement markets on the East Cost, they had seen themselves as cement producers, and conducted their business strategies accordingly. However, as has been stressed, the new business approach relied upon the setting up, and rationalisation, of new distribution networks. Thereafter, the sphere of production lost its dominance, as cement companies had not only to be cement producers, but also managers of distribution network.

Finally all producers knew that there would be no return to the former localisation of markets. The interconnection of local markets had been

---

6. *'...in this manner, the large new entrant avoids having to obtain a substantial share of any one market, thus minimising the prospects for major retaliatory responses by established firms.'* (US Federal Trade Commission, 1966a: 44).

achieved through the setting up of terminals, either by Dundee, Atlantic Cement or their competitors. It was an inroad for imports and the globalisation of the markets. Paradoxically, whilst the cement distribution networks were being set up, the production sphere of the US cement industry was collapsing.

Change in business perspective

As managers of distribution networks, the cement producers began to think of their business differently. They were no longer only producers, but were also potential arbitrageurs. They faced the choice of either continuing to produce cement, which would require sustained and important investment, or of buying cement from distant producers. The first prerequisite condition for setting the globalisation process into motion was met.

The 1960s were, as noted, marked by the increased advantage taken of economies of scale in production. In the Mississippi valley, as in the Great Lakes area, and in all of the North East Coast area, local markets were linked. By the time the effects of this had been passed on in full, demand for cement had reduced. The industry fell into deep crisis throughout the 1960s and 1970s. The price of cement collapsed in all markets, and particularly so in New York, and the profitability of cement producers deteriorated. The response taken to this low profitability was low investment. As a result, the over-capacity in production of the 1960s was transformed into under-capacity in the 1970s, with cement shortages appearing in some regional markets.

The cement producers were doubtful about the prospect of any economic recovery in the industry. Facing falling profits, *'not being stuck in cement'* was the slogan of the day (Allen, 1978). The strategic matrices used by business consultants hammered this message across the industry. The "market appeal/competitive position" McKinsey matrix dates back to 1968, and the Boston Consulting Group matrix to 1969. Both provided the same picture. In particular, the BCG matrix ranked cement in the cow industry category - important cash flows without growth prospect. The conclusion seemed simple: to withdraw cash from the industry and to invest it elsewhere, in technologically advanced industries (Collomb and Ponssard, 1984).

The 1968 Lehigh Cement report explained: *'In charting our course for the future, we take the position that we are not manufacturers of cement, concrete, furniture, and rugs, but managers of assets -currently some $175*

million -all of which belong to those who have invested in this company.
As managers of assets, not producers of specific things, it behoves us not
only to employ the tools at our command in the most productive way
possible, but also to recognise the variety of opportunities available for
their employment.' (p. 7). Actually, in 1968, Lehigh diversified into the
furniture, carpet and weaving industries. Later this diversification strategy
proved to be a complete failure.

An extreme case was Penn-Dixie. Established in 1926, it became the
tenth largest American cement producer in 1951. In 1967, it was solely a
cement producer. Its turnover was $50 million, and it had no debt. The
management had been wise and cautious. In April 1966, raiders acquired
10 per cent of the shares quoted on the Stock Exchange. The leading
figure was Jerome Castle, who stated: the cement industry has the lowest
return of all the American industries. It seemed like the right moment to
invest. On 9 May 1977, he declared to the New York magazine: *'you have*
to accept the fact that steel and cement are not growth industries, but
mature and stagnating.' The financial strategy was therefore to milk the
cash from the cow industry, and to invest it in promising activities. The
financial battle lasted for a year on the Stock Exchange, after which time
the raiders had won. The management of Penn Dixie was dismissed on 26
April 1967, and Jerome Castle took over. A massive plan of
diversification was quickly launched, and was accompanied by a dramatic
increase in debt. It seemed that Castle could raise whatever funds were
necessary. The cement branch of the business soon only counted for a
quarter of turnover. The company invested very widely, including in
plaster, chemicals, steel, insurance, and leasing (Stearn, 1971). In 1974,
"cement" ceased to appear in the name of the company. But the company
could not survive the extensive acquisition programme on credit, and, in
financial trouble, and Castle started selling company assets. In particular,
he sold a cement plant to Medusa, and invested the money in highly
speculative and volatile ventures. In November 1976, the *Securities and*
Exchange Commission began to investigate Castle's financial dealings. He
was sacked on 27 May 1977. Following the ten year frenzy of acquisitions
and diversification, one of the leading US cement company was declared
bankrupt. Its cement plants had become obsolete and badly run, and
identified as "slums" by some of the profession (Grancher, 1977).

Although Penn Dixie was an extreme case of unsuccessful
diversification, it encapsulates many of the ingredients of the time. Wall
Street was particularly oriented towards diversification, as it was a policy
favoured by financial analysts, who also made use of business strategy

matrices. The Allen study (1978) established that the shares of American cement companies had exhibited a similar profile in the 1970s: at first, the undiversified companies had a low share price; the share prices then rose, when the intention to diversify was made public; they steadied at this high level for about one year after diversification; the share prices then fell below the pre-diversification level. Thus, the capital invested in diversification did not contribute to the modernisation of the cement industry. Little by little, diversification eroded the competitiveness of the US cement industry, and left it bloodless.

The situation was aggravated by unforeseen events. The Clean Air Act hit the cement industry badly, with a billion dollars having to be spent to meet the new anti-pollution requirements, increasing investment by 10 per cent (US Department of Commerce (1987), Ch.7). Many obsolete kilns had to be shut down, as the cost of modernisation was too high. Some States, such as Texas, went further than the federal administration, and adopted even more restrictive anti-pollution legislation. Simultaneously, as spending and costs increased sharply in order to meet the new requirements, the Nixon administration froze prices (on 15 August 1971), and profits were further reduced.

In some extreme cases, cement producers renounced investing.[7] Thus, from January 1968 to January 1971, fifteen cement plants were shut down, while only four new ones were started up. Concern grew that about 37 cement plants, that is to say one fifth of the industry, were either obsolete, or on the verge of obsolescence, with kilns that were over forty years old. (*RP*, Anonymous, May 1972). In 1972, the only four new cement plants that were built, were done so by concrete companies rather than cement

---

7. This corresponded with the surge of diversification. Journalists' comments on the industry show that "pessimism" in the industry was growing. In their annual review of the industry, Walter E. Trauffer wrote in 1965 (*P&Q*, July 1965: 79): *'in spite of discouraging conditions now existing in the industry, and the probability that most of these will continue for some time, there is a general spirit of optimism about the long range future.'* Later, in July 1966, he wrote: *'There is still optimism about long range prospects for the future'* (*P&Q*, July 1966: 87). Then in July 1967, when an article was dedicated to the inauguration of the Clarksville cement plant, he wrote: *'Productive capacity continues to increase more rapidly than demand, and this condition will apparently continue well in 1968'* (*P&Q*, July 1967: 71). But in July 1968, in the editorial, Walter E. Trauffer noted that many past scheduled investment plans had not been carried out, and that no significant project had been announced for the year to come (*P&Q*, July 1968: 71).

producers (in particular, the Ready mix concrete Texas Industries company and Gifford-Hill company).

Whilst the US industry stopped investing, cement producers from other parts of the world, and particularly from Europe, remained active. They expanded their production capacity, often aiming at strengthening their position in the US cement market. In 1968, Holderbank enlarged their Saint Lawrence cement plant in Canada which served the Great Lakes market. Lafarge invested in Quebec and acquired a stake in Ocean Ltd, in Vancouver. The following year, the French cement company started up a new plant in Vancouver, and acquired Canada Cement Corp., leaving them accounting for a third of Canadian cement production. Two years later, the State of Michigan adopted new anti-pollution regulations. As a result, Martin Marietta shut down four obsolete kilns at its Bay City cement plant. In order to stay in business, and maintain its market share in the local market, Martin Marietta began to import cement from Canada. Therefore, it was as if at the fringe of the US market, foreign investment had made up for the lack of commitment of US producers in terms of production investment. However, trade between Canada and the US provides only a limited example of globalisation. Imports only developed in a few regional markets close to the US/Canadian border (Buffalo, Detroit, Seattle and Ogdensbourg accounted for 70 per cent of the Canadian imports). Only a few shipments reached Tampa and Miami in Florida.

At the other end of the scale, the gap between the production capacity of the US industry and that of the rest of the world, and in particular Europe, had expanded. This set a movement of very different magnitude into motion.

In Europe, at the end of 1968, the three leading Norwegian cement producers merged to make one company, Norcem. In 1972, the ship "Bradu" unloaded its first Norwegian cargo of cement at the Rinker terminal of Port Everglades.

In 1969, four small Spanish cement producers regrouped to acquire four ships that were specially equipped for shipping cement in bulk. Another Spanish producer bought a Norwegian ship that was equipped with unloading systems in order to export to the US.

The French group **Lafarge** extented its Le Havre production capacity to 1.250 million tons in order to supply the West Indies and US markets.

The UK cement producer Blue Circle, made its North Fleet plant in Kent the largest in the world (4.2 million tons) with the explicit aim of exporting to the US. Blue Circle became the second largest exporter to the US with 1.1 million tons.

Dealing with production over-capacity quickly became a major issue for cement producers. Of course, as seen, having local over-capacity does provide a means of deterring new entry into the market, even if the success of the strategy is questionable (Lieberman, 1987). Conversely, trying to keep capacity closely in line with demand fluctuations usually results in temporary shortages when demand is significantly higher than expected. In this situation, cement producers run the risk of encouraging imports and initiating an entry dynamic in their local market. This is particularly so if the producer cannot react swiftly in order to make up the shortage, and this tends to be the case when new investments in production capacity are required, as it takes time for them to become operational and if terminals can easily be built and made profitable. This is underlined by Porter and Spence (1982): '*If a firm fails to add capacity at the appropriate time, it not only loses immediate sales and market shares but also may diminish its long-run competitive position.*'

Thus, a sequence of events set in motion the globalisation of the cement industry. Firstly, some local producers neglected cement production and concentrated on diversification, investing their cash in allegedly more profitable activities. Others lost confidence in their business and failed to invest. Concurrently, foreign producers were investing heavily in the industry, and gradually supplanting local producers in their domestic market. The market became unified in terms of distribution network systems that link regional markets (at least in the East of the US). As a result, the gap between local and foreign competitors widened. New economic agents entered the market and made full use of the new distribution networks, arbitraging between local and overseas production, and bringing about the globalisation of markets.

The rise of independent purchasing power

Concentration in the cement industry, due primarily to the capital required for the modernisation of plants, has been matched by concentration in the concrete industry.

Since 1945, the Ready Mix Concrete industry has gradually become the largest buyer of cement. In 1959, in the US, the concrete industry accounted for 53 per cent of the cement orders. The figure was 70 per cent for 1985. The industry is widely dispersed geographically. It is fairly normal for a concrete company to deliver within a 30 mile radius of their location. In urban zones, most trucking deliveries (concrete mixer trucks) occur within a radius of between 5 and 10 mile. In 1964, there were 4000 RMC companies, and in 1982 there were 4161. It would seem from these figures that the industry had not seen any significant rise in concentration. The figures indicate that the concrete industry has remained scattered and one would expect that its purchasing power was no match for the cement industry. However, the situation is, in fact, more complex than this. Urban zones, where cement consumption is the highest, are usually dominated by one or a few powerful independent RMC companies. They have a lot of cash, and are the most significant cement buyers (in the 60s, 12 per cent of the RMC companies accounted for 60 per cent of cement consumption; it has been reported that, on average, one significant RMC company accounts for about 10 per cent of the regional market of a cement plant). In the early 1960s, four RMC companies accounted for three quarters of the cement sales in Memphis, Phoenix, Norfolk, Portland (Oregon), Baltimore, Richmond, Jacksonville. High transportation and delivery costs discriminate in favour of the largest concrete companies. Cement plants are better off selling to large buyers compared with small scattered buyers with regard to delivery costs. As a result, cement producers compete for the business of large concrete firms. The latter exert significant purchasing power over the cements producers. The cement producer who strikes the deal secures a large and regular demand for cement, that can be supplied at low delivery cost. Thus, the competitive advantage over unsuccessful competitors is significant.

At times of low demand, the largest concrete companies have considerable purchasing power over cement producers, even if it is primarily local. From then on, large independent cement buyers have played an active part in the globalisation process. They grew financially such that they were able to buy or to set up cement plants, and they remained independent throughout the 1960s, thanks to the FTC opposing vertical integration from the cement industry.

Thus the conditions for globalisation were met.

Throughout the period, the distance between US producers and their foreign counterparts increased with regard to production and productivity.

Distribution network systems linked and unified local markets.

Room was being made for the entry of new economic agents who could supply the market by arbitrating between local and the foreign producers.

This was facilitated by the rise of an independent and significant purchasing power that developed a strong bargaining position with cement suppliers.

CHAPTER 7

The globalisation process

The conditions for globalisation have been met, then, but how has the globalisation process developed?

US cement producers moved from being pure producers of cement, to being distribution network managers. They relied on imports to make up for domestic cement shortages. At first, they had control over imports, and managed them with respect to local markets.

However, once the local markets became connected, imports developed within the context of a global market, independent from the needs of local producers.

Controlling imports

The US cement industry was mistaken with its economic forecasts, and it did not invest sufficiently in production capacity. As a result, periods of shortage arose. The first significant shortage came in 1955 and 1956. The rate of capacity utilisation was at an all time high (respectively 94.3 per cent and 90.6 per cent in each year), and 980000 and 840000 short tons were imported in each year respectively.

The second period came at the beginning of the 1970s. We have already discussed the circumstances under which Lone Star had contracted with the French producer Lafarge in the early 1970s. In 1970 and 1971, while under the threat of having to close its Tampa cement plant as it did not conform to anti pollution regulations, General Portland turned towards foreign markets. In July 1972, it announced that it was discussing the acquisition of a 49 per cent stake of Cimentos Anahuac SA, the second largest Mexican cement producer. The negotiations failed. However, in October, a supply contract was signed with the Mexican producer for 280000 tons to be delivered in 1973, and 750000 tons to be delivered between 1976 and 1979. A supply contract was also signed with CA Venezolana de Cementos. In their 1973 annual report, General Portland disclosed: *'This imported cement will produce additional earnings since it can be purchased on significantly more profitable basis than cement acquired last year from domestic competitors and Canada.'*

In November 1972, Ideal Cement signed a supply contract for 2.5 million tons per year with Venezolana de Cementos, the largest Venezuelan producer. In doing so, Ideal aimed to strengthen its market position in Alabama, Florida, Houston, Louisiana and North Carolina.

Atlantic Cement had a terminal network which had a two million tons distribution capacity. In 1972, it noted that production costs had risen by 50 per cent at Ravena since its opening, and declared that it intended to ship cement from Spain. A supply contract was signed and agreed for ten years with Cia Valenciana de Cementos Portland, for a total amount of $120 million.

The third period covers 1978 and 1979, when the construction industry was booming, particularly in some States. Concurrently, anti-pollution regulations became more restrictive and lead to lawsuits and litigation. Universal Atlas settled with the EPA for $4.2 million regarding its Buffington cement plant. The State of Texas forced General Portland to close its Houston cement plant (April 1977). The State of California, where shortages were particularly acute, forced Kaiser Cement to shut down two of the six kilns at its largest plant, in Permanente (1977). Three quarters of the flow of imports at this time was under the control of the US cement producers. At their peak, they accounted for 10 per cent of US cement consumption.

Therefore, when, in the 1970s, the US cement producers turned towards foreign producers for imports in order to make up for shortages, it was with a view to maintaining the stability of their local markets. Imports were not a threat to national local producers, and this was reflected in cement prices. In 1979, when imports surged, cement prices (corrected for inflation) were at their highest, and cement imports were sold in the market at that price. This indicates that imports were being managed under a local rationale.

However, the apparent control over imports by local producers only managed to conceal the dynamic process that was at work, and would lead to globalisation, in a short time. The local strategy adopted has had key consequences for the long run.[1] This can be seen in the imports curve from 1945. After periods of shortages, imports declined, which is rational in so far as the imbalance between supply and demand had reduced, either due to producers having invested more in production to meet the new demand levels, or because demand had fallen. However, the reductions in imports were not symmetrical to their increase during the shortage periods. That is, imports did not disappear from the market once local production capacity was sufficient to meet demand. There were significant imports in 1955 and 1956, a time when cement plants could not meet increased demand. However, during the following decade, when the rate of capacity utilisation was low (below 75 per cent), the level of imports, was on average steady, and at a level comparable to that in 1955 and 1956.

In 1973, US cement domestic consumption peaked at 85 million tons. The three following years were marked by a big fall, including of 67 and 70 million tons respectively for 1975 and 1976. Imports also dropped dramatically. However, they remained more than double what they had been at the time of the shortages in 1969, and they stabilised at 5 per cent of domestic consumption. Therefore, imports settled in the market, increasing to successive thresholds. It was as if the cement producers that used and controlled imports for domestic purposes had gradually opened the market up to permanent imports, and gradually eroded domestic production.

The fact that imports proceed in stages can be explained from different perspectives.

Firstly, imports required specific investments, notably in loading and unloading facilities at harbours. Once these investments had been made, it would have been costly to shut the facilities down when the economic

---

1. As Roy Grancher has pointed out, short-term import decisions cause the industry long term risks (*RP*, May 1975: 109): '*These and other examples of import utilisation and purpose form a matrix of both short and long term adaptability. The dumping philosophy that once existed has largely given way to recognition as a business investment, a flexible marketing tool, and a profit opportunity. However, it is a mutual two-way street. Volumes from other countries cannot be expected to be turned on and off by domestic buyers like a faucet, as a necessity arises. During last year's drop it was those long term contracts that did hold up purchased tonnages. But isn't that the market mechanism work? If imports are to form the auxiliary, adjunct, or quite possibly the sizeable portion of operations here, that implicit risk of the enterprise must also form a definite cost calculation and negotiable contract point?*'

boom waned. Instead, their profitability was exploited. Equally, imports had meant that the domestic lack of investment in production capacity had been off-set by investment in production capacity overseas. Thus a long-term trend developed with a building up of harbour facilities and terminals abroad that made it easier to import. This factor was then incorporated into local producers' decision making. Thus, there was a feedback effect from imports to local producers' investment plans.

Secondly, because imports were mostly channelled by US cement producers, and therefore came within the scope of market localisation, they were, in part, left uncontrolled. From the 1970s, the RMC companies, which had increased their purchasing power, played a part in the development of imports. For RMC companies, the cement shortages of 1978 and 1979 were dramatic. Some of them, independently run RMC companies, had to close at a time when the demand for construction was high. They claimed that the cement producers gave preference to particular customers, and notably to their concrete subsidiaries. Governors of a few States expressed their concern, and put the issue in the political arena. The case finally ended up at the White House on the desk of President Jimmy Carter. The largest concrete companies, such as Rinker and Maule in Florida, adopted a twofold strategy. They invested in the construction of their own cement plants, and, at the same time, they signed supply contracts with foreign cement producers, the latter gaining a foothold in the US market. Thus, from the 70s, in arbitrating between local and foreign producers, the independent RMC companies prepared the ground for globalisation.

The rise in imports also represented a change in attitude by international cement producers. When the technical conditions of transportation required to interconnect local markets were met, the management of the largest producers evolved towards a global way of thinking. For instance, the Swiss Holderbank group, acquired Ideal Cement in 1986. Ideal, as noted earlier, operated a terminal in Tampa, Florida, and had imported cement from Mexico since the mid-1980s via this terminal. From 1986, Holderbank stopped importing Mexican cement and supplied its newly acquired terminal from its cement plant in Theodore, Alabama.

Finally, it was much easier for local producers to control cement imports than clinker imports. The transformation of clinker into cement requires a grinding unit, and local cement producers were the only ones who possessed such facilities. By importing clinker, they made sure that they would control cement distribution. It is far less obvious in the case of cement imports, as a customer would be able to get their supply directly from harbour terminals, before it had arrived at the cement producers storage facilities.

Globalisation

The concept of globalisation entails a renewed approach to business, with local and regional markets no longer seen as dependent upon local market conditions. The globalisation of the US cement industry began a long way away, in the Middle East.

Technical limits

The shipment of cement is not a new phenomenon: the New York Stock Exchange, Wall Street, was built with French cement supplied by Lafarge, and the Waldorf Astoria, the Metropolitan Opera, and the pedestal of the Statue of Liberty were built with cement produced by Dickerhoff in Germany. Cement was used by ships as ballast when they crossed the Atlantic, so transportation was not expensive. However, for a long time, a technical constraint prevented cement from being shipped on a significant scale, that is, in bulk. Cement freight would accentuate the wavering of boats caused by the movements of the sea, and increase the risk of capsizing. As a result, cement was transported in sacks until the early 1970s, and incurred the additional costs of packaging, and of handling to load and unload. Clinker, which is more solid than cement started to be shipped at that time. Producers who imported cement could shut down their kilns, but they would leave their grinding mills in operation. In the 1970s, a technological breakthrough overcame the main problems of shipping cement in bulk, and drastically changed the competitive process in the industry.

The oil crisis

The world oil crisis of 1973-74 transferred tremendous amounts of money to the arab countries. They invested in economic development, and, in particular, in infrastructure and cities. Between 1974 and 1979, world cement consumption increased by 20 per cent, and in the Arabian Peninsula it doubled. However, the Arabian countries lacked their own cement plants, and had to import cement in order to carry out their construction plans. As a result, international trade in cement rose sharply, accounting for 3.6 per cent of world cement consumption in 1960, 4 per cent in 1970, 5.4 per cent in 1975, and 7.6 per cent in 1980. In 1975 and 1976, there were so many bottlenecks in Red Sea harbours resulting from the delivery of sacks of cement, that ships were sometimes unloaded at sea, by helicopter. The major cement importers at the end of the 1970s, then, were the Arabian countries, and the US (as a result of shortages in US markets). In response to this increase in international trade, some countries decided to specialise in cement exporting. Spain was the first,[2] followed by Japan, and then later, Greece.

Traders were the main new economic agents that developed and organised international trade.

The traders

The traders were not cement producers. Rather they bought cement surpluses in order to meet shortages elsewhere. At first, they confined their activities to the Middle East.

REDEC (Saudi Research and Development Co.) is a good example. They were set up in 1967 as a subsidiary of the Saudi group Pharaon, and specialised in the trading of building materials. REDEC had tried to provide for the cement shortages in Saudi Arabia in 1975-1976. With the help of the Norwegian ship manufacturer Gearbulk, REDEC developed a new cement silo ship, a 50-75000 tons freighter converted into a floating terminal. It was moored at a harbour, and simultaneously allowed trucks to load both bulk and sacked cement. The silo ship was also equipped with a packaging unit. The first silo ship was moored at Jeddah, on the Red Sea. At the time when the Arab economies were booming, REDEC channelled half of the Saudi Arabia cement imports, a total of 6 million tons, through 4 terminals, three of which were floating. Concurrently, REDEC set up two floating terminals in Egypt (Alexandria, and Aboukir) that had a distribution capacity of 2.5 million tons. It took six to eight months to get authorisation from the harbour, and to position the terminal. The total cost of the operation was $975000. Building on their experience, REDEC expanded, and started setting up terrestrial and floating terminals all over the world, such that in 1983, it traded 7 million tons. By 1984, it owned 10 to 15 ships, and were hiring a further 20 to 30. The Company also had

---

2. In Spain, exports accounted for 5 per cent of cement production in 1972, but 40 per cent in 1981. In Japan, they accounted for 6.6 per cent in 1975, and 12 per cent in 1981 (10 million tons).

seven silo ships. The management stressed that they were not interested in cement production, and that the main bulk of their trade was in cement produced in European countries.

The globalisation of the US cement markets

In the early 1980s, after a severe slump, the US economy recovered. The recovery benefited the construction industry, and, as a result, US sales of cement multiplied,[3] and the rate of capacity utilisation in the cement industry increased. But, in the middle of the 1980's as the US economy continued to grow, the economic situation in other significant cement producing countries (Mexico, Venezuela) deteriorated, creating domestic over-capacity. As a result, the cement producers in these countries targeted new markets.

The US cement producers and traders had set up inland and harbour distribution networks, including silo-ships and terminal facilities. The regional coastal and inland markets interlinked with the overseas markets. The over-capacity in various parts of the world matched the increase in US cement demand.

The economic conditions were propitious.

Firstly, the dollar appreciated against other currencies, making exports to the US more competitive, and profitable. For example, for Greece and Spain, two of the major countries that had specialised in cement production, the dollar exchange rate moved form being 63 pesetas and 30 drachmas respectively in 1976, to being 155 pesetas and 150 drachmas in 1986 (*RP,* Uding, April 1986). Overall, from the first quarter of 1986 to the first quarter of 1990, the nominal value of the Mexican peso depreciated 84 per cent relative to the US dollar.[4]

Secondly, shipping costs noticeably lowered in the 1980s, due to world over-capacity of freighters. It has been estimated that, on average, shipping costs reduced by approximately 50 per cent between 1982 and 1985 (US Department of Commerce, 1987). A shipping imbalance compounded the situation. The US exported products such as coal[5] and

---

3. Cement consumption was 91 million tons in 1979. It gradually fell to 69 million tons in 1982, and then increased to 97 million tons in 1988.

4. However from January 1986 to December 1990, the nominal value of the Japanese Yen appreciated 43.7 per cent overall relative to the US Dollar.

5. In the early 1980s, the US exported 60 million tons of coal by ship, but there was no equivalently sizeable or homogenous product to be imported when ships returned from their delivery locations. This left room for cement imports.

grain, but rarely imported commodities. Since it was uneconomical to position empty ships in US harbours, traders were always on the look-out for opportunities, and used to offer special freight rates to the US. In this regard, cement was the perfect product to deal with. Ships loaded with cement would sail from Spain to Houston, be unloaded, sail to the mouth of the Mississippi, be cleaned and loaded with grain, and then sail back to Spain. Norwegian cement shipments would be unloaded in New York, and coal shipments would be conveyed to Norway (US Department of Commerce, 1987).

In this advantageous economic context, traders were able to put into place the globalisation of the US cement market,[6] and break away from the local market rationale which had prevailed before that time. However, it is worth noting that they did this without such a specific intent in mind. At first, they did not seek to distort the local markets. Two examples will help illustrate this, the first relating to the West Coast of the US, the second to the East Coast.

At the beginning of the 1980s, Stinnes, a long established operator in international trade, set up a trading cement subsidiary, Delta cement (*RP,* Huhta, May 1981). A small team from Delta cement settled in New York, and reviewed all of their opportunities to gain a foothold in the US. It divided the US territory into three geographical zones. The East Coast was soon discounted, and North California was selected as their final choice, as the cement market there seemed large enough (3 million tons), and there were imbalances between supply and demand. Local producers supplied 2.5 million tons, and the remaining 0.5 million tons were ordered from distant inland cement plants in neighbouring states, particular Nevada. This entailed high trucking transportation costs. The business strategy of Stinnes was simple: it aimed to smoothly take control of this latter part of the market. The goal was to import in substitution for the distant un-economical producers' cement without disturbing the market price, and in doing so secure comfortable margins.[7] There were several different possible locations for the investment. Some, such as Redwood, were disregarded because of the restrictiveness of anti-pollution regulations.

In the 1980s, Norwegian freighters shipped cement to US East Cost harbours, and loaded coal to be delivered to Norway on their return journey (*RP,* Huhta, April 1982: 41).

6. In the 1980s, the US accounted for a quarter of the world cement market.

7. This supply/demand imbalance stemmed from unexpectedly strong economic growth in the market, and the lateness of efforts of local producers in terms of plant modernisation and production capacity increases.

Stinnes probably made the others compete in order to get the best deal. The harbour authorities of Stockton reacted as any private company would: they agreed to spend money on harbour facilities, and to subsidise Stinnes. The construction of the terminal and the loading and unloading equipment were the responsibility of the harbour authorities. Stinnes moored its ships at the quayside, and had the cement transported to the terminal, where it was trucked and delivered to customers that had already been visited. The cement itself came from Japan, and Stinnes, as a trading company, took advantage of back-hauling to reduce shipping costs.[8] However the Stinnes attempt to gain a foothold in the US market failed for technical reasons.[9]

REDEC adopted an identical business strategy. It opened its Falcon cement terminal in Houston (Texas), in 1984. There was no quarry from which to produce cement in the Houston area, but up until 1973, there had been four cement plants in operation that used oyster shells, dragged from the bottom of the sea in the Gulf of Mexico, to produce cement. However, production of this Houston cement had to be stopped as the dragging devices damaged oil pipelines at the bottom of the sea. Hence, cement had to be conveyed from distant inland Texan plants, particularly those located in the San Antonio area where limestone quarries were available. In the early 1980s, the Houston market accounted for 3 million tons, and the nearest cement plants were 200 mile away. The REDEC terminal could deal with 50000 ton ships. In order to stay in line with the local market approach to trading cement, REDEC set up a terrestrial cement terminal rather than a floating one. This was to avoid what a REDEC representative referred to as the *'float in, float out'* psychosis (*RP*, Rich, April 1986), and

---

8. For this complex system, Stinnes were not able to calculate precisely what the shipping costs were, but they were noticeably low (*RP*, Huhta, May 1981-63). In the mid-1980s, an internal memo from Blue Circle estimated the shipping cost of a ton of cement to be $7.5 for a Greece-USA journey using a 25000 tons freighter. Other estimates are lower than this, with the lowest figure being $4. Therefore, the f.o.b. price of a ton of cement at a US terminal would, on average, be the cement price quoted by the foreign cement plant plus $6 By comparison, a US inland cement plant would charge 8 to 10 dollars transportation cost within a 60 mile radius. When their production costs were higher than those of the foreign cement plant, they could not align their price.
9. The Terminal opened in February 1981. It was closed after a short time because of technical running problems that were due to the ill-conceived nature of the terminal.

to demonstrate a long-term commitment to the local market.[10] The REDEC cement was shipped from Spain and supplied by Cementos Rezola, Bilbao. In order to guarantee the consistency of its quality, REDEC committed itself to only delivering cement that had been produced by a single cement plant, and, as a result, was from a single kiln and a single quarry. However, as can be observed in industrialised countries, although low prices appeal to buyers, they are cautious about traders. They are willing to do business with them only if they discern a long term commitment to supply. They do not want to face a loss of supply because of the trader's withdrawal from the market, and suddenly to have to secure a supply contract at short notice. Also, they are attentive to the trader's commitment to regular supplies, to its terminal, and to the quality of the product. REDEC explained that its trade had been concentrated on under-developed countries until then, and that it saw its entry into the US market as exceptional, and as having been prompted by the lack of investment in cement production in the country. The cement industry of the US lagged behind that of other countries. In 1982, while there was an economic slump, the US imported 3 million tons of cement.

Thus, in both cases, the traders' strategies displayed what Chen and Miller (1994) characterise as a "subtle attack". Competitive aggression was limited in scale, and at the fringe of the main market. At the outset, the traders competed solely with distant cement producers in supplying shortages. The examples referred to cement supply by Nevada plants in the Californian market, and to distant inland Texan plants supplying the Houston market. There was no question of frontal competition with the dominant local producers. The local markets were preserved from outside influence.[11]

Another factor was that the business relationship between cement producers and large independent concrete companies was tense. As has already been mentioned, in the 1970s the largest concrete companies bought terminals and used them to import cement, particularly in Florida.

---

10. Traders could not allow themselves what inland cement producers could: the first siloship, or floating terminal, was set up by Medusa in the Great Lakes region in 1982 to supply the Chicago market (*RP*, Robertson, October 1986).

11. Local producers did not view the entry of traders into their traditional cement markets favourably. W.E. Ousterman Jr, Chairman of the board and CEO of Kaiser Cement, was representative of the general opinion expressed in the industry about traders, when he refered to them as "peddlers" (*RP*, Ousterman, April 1982).

This was also an ongoing process in the 1980s.[12] An often quoted and particularly striking case is that of Apple Ready Mix Concrete, a Saint Paul Minneapolis firm that operated inland, in the centre of the US. In 1985-86, it arranged a joint venture with Cementos del Mare, with the aim of importing Spanish cement via the Mississippi river network. Prior to the move, the Minneapolis market had had a reputation of steady and profitable cement prices, with local producers benefiting from this. Although Apple Ready Mix quickly put an end to the joint venture, the knock-on effect in the market was to the advantage of local concrete companies, with regional cement producers becoming exposed to increased price competition.

At the end of 1987, traders controlled most of the cement import terminals and ships (26 ships, 62 per cent of the sea fleet) (*RP*, Huhta, March 1988), but the internal distribution networks were still operated by US cement producers. In 1987, imports peaked at around at 18 per cent of US cement consumption, but three quarters of these imports were under the control of US cement producers (US Department of Commerce, 1987). Facing the emergence and development of cement trading, the national producers tried to turn the new form of competition to their own advantage. As with the late 1970s, the late 1980s was a time of cement shortages, and the US cement producers responded to the new market entry and trade by signing import supply contracts with overseas suppliers in order to maintain their local market share.

The concept of globalisation is now more focused.

Globalisation does not equate to the disappearance of local markets, but rather to a struggle (head to head competition) between a traditional local way of thinking about how the market operates, and a "non-local" or "de-local" approach. In 1987, when imports were at their peak, they were said to account for 18 per cent of cement consumption. However, there were important discrepancies between regional markets, and imports were, in fact, concentrated in a few circumscribed areas, and originated from only a few overseas markets (*RP*, Ullman, April 1989).

---

12. When investigating the conditions in which Venezuelan imports occurred in the period 1988-91, the USITC discovered the key role of the large independent concrete companies in channelling Venezuelan cement through the Florida market. The large concrete companies claimed to have been forced to do so, as they were competing with concrete companies that were integrated with local cement producers, and, therefore, could not expect arm's length competition with regard to their cement orders (USITC, July 1991).

Half of the imports of clinker were shipped to the following locations (annual figures, in millions of tons): North Florida (2.2); Los Angeles (1.8); South Florida (1.4); New Orleans (1.1); New York (1.3); Buffalo (1).

In 1988, four regional markets accounted for two-thirds of US imports (17 million tons): Florida, California, New York, and Texas/Arizona.

The concentration of imports in only a few destinations conformed with the supply of imports from only a few foreign markets. A third of the cement shipments to Florida, and Texas/Arizona (transported by train transportation), came from Mexico. The other main destination for Mexican cement was San Diego, in South California. Half of the cement imported from Canada was shipped to the States of New York and New England. The third largest source of imports was Greece (accounting for 13 per cent of the US imports). Most of the Greek cement was shipped to Florida and New York via Greek cement producers Titan and Heracles. Japanese cement was only shipped to California, and was mostly shipped to South California.[13]

This data is consistent with the traders' strategies that were outlined earlier. REDEC and Stinnes both set up terminals that targeted particular regional cement markets. As a result, the globalisation process did not mean the nullification of the regional dimension of markets: regional disparities were maintained. The standard deviation of cement prices in the US -calculated from the average cement price in different States, as recorded by the US Bureau of Mines- increased as imports into the market grew. It was, respectively, 15 per cent and 30 per cent for 1957 and 1973. In 1973, at a time of cement shortages, it was 22 per cent, and after that, it

---

13. Up until 1983, 60 per cent of Japanese exports were shipped to the Middle East. In 1983, Middle East markets collapse, and Japanese cement producers concentrated on selling cement in California, and, in particular, in South California. The latter accounted for 67.9 per cent of Japanese cement exports to the US in 1986, 70.8 per cent in 1987, 73 per cent in 1988, and 73.7 per cent in 1989, but only 61.2 per cent in 1990, when cement consumption fell. In 1990, the South Californian market absorbed 40 per cent of Mexican exports to the US. In that year, Japanese and Mexican cement accounted for 25.3 per cent of South Californian cement consumption. The cement imports to South California were shipped to two terminal depots located in Los Angeles and San Diego (USITC, 1991a). Florida was the most frequently targeted US State with regard to exports (accounting for 31 per cent of US cement imports in 1991). 64 per cent of these cement imports were shipped through the Tampa Customs District. 53 per cent of the Florida imports came from Venezuela. Imports, then, were concentrated (US Bureau of Mines).

went up steadily to 55 per cent in 1978, as imports increased. Overall, from 1978 to 1990, the spread of US state prices fluctuated between 45 per cent and 60 per cent (Source US Bureau of Mines). This difference in cement prices between States provides evidence of the persistence of market localisation. It is useful, though, to compare the 1978 period with the early 1990s. In 1978, imports were shipped through, and under the control of, local cement producers, who had taken recourse to imports in order to cover production defects. In 1978, the average cement price reached a record high of $58.28, at constant dollar value.[14] In 1990, the spread of US cement prices was similar to that in 1978, but the average cement price, at constant dollar value, was at its lowest, at $48.72. This summarises the main impact of globalisation: low average prices, but a preservation of the local dimension of markets.

In this head to head confrontation between local and global, geographical factors are pivotal. As has been outlined, harbour facilities and the size and potential of river networks, including the Great Lakes, determined the extent, and speed with which distant local markets were interconnected. Over the period 1986-90, cement prices in South California fell as a result of Japanese and Mexican imports. However, at the same time, prices in North California rose (USITC, 1991b).

A second crucial point to be emphasised relates to the potential effects of the globalisation process. Globalisation has more of an economic impact than simply the interconnection of distant local markets. There is also an economic impact relating to the potential threat that hangs over local markets, and this provides some insight into the progress of globalisation. The globalisation process develops by overcoming successive steps without looking back, as though a "pawl effect" was at work. This dimension was analysed earlier. Once an economic boom ends, the imports that had been necessary in order to supply for shortages do not disappear. They do reduce, but not as one would expect. This is particularly notable during an economic slump, such as in the US cement market in 1982. Globalisation remains a potentiality, still alive underneath the working of local markets. In this way, it exerts a strong influence on local business strategies: *'With the cement industry now internationalised,*

---

14. The price data consisted of the average cement prices published in the yearly issues of the Mineral Yearbook, edited by The US bureau of Mines. Price at constant dollar value, means that the cement price series have been adjusted for inflationary effects, using the US producer prices index for all commodities (with a base of 100, in 1982) as a deflator.

*why should a company build or modernise a local cement plant? The
investing company now must expand its horizons beyond the local market.
The new or modernised local plant must be able to compete successfully
against foreign imports, as well as other local suppliers. The company also
needs to consider the potential of building an import terminal of its own,
and comparing its economics against those of the new or modernised local
plant.'* (*ICR*, Roy, June 1993: 54). Therefore, globalisation also needs to
be taken into account in local investment decisions in terms of its potential
threat.

The Japanese case

The Japanese case is consistent with the analysis of US cement markets.
The similarities of the situation include the presence of peripheral
investments, currency rate fluctuations and independent purchasing power.

The 1980s were marked by an economic crisis, and the enforcement of
capacity rationalisation schemes. Cement production peaked in 1980, and
then declined. In 1983, there was fall in both domestic and export
consumption. As a result of successive structural adjustment plans that
continued until 1986, capacity reduced drastically, with 31 million tons
being scrapped (to be fair, 25 million tons were obsolete). However,
despite the adjustment plans, production over-capacity remained. In 1987,
the average rate of capacity utilisation was 65.5 per cent far below a
profitable level. With the agreement of MITI, and backed by regional
cartel-type agreements, Japanese cement producers tried to keep cement
prices up. Despite the economic crisis, and continued over-capacity, then,
the average cement price went up from 14150 yen per ton in 1983, to
14254 yen per ton in 1986. As a result, the profitability of Japanese
cement producers improved, providing the basis from which they could
globalise.

Firstly, new effective production capacity had built up in the proximity
of Japan. This mainly pertained to Korean investment. While Korea was
experiencing an economic boom, Korean cement producers anticipated a
continuous increase in cement demand, and built huge plants near deep
coastal waters. They thought that they would be able to temporarily
compensate for a production capacity surplus in terms of home cement
consumption, by exporting to overseas markets. By 1984, overall Korean
cement production capacity was 23 million tons, and Korea was exporting
5.5 million tons (i.e. 24 per cent of production capacity). Donghae, the

largest cement plant in the world, has a capacity of 8.8 million tons, 4.5 million of which is exported (*RP*, Tak, August 1984).

Secondly, the yen increased in value after 1985. In 1987, after taking into account exchange rates, and even after adding on shipping costs, Korean plants were able to deliver cement in Japan 2,000 yens per ton cheaper than local producers.

Finally, the downstream market in Japan was (and still is) by concrete buyers that accounted for 70 per cent of cement consumption. 5000 Ready Mix Concrete companies were owned by Keiretsus,[15] a company that also had stakes in cement companies. In addition, there were large independent concrete companies, and at the fringe, concrete companies run by Korean families that had settled in Japan. It was this independent purchasing power that set the globalisation process in motion in the Japanese cement industry. Korean cement producers used the independent buyers as a tool for securing entry into the market. Thus, Ssang Yong Cement of Korea set up six terminals in Japan between 1986-88.

The globalisation of Japanese cement markets occurred between 1985 and 1989. In 1984, imports were negligible (0.2-0.3 per cent of home consumption). After 1985, imports rose, backed by the yen appreciation. In 1989, 3.7 million tons were imported exclusively from Taiwan and Korea. Imports nearly stopped in 1990, following a sharp increase in Korean cement consumption, but the potential threat remained.

Competitors who see their business interests in a local perspective but face globalisation have nevertheless a few competitive and institutional strategies they can adopt to try to counteract it. These will now be discussed.

---

15. Japanese financial groupings were usually vertically integrated, diversified, and backed by a large bank.

CHAPTER 8

Strategic responses to globalisation

The effective or potential competitive disruption that producers face in their local markets, due to globalisation, increases their business risk, as there is greater uncertainty over financial returns when making long-term decisions. In order to reintroduce stability into their market place, there are two types of strategic response that local producers can adopt, competitive and institutional.

Competitive strategic responses

The globalisation of local cement markets has resulted in the development of a number of strategic responses. Some of these have focused on controlling the upstream side of the market, others, the downstream side. Also, local producers have attempted to stabilise competition by securing market positions that enable them to retaliate against competitors in a multi-market competitive game.

Entering the trading market

From the outset, cement producers attempted to control the factors that were leading to the disruption of their local markets. The main factor was the entry of traders.

The largest cement producers responded to this new form of entry by creating their own trading companies: Holderbank, the world leader, set up

141

a subsidiary called Umar (Union Maritima Internacional S.A.); Lafarge, the world number two, set up Lafarge Overseas, later renamed Cementia Trading; Cemex, Cemex Trading; CBR-Heilderberger Zement, NC trading BV; Scancem, International Scansem; etc. These moves were based on some clear objectives. Firstly, cement producers had to think of a riposte. Their local market positions and dominance had suddenly become threatened throughout the world. Market globalisation had got under way, and local producers could no longer remain passive. An immediate response was to move with the changes in the hope of later controlling them. Also, importantly, the setting up of trading subsidiaries created market conditions that enabled producers to compete at arm's length with independent traders, but provided them with a means of retaliation. Aside from this, the move involved the confiscation of part of the traders' upstream profit, that could compensate producers for local losses, even when, at least at first, they could not expect to gain control of a significant share of the trading.

A clear assessment of the benefits of this strategic response is not available. In particular, it is difficult to know how (and if) the largest cement groups have been able to cope with the fact that their trading subsidiaries are bound to seize on any profitable short term opportunities, while their production and distribution activities require a long term view of the industry. The financial balance between profits from trading and the corresponding losses from production, is equally difficult to draw. However, it does appear that in the medium term, the largest cement producers did succeed in taking a significant proportion of business from independent traders.

Strategic alliances

While entering the trading market at the upstream level, cement producers also attempted to gain greater control at the downstream level, in order to counter the disruption of local markets. As a result, in the 1980s, several joint ventures were signed with the new entrants. This type of strategy had advantages for both participants. The new entrants did not have to cover the costs of setting up their own distribution network and canvassing potential buyers. Market entry was relatively easy, and immediately involved a significant volume. For the incumbent producers, joint ventures were a way of keeping new entrants at bay, as they would control the delivery of cement's new entrants through their distribution networks.

Cemex was the first Mexican producer to make its intention of entering the US market known. On the one hand, it bought import terminals. On the other, it signed supply agreements with local producers. For instance, it set up a joint venture with Texas Lehigh, called Texas Sunbelt, that managed terminal depots at Corpus Christi, McAllen and San Antonio. Cemex also signed supply contracts with Centex and Southdown: *'In early 1986, [Southdown] entered into various agreements with Cementos Mexicanos SA (CEMEX), the largest producer of Portland cement in Latin America, under which cement is imported and marketed in areas of the United States contiguous to the Mexican border. The arrangement includes the operation of cement terminals in El Centro and San Diego, California; Phoenix, Arizona; Albuquerque, New Mexico; and El Paso, Texas. Marketing operations are conducted by Southwestern Sunbelt Cement (Sunbelt), a general partnership organised under the Texas Uniform Partnership Act, which is a joint venture 50 per cent owned by a subsidiary of Southwestern[1] and 50 per cent owned by a subsidiary of Cemex. The joint venture agreement provides for a term of twenty years, but may be terminated at any time by mutual agreement of the parties.*

Under term of the various agreements, Cemex supplies clinker and finished cement to Sunbelt to be marketed from the various terminals. South-western also supplies cement to Sunbelt if requested. Southwestern is responsible for management of the terminal facilities and marketing of cement for which Southwestern receives a management fee from Sunbelt based on the quantities of cement imported. Earnings from the sale of cement by Sunbelt are shared equally between Cemex and Southwestern after deducting all costs and expenses of Sunbelt, including the management fee to Southwestern.' (Southdown Incorporation, *Annual Report*, 1986, pp. 32-33). It is clear, then, that the joint venture left Southdown in control of both destination and pricing stategy relating to cement imported from Cemex.

These joint ventures, however, proved unstable, and frequently resulted in conflicting views between parties. For example, on the 8th of September 1989, three years after its creation, Cemex put an end to its alliance with Southdown. It bought out the joint venture and decided to manage the terminals itself.

---

1. South-western was itself a subsidiary of Southdown Inc.

In order to maintain control over the distribution of cement, local producers also signed co-operative alliances[2] as a strategy to delay independent entry.

Local producers also tried to control the downstream market more directly.

After forging strategic alliances with local producers, the Mexican producers invested in terminals and captive users.[3]

In California, the Japanese adopted a similar strategy. In 1987, Onoda signed a joint venture with Lone Star. The joint company, Calmat, acquired terminals, concrete companies and sand and gravel firms in Oregon, Washington, and Alaska. Entry here was twofold, as Lone Star did not have a cement plant in these regional markets. The cement was imported from Japan, and supplied by Onoda. In 1988, shortly after it was set up, Onoda bought out Calmat, and entered the markets independently.

The general move towards the signing of agreements and joint ventures between overseas and local producers, therefore, has to be analysed in a dynamic perspective. It simultaneously represents a means of entry for the outsiders, and a defence strategy for the regional insiders. Defence can overcome the attack, and vice versa.

Vertical integration

In the mid 1980s, lawyers pointed out to cement companies that the interdiction on vertical integration that had been formulated twenty years earlier had been rescinded. The FTC did not comment on its motives in not renewing the interdiction. There is not clear evidence as to whether a debate took place within the agency, or whether the cement industry had been the subject of a particular investigation or assessment.

This new legal context arose at a time when US cement imports were at their peak. Cement producers (US producers and subsidiaries of

---

2. For instance, Riverside (ex-Gifford-Hill, acquired by Beazer-UK) owned one terminal in Los Angeles under a joint venture with a Japanese cement producer, and one terminal in Stockton (North California) under a joint venture with the Korean cement producer Ssang Yong. As noted, Lone Star entered into a joint venture agreement in 1988 with the Japanese cement producer Onoda Cement.

3. *'During much of the investigative period, Mexican cement was imported by or in connection with US cement companies. Mexican interests now hold substantial interests in importing operations, as well as downstream captive users.'* (USITC, 1990: 91).

overseas producers that had been long established in the market) again began buying downstream concrete interests. This occurred mostly in the areas that were most vulnerable to imports, with the aim being to keep control of the market (*RP*, Huhta, February 1990; March 1990). The first to move was Blue Circle (UK), in 1987. It acquired a large RMC company in Atlanta, Williams Brother. Lafarge soon followed, and in the same year bought the Texan RMC company Bryco Inc. (Bryan, Texas), in which it had had a 45 per cent stake. Bryco had a fleet of 75 concrete trucks. In 1988, it did the same with Jimco, the largest RMC company in New Orleans, another company in which it had a minority stake. Then, at the beginning of 1990, it acquired Beyer's Cement Inc., a large cement distributor in North Dakota. The acquisition gave Lafarge a key network of terminals in the region, and a fleet of 70 semi-tractors and 100 trailers.

Although the 1960s wave of downstream buying of concrete companies had proved disappointing, it was still thought that vertical integration could enable the revival of the US cement industry: *'Today, after examining the subject more closely, we believe vertical integration may be the only hope US cement producers have of breathing new life into their industry-the only hope of ensuring an economically viable future for the American cement manufacturer.'* (*RP*, Huhta, March 1990: 14).

Multi-market rivalry

In a multi-market competitive environment, a new entrant can be disciplined by imposing a credible threat of retaliation in its home markets. This can be done by setting up terminals in its territory. A dynamic equilibrium can ensue, with each competitor under threat from the other. However such an equilibrium generally requires a limited number of competitors, and potentially symmetrical retaliation. In the case of the globalisation of US cement markets, this did not work. The production capacity and financial strength of the US cement producers did not match that of the entrants. Aside from this, none of them had experience of foreign markets, or had ever tried to set up and export abroad.[4] Rather, as has been mentioned, the financial condition of the US cement industry led to its take over by overseas producers. Geographical obstacles also prevented a US retaliatory strategy from developing. For example, large cement plants were set up along the Mexican coast. From there, they could export and ship cement to any distant location, and, in

---

4. There was only negligible US trade with the Caribbean Islands.

particular, they could target the cities and urban zones of the US East Coast. By contrast, the largest Mexican cement market was inland, and situated well inside the Mexican territory. As a result, direct entry into the Mexican market would require the setting up of terminals in Mexican harbours, and the conveying of cement, by truck or rail, to Mexican urban markets. Such a venture would be extremely costly, and the outcome uncertain. Thus, the balance between exporters to the US and local producers lay very much to the advantage of the former.

This explains why US cement producers had to resort to institutional responses in order to counter the globalisation of their local markets.

Institutional responses to globalisation: antidumping and countervailing duty

In December 1986, a group of US cement producers lodged a formal dumping complaint[5] against Colombia, France, Greece, Japan, Mexico, South Korea, Spain and Venezuela. US legislation stipulated that the reference market could be the whole of the US, or part of it: a regional market. In their accusation, the plaintiffs referred to the US market as a whole, made up of regional markets that had been subject to the dumping of cheap cement imports. Nothing came of the complaint, as it did not convince the anti-dumping authorities.

As has already been mentioned, at the beginning of 1986, Southdown, one of the last remaining independent US cement producers, had entered into a joint venture agreement with Cemex to import cement from Mexico, and distribute it in the US through a network of terminals. On 8 September 1989, Cemex bought out the joint venture,[6] and from then on managed the terminals independently. On 26 September 1989, a new dumping complaint was lodged to the Department of Commerce and the International Trade Commission, by the Ad Hoc Committee of Arizona, New Mexico, Texas, and Florida producers of Grey Portland Cement. The complaint was against the imports of Mexican cement. Southdown had

---

5. To get a better understanding of how to initiate an antidumping complaint, and how the process works, see Congressional Budget Office (1994) and USITC (1995).

6. Southdown complained that Cemex gradually reduced the joint venture's management fees, and increased its imported cement price, in order to squeeze the profits of the joint venture, and therefore of Southdown.

been behind the setting up of the Ad Hoc Committee,[7] which included other US cement producers,[8] and mining and material unions. On 18 May 1990, the Ad Hoc Committee of Southern California, which also had a Southdown subsidiary, Southwestern Portland Cement, among its members, petitioned against cement importers (USITC, 1991a). On 21 May 1991, the Ad Hoc Committee of Florida petitioned against Venezuelan imports for antidumping and countervailing duty (USITC, 1991b).

Thus Southdown was a key figure in these legal disputes (*RP*, Anonymous, February 1992).

The economic arguments had been carefully worked out, and relevant markets defined on a regional basis.[9] In the case of Mexican imports, the regional market was made up of the Southern Tier: California, Texas, Arizona, New Mexico, Alabama, Louisiana, Mississippi and Florida.[10] In the case of Japanese imports, the relevant market was South California. With regard to Venezuelan imports, it was Florida. The authorities agreed on these market definitions. For example, 95 per cent of Florida cement production was sold in Florida. Only 10.5 per cent of Florida cement consumption came from other US States, and this cross-border trade was confined to the North of Florida, the inland part of the State. Also, in

---

7. The chairman of the Committee, Clarence C. Comer, was chairman and CEO of Southdown (*USITC*, 1990).

8. Texas Industries, Florida Mining and Materials, Phoenix Cement Company, National Cement Company of California.

9. The 1930 Tariff Act allowed a regional US market to be considered in isolation only '*in appropriate circumstances (...) if:*
   (*i) the producers within such market sell all or almost all of their production of the like product in question in that market, and*
   (*ii) the demand in that market is not supplied, to any substantial degree, by producers of the product in question located elsewhere in the United States.*'

10. Commissioner David B. Rohr argued that the relevant market should have been more narrowly defined. He pointed out that the cement plants situated in the Northern and middle parts of Alabama and Mississippi '*ship predominantly northward and, thus, do not market their cement in the same areas as the other plants in the region. Further, only a very small portion of Mexican cement enters the areas in which these plants do sell their cement.*' (*USITC*, 1990: 71). He also considered that the state of Louisiana did not form a relevant geographical market: '*Mexican imports into Louisiana generally are not shipped more than 100 mile from the import terminal.*' (*USITC*, 1990: 13-14). As for the petitioners, making use of this rationale, they argued that only the coastal counties of Alabama, Mississippi and Louisiana could be included in the relevant market.

1990, 82.6 per cent of South Californian production was sold in South California, and 93 per cent of total California production within the boundaries of the State. Producers from other parts of the US supplied 1.6 per cent of South Californian cement consumption, and 3 per cent of the Californian cement consumption. By the same token, in the Mexican case, more than 89 per cent of shipments occurred within the region where the product was produced (91 per cent in 1986). However, these average figures do not give a fair account of the impact of the cross-border trade. They do not include Mississippi and Alabama cement producers situated on the banks of the river, that shipped cement over distances well above average for delivery by inland producers in Alabama, New Mexico or Texas.

With respect to the relevant markets mentioned above, imports appeared concentrated. From 1986 to 1989, 93 per cent of Mexican imports were sold in the Southern Tier market, and a similar pattern was discernible with regard to Japanese imports in Southern California.[11] As for Venezuelan imports in the US, Florida accounted for 63.5 per cent in 1989, 83.2 per cent in 1990, and 100 per cent in the first quarter of 1991.

The ITC, which had previously refused to consider the US cement market as a competitive entity, agreed on the regional relevant market definition, and on dividing California in two separate relevant markets when dealing with Japanese imports in Southern California.

In economic terms, a new factor had come into play compared with the 1986 situation. This was linked to the passing of the Omnibus Trade and Competitiveness Act, in 1988. The Act requested the USITC *'to examine all relevant economic factors (...) within the context of the business cycle and conditions of competition that are distinctive to the affected industry.'* From this point on, the US cement producers argued their case in line with the business cycles of the cement industry. They were most pronounced in the Mexican case. The Southern Tier market had experienced two contrasting economic developments between 1986 and 1989: Florida, an economic boom; Arizona, New Mexico and Texas, an economic slump. In Florida, the US cement producers argued that Less Than Fair Value (LTFV) Mexican cement imports *'have suppressed prices and prevented regional producers from realising an adequate return on investment and from achieving the profits they would otherwise have achieved during the expansion phase of the construction and cement cycle.'* (petition p. 37). In Texas, Arizona, and New Mexico, they pointed out that imports *'have*

---

11. See data provided in the earlier chapter.

increased and have maintained significant market share when regional producers are most vulnerable during the contraction phase of the construction and cement cycle.' (petition, p. 37). The ITC agreed that the cement industry was governed by the business cycles of the construction industry, and also that, at times of economic boom, the rate of capacity utilisation reached high levels, as did increases in prices and profitability. They recognised that the high financial returns in boom periods were necessary if producers were to invest in plant modernisation. They also compensated for losses made in economic slumps, when the rate of capacity utilisation, prices and profits were low. As a result, at a time of economic boom, LTFV imports could cause material injury to local producers even if prices did not go down, and if local producers did not make losses. The fact that they prevented prices from going up, and that local producers had only been able to secure low profitability under unfair price competition, was sufficient to prove material injury.[12] Such circumstances stripped local producers of financial resources to invest in the long run, such that they ran the risk of failure when the business cycle entered its downside phase.

The ITC was cautious not to be dragged down this road. Very sensibly, in 1986, it upheld that the business cycle was difficult to use in practical terms. *'The question of where an industry is in its business cycle at any given time, as well as the question of the length of the cycle, is one which is not readily answerable.'* (1986 Cement, quoted in USITC, 1991a: 28). However, the enactment of the Omnibus Trade and Competitiveness Act (1988) forced the ITC to take into account the business cycle in its assessment of material injury.

Thus, the anti-dumping and countervailing duty procedures call for a few important comments.

---

12. This was the case in Southern California in spite of Japanese and Mexican imports: *'The industry operated profitably throughout the period of investigation'* (USITC, 1991a: A-32). The cement deliveries of local producers increased in the period 1986-89, as did their rates of capacity utilisation (26 per cent of local plant capacity was being operated at full speed). Conversely, the deliveries did not increase in value. They even fell slightly, with cheap imports preventing the cement price from going up. *'A loss of market share during a period of growing demand in this industry indicates injury'* was the main finding of Commissioners Seeley G. Lodwick and Don E. Newquist (USITC, 1991a: 28-29).

Dumping evidence

Between 1988 and 1992, the Department of Commerce concluded that there had been material injury in 97 per cent of the cases that had been put forward.[13] The procedure appeared *'severely biased'* (CBO, 1994: 49).[14] Earlier chapters indicated that price discrimination is economically rational for a producer when he is trying to enlarge his natural market, if that market is sufficiently secure against price competition from other local producers. The Mexican cement industry was in such a competitive situation with regard to the US cement industry. Economic and geographical conditions made retaliation by US producers in Mexican cement markets unworkable. The prices of Mexican cement imports into the US could therefore be viewed as being based on price discrimination at the expense of US local producers, within the framework of a normal competitive process. The analysis of the price fluctuations in the various markets shows that Mexican producers did not systematically undersell. On the contrary, market situations contrasted greatly. In New Orleans, between January 1986 and December 1987, Mexican import prices were consistently lower than the US cement price: between 7.2 per cent and 18 per cent. Conversely, in Albuquerque, they were consistently higher than the prices quoted by US local producers, with the difference ranging from 0.04 per cent to 23 per cent. In Tampa, based on a 51 month reference period, Mexican cement producers undersold the domestic product for 33 months, with margins ranging from 1. per cent to 13.7 per cent. In the remaining 18 months, the Mexican product was between 0.1 per cent and 9.5 per cent higher in price than the domestic product (USITC, 1990).

However, some countries had subsidised their industry in order to make it stronger in US markets, particularly with to view of increasing its dollar reserves. Douglas M. Queen, a highly regarded consultant who

---

13. The US procedure is as followed. A petition is addressed to the ITC. The ITC issues a preliminary determination. If it finds no material injury, the case is closed. If a material injury is thought to exist, it is passed on to the Department of Commerce. The latter decides whether or not imports have been helped by dumping at subsidised prices. If, in its final determination, it concludes that dumping or subsidisation has prevailed, the case goes back to the ITC for a final determination.

14. The situation is even worse in the EEC, as the dumping determination is more politically biased than in the US, even if this is less the case with regard to material injury (Tharakan and Waelbroeck, 1994).

specialised in the cement industry, studied the cost structure of the Mexican producers at that time. In his opinion, the Mexican government subsidised its cement industry by supplying it with oil at prices less than 20 per cent of the spot market price. Energy, and particularly oil, is by far the main cement production cost (US Department of Commerce, 1987: ch. 6).

The income made from Venezuelan cement imports was transferred to a Venezuelan fund, the FINEXPO. When an exporter brought back dollars, the fund exchanged them for bolivars with a premium for the exporter. Cement exporters also benefited from preferential finance and tax allowances.

Specialising in exports

Did the cement producers situated alongside US boundaries specifically invest in production capacity in order to export to the US? The answer to this is not that obvious, but a few insights can be drawn.

First of all, it is undeniable that the Northern US and Canadian cement markets have been connected. Since the late 1950s, Canadian investments have taken into account the opportunities of exports to the US, particularly in the Great Lakes area where cement distribution networks had been set up.

By comparison, the Mexican case is not as straightforward. Over the period 1978-1982, Mexican cement consumption increased by 47 per cent, a growth rate of more than 11 per cent per year. At the end of 1989, the Centre for Econometrics Research on Mexico (CIEMEX) - a Mexican economic institute associated with Wharton Econometric Forecasting Associates (WEFA) - forecast a growth in Mexican cement demand of 10.3 per cent in 1990, and 12.4 per cent in 1991. If the forecast was credible, increases in production capacity in the Mexican cement industry were in line with the expected development of local markets. A more detailed study supports this view: *'I note that there is also a considerable amount of new capacity coming on line in Mexico in the near future. Much of this capacity is coming on line in areas within easy reach of US markets. By the same token, these plants are within easy reach of the fastest growing areas of the Mexican economy, and are located where one would naturally expect, within easy reach of the raw material deposits which are essential for them. Certainly, if the Mexican economy were to "turn sour", these facilities would easily be able to export what they could no longer sell in Mexico to the United States. However, the evidence does not support the conclusion that these facilities are intended principally for additional export to the United States.'* (USITC, 1990: 90). The only Mexican project that could be isolated as specifically targeting US markets relates to the Cemex cement plant situated in Hermossillo, Sonora, in Northern Mexico.[15] In 1987, Cemex indicated that the vocation of the plant was *'to supply a larger volume of cement to the United States.'* It is worth noting that at first, there was no mention of delivering cement by ships: the exports were planned by rail. In other words, in Cemex's thinking, the plant was simply aiming at expanding its Mexican inland local market into the neighbouring US territory. Cemex set up new production capacity according to the local market rationale, as the targeted area was not open to competition from river or sea cement shipments. A similar strategy was at work in the urban zone of El Paso, where Mexican producers drove out the US local producers, by exporting cement to the US by rail.[16] The business relationship between Cemex and Southdown, already touched upon, seems to indicate that Cemex chose to enter the market by underselling, with the prospect of raising prices when entry proved successful. It seems that it was in the latter period that the relationship deteriorated. In this competitive framework, Mexican exports by ship, going further than the Gulf of Mexico area, were probably based on a very different rationale. They can be interpreted as the result of potential or effective competition among exporters adopting "hit and run" strategies.[17] But, on the whole, even if Cemex took part in "hit and run" exports, its investments in distribution networks and concrete assets indicate that it entered the US market with a long-term development policy in mind.

The strategies of the US cement producers

---

15. 125 mile from Tucson, Southern Arizona.
16. The ITC figures show that Cemex consistently undersold in the State of New Mexico between 1986 and 1989. The Mexican cement that was sold in El Paso, came from Torreon (475 mile) by rail. Cemex acquired a cement plant from Southdown in El Paso, which it converted into a terminal.
17. At the beginning of 1990, Cemex neither owned a cement terminal in Florida, nor in the East Coast. However, Cemex had bought sand and gravel terminals from Blue Circle, and RMC companies in Arizona. In September 1989, Cemex acquired Houston Shell and Concrete, a large RMC unit, and leased the Lone Star/Falcon Cement terminal (*RP,* Ullman, April 1990).

In the 1986 Cement investigation, the ITC found that domestic producers dealt with 30-50 per cent of cement imports, and virtually 100 per cent of clinker imports. Given that this was the case, how could the Commission accept that the US cement producers were suffering "material injury" due to cheap imports? For instance, the Cemex joint venture with Southdown yielded $3.9 million dollars in 1987, $1.2 million in 1988 and $0.676 million in 1989 (*Annual Report,* 1989).

Cemex pointed out the paradox. *'At the hearing counsel Cemex stated that: "US cement producers rely on imports in this market. As a decision, a strategic decision to maximise income, they rely on imports to supplement their own production. They go out and get the imports. This is not a case in which foreign producers are coming into the United States and seeking customers to expand market share here. It's a case of an importer constituency, primarily composed of domestic producers, that uses imports, that relies on imports, and goes to the foreign producers, whether it is Mexico or somewhere else, to bring in those imports. When they do it, they control the prices".'* (USITC, 1990: A-23, note 40).

Nevertheless, the Commission considered that facing Less Than Fair Value imports, as had been deemed the case by the Department of Commerce, local cement producers had no choice but to take part in the import process if they were to preserve their market share. Therefore, the fact that most of the cement imports were channelled through US producers did not contradict the existence of material injury. The latter consisted of financial losses, or, more accurately, profits that had not materialised, and production capacity that had been unduly shut down.

Business cycles

From 1988, the ITC was legally bound to assess material injury with regard to the business cycle. It has been noted that such an approach can mean that local industry could be profitable, benefiting from increases in prices and market shares,[18] and simultaneously be declared injured on the grounds that its economic situation should have been better, given that it was in an upward phase of the business cycle. At the same time, the cement industry in a different geographical market could be declared

---

18. In the Venezuelan case, during the period of the investigation, the market shares of local Florida producers increased steadily. The domestic producers' share of the total market was 47 per cent in 1988, 48 per cent in 1989, and 56 per cent in 1991.

injured by Less Than Fair Value imports while its economic situation was the opposite, such that it was in the downward phase of the business cycle. Although the ITC was very reluctant, it had to commit itself to the business cycle approach, given the 1988 Congress vote.

The effects of the institutional strategies

What has the impact of antidumping and countervailing duty petitions been on market conditions?

In a nutshell, it has been tremendous. The first ITC decision related to Mexico, and was made in August 1990. In 1991, Florida stopped importing Mexican cement, with Venezuelan cement imports replacing the Mexican ones. At the beginning of 1990, Mexican imports accounted for 18 per cent of total imports in the State of Florida. In December that same year, they fell to 6 per cent. Venezuelan imports were steady in 1988 and 1989, totalling 414000 tons and 444000 tons respectively, and accounting for approximately 6 per cent of the market in both years. In 1990, subsequent to the ITC decision, Venezuelan imports surged to 1.121 million tons (18 per cent of the market, a 152 per cent increase in comparison with 1989). Although Florida cement consumption dropped at the beginning of 1991, imports of Venezuelan cement continued to rise, and soon accounted for 20.7 per cent of the Florida market. On 12 May 1991, the cement producers of Florida petitioned against Venezuelan producers. In July 1991, the ITC issued its preliminary determination. It concluded that there were grounds for material injury. However, ultimately the case was dropped. The Venezuelan producers engaged in a sort of voluntary restraint with regard to their exports to Florida, both in terms of price and volume. Thus after the antidumping decision, and the potential threat of renewed action, cement exports to Florida fell by 43.9 per cent in 1991, and by 33.9 per cent in 1992 (*ICR*, Roy, November 1993).

Overall, cement imports into the US fell by 60 per cent between 1987, when they were at their peak, and 1993. The ITC decisions coincided with a short term market slump in 1990 and 1991, when US cement consumption dropped by 13.9 per cent. However, over the period 1991-93, cement consumption increased by 10.7 per cent: 6 per cent in 1992, and 4 per cent in 1993 (see Appendices to the Chapter).[19]

The crucial point is probably not the nominal decrease in US cement imports, but rather the impossibility of returning to the previous market situation. Prior to the ITC decisions, imports increased with US cement shortages, and in recession phases they decreased (although, not as strongly as one would have expected). Once the ITC decisions were enforced, however, the market situation was totally different. The duties imposed by the Department of Commerce on LTFV cement imports that were deemed to have caused material injury are irreversible. The duty has no time limit, and is quasi definitive.[20] Moreover, the ITC decisions are deterring, as illustrated in the Venezuelan case. The Venezuelan producers preferred to give up once the preliminary decision had been made known.

Therefore, in future, US local cement producers will probably regain control over cement imports. The difference with the past situation will be the increased internationalisation of the largest cement producers that adopt a global strategy towards local markets. *'Such supply will tend to be a more controlled sourcing, as tonnages move from group-owned export plant, through trading arm, into company terminals, passing within its distribution network, often to a vertically integrated customer base. Imports will be back as a factor in this decade, serving both for competitive advantage and for profit.'* (*RP*, Grancher, April 1993: 59).

On the whole, the US antidumping actions have had the effect of reinstating local market competition in a "continental" context. As before, US cement imports will mainly occur in the North from Canadian producers, and in the South from Latin American producers, particularly the Mexicans. The Canadian cement plants in question are owned by the two largest world producers, Holderbank and Lafarge. In addition, through their acquisitions, they are both the largest producers in the US. In the South, Cemex has taken over a few local markets near the border, and is now a US cement producer following its acquisition of Balcones. The plant itself had been modernised by Lafarge and expanded to have a 950000 tons capacity. It is said to be the finest US cement plant. Lafarge sold it, together with its distribution network, to Cemex in 1994 (*ICR*,

---

19. Due to regional differences, cement consumption fell in 1993 in California, New York and Pennsylvania, while it increased more than the average in Florida and Texas.

20. The duties imposed on Mexican producers amounted to $60 million. They appealed before a US court of Justice, but lost. Then, they challenged the USA before the GATT.

Roy, August 1994). The acquisition cost was about $100 million (*ICR,* July 1994: 16). Presumably, building up a US market position via the ownership of plants was the long run strategy of Cemex from the beginning, and this has been accelerated by the ITC decisions on antidumping and countervailing duty. Moreover, from 1993 to 1995, Cemex, Lafarge and Holderbank acquired Venezuelan cement producers.

Other institutional strategic responses: quotas

In an earlier chapter, it was illustrated how South Korean imports developed in the Japanese market in the 1980s. They did so when cement consumption dropped, and the Japanese producers had entered into a restructuring deal with MITI with plans to shut down excess capacity. In order to fend off these imports, Japanese producers organised a boycott of Korean cement. Arguing that it was impossible to guarantee the quality of a mix of Korean and Japanese cement, they refused to sell to RMC companies that were supplied by Korean producers. The boycott angered the Japanese Fair Trade Commission, which opposed some aspects of the MITI restructuring deal.

In a second move, the Japanese producers adopted a new strategy. They negotiated directly with Korean producers on import quotas. The "voluntary restraint" agreement that resulted was twofold:

1. cement imports from Korea would not exceed 2.2 million tons per year, starting with the year September 1986 to September 1987. 1 million tons of this would be bought by Japanese producers.
2. imports bought directly by Japanese producers would be managed via the Ssang Yong Group of Korea's subsidiary, Ssang Yong Japan.

The agreement did not bear fruit. The economy of South Korea boomed, and the Olympic games in Seoul increased cement demand in the domestic market. As a result, Ssang Yong did not make full use of their quota, and only 1.53 million tons were imported from South Korea in 1987. However, the Japanese cement price fell slightly, partly due to cement imports from Taiwan, confirming the substitution phenomenon with regard to imports (such as with the substitution of Venezuelan cement for Mexican cement in the US).

Conclusion

Defensive strategies against globalisation are primarily delaying strategies which allow the producers to take an active part in the globalisation process rather than to simply endure the phenomenon. Only the antidumping/countervailing duty device seems able to put a halt to the process, and bring a return to previous local market equilibria, where imports are under the control of the local producers. One important feature of this strategic response is its deterrent effect, which works for a period of time that does not have fixed limits and is more or less left undefined.[21] The procedure is extremely effective for local producers.[22]

---

21. The AD/CVD policy, like other policies, has been cyclical. It fluctuated according to the appointments of ITC Commissioners and heads of Department of Commerce divisions, and to changes in the membership of competent subcommittees. On the influence of changes in the majority in the US Congress, and the policies carried out by the Federal Agencies, see the FTC case - Weingast and Moran (1983).

22. *'The protective capture of CVD and AD processes is clear.'* (Bhagwati, 1990: 52).

Appendix 1

US IMPORTS WITH "PAWL EFFECT"

US Cement Imports (Thousand Short Tons - US Bureau of Mines)

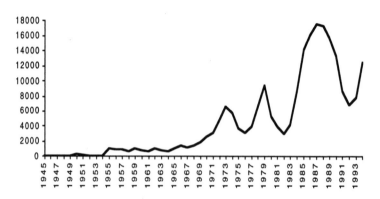

Imports as % of Domestic Consumption (US Bureau of Mines)

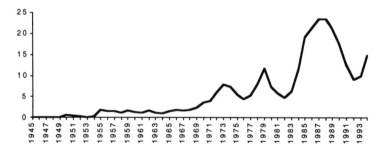

Appendix 2

IMPACT OF AD/CVD ON IMPORTS SUBSTITUTION (MEXICO/VENEZUELA)

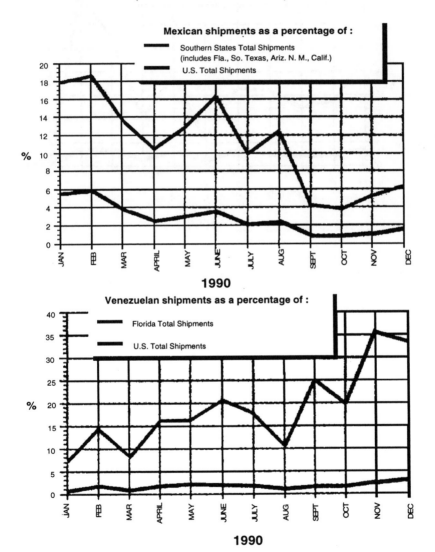

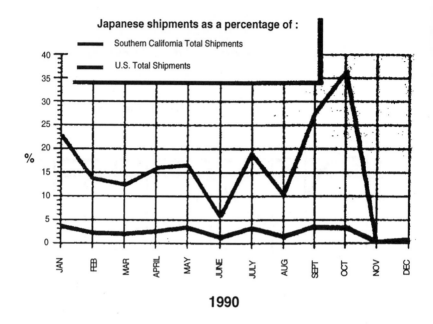

1990

Mexican, Venezuelan and Japanese shipments of Portland cement as a percentage of total US and regional or state shipments in 1990.
Source: US Bureau of Mines.
(*P&Q*, Dorn, april 1991: 43)

Appendix 3

ANTIDUMPING IMPACT ON US IMPORTS

US IMPORTS OF CEMENT AND CLINKER short tons
(thousands)

	1988	1989	1990	1991	1992	1992 (Jan.-June)	1993 (Jan.-June)
VENEZUELA	627	744	1,486	898	60	22	117
JAPAN	1,758	2,415	2,101	331	306	138	15
MEXICO	4,928	4,320	2,228	997	860	431	370

AVERAGE C. I. F. VALUE PER TON OF U. S. IMPORTS OF HYDRAULIC CEMENT
$/Short ton

	1988	1989	1990	1991	1992	1992 (Jan.-June)	1993 (Jan.-June)
MEXICO	$ 29,98	$ 32,14	$ 35,40	$ 38,64	$ 39,04	$ 39,38	$ 38,69
JAPAN	32,91	32,59	36,06	39,99	44,27	42,07	54,92
VENEZUELA	34,99	40,28	38,34	42,21	47,39	45,43	41,05
AVERAGE	32,63	35,00	36,60	40,28	43,57	42,29	44,88

(Source: *RP,* Turley, november 1993)

Overall figures (thousands tons):

	1988	1989	1990	1991	1992	1993
Imp	17,3	14,3	12,0	7,9	6,1	7,0
Cons	93,2	82,3	81,3	74	75,4	81,7
per cent	18,5	17,3	14,7	10,6	8,0	8,5

(Source: US Bureau of Mines)

CHAPTER 9

Concluding comments

Making use of institutional mechanisms, some countries have been able to delay or fend off the globalisation of their local markets. Other countries brought the process to a halt by imposing quotas. Companies themselves adopt defensive strategies in response to globalisation, such as forging business alliances, controlling local distribution networks, or setting up potential and effective means of retaliation within a multi-market competition game.

But the process has its own internal dynamic. In the cement industry, the root cause of market globalisation lies in the needs of construction and infrastructure activities in countries experiencing rapid growth. Important cement production capacity is set up in the anticipation of sustained economic development. In the interval, the capacity is used to export. This was the case in South Korea, and has also been the case in Greece, as will be seen later.[1]

Subsequently, coastal urban markets come under the threat of rapid globalisation, that is to say, a sudden disruption of the local competition

---

1. In specific circumstances, the structural imbalance between capacity and demand can be amplified. A particular case would be where a government subsidises or gives financial advantages to its industry in order to make sure that it will deliver. This is all the more the case for less developed countries, where exports result in vital foreign currency reserves. Also, a country may have geographical characteristics, such as coastal sides close to industrialised countries, that allow it to perform better in particularly profitable exports markets.

game. New economic agents enter the market, that convey a different approach to their business. Their economic rationale rests on making the most profitable use of production over-capacity in various parts of the world, given shipping costs, currency rates, and technological progress in loading and unloading systems. Yet, the local competition rationale does not fade away. It holds on under the pressure of market globalisation As it stands, the process seems irreversible. A world production shortage would probably bring about the setting up of new coastal plants, which in return would strengthen the globalisation process.

The mark of the globalisation of cement markets is embraced in the formation of a world fleet of cement silo ships in the 1990s (*ICR*, Anonymous, March 1994).

At the beginning of 1994, it was estimated that, throughout the world, the number of cement silo ships in operation was about forty. The use of silo ships has been speeded up by the 1992 cement shortages in Taiwan. Since then, strategic moves have been disparate. Some silo ships have set off to China (Pharaon has moored its Golden Arrow at Guadong). Other targeted destinations have been the Middle East (Libexim has located one silo ship in Aden, Yemen,[2] and one in Beirut, Liban; Lafarge has located a silo ship in Istanbul, Turkey), and South America (Heracles has moored its Heracles Spirit at Santos, Brazil). The Eastern Falcon, owned by Pharaon, had set off towards Karachi, Pakistan.

In 1994, the leading trading firm was the Greek company Libexim, which owned fifteen silo ships, and was about to increase its fleet in February 1994 by acquiring the Eagle, then located in Egypt, from Pharaon.

Since then, loading and unloading techniques have progressed. Today, it is possible to equip any ship with an unloading system for trucks, within a few days, for less than $1 million.[3]

---

2. This is supplied by Romanian Cement (*IBJ*, Beechener, January 1993).
3. One such system has been worked out by H.W. Carlsen, the Swedish cement handling specialists. They took their successful 180 tph CSP compact (the Carlsen road mobile mini-terminal), and modified it. The CSP Compact previously sat on the back of a trailer, but here it was to be used as a gantry on deck, and changes had to be made to enable it to travel on rails instead of tyres. The gantry allowed combined ship-unloading/truck-loading. To ensure that the system is as clean as possible, all unloading is done by means of suction. In this particular case, it is done by means of a hydraulic suction arm installed on the gantry unit. When a bulk truck pulls alongside the terminal, cement is automatically unloaded via the special truck loading system on the gantry. This

It is this globalisation process that is in progress, and has entered into conflict with the local market competition rationale, that the competition authorities (in the broad sense: antitrust and antidumping/countervailing agencies) have to come to grips with, and regulate.

---

concept is cheaper, as the ship itself does not need to be converted. This saves money, both in terms of the investment, and in terms of the length of time that the ship needs to be out of service. It is fully self-sufficient, so no connections need to be made on shore. (*ICR,* Anonymous, October 1993).

PART 3

UNDERSTANDING AND REGULATING MARKETS AT A TIME OF GLOBALISATION

When investigating cement producers' business practices at the end of the 1980s, the Japanese Fair Trade Commission had to deal with two issues: anti-competitive practices that pertained to local competition, and practices that related to the globalisation process (the competitive behaviour of Japanese producers who had to cope with Korean and Taiwanese cement imports).

Another case, and certainly the most prominent one, is the EU cement antitrust case, which has not yet[1] been settled as the European cement producers have appealed against the decision of the EU Commission to the European First Instance Tribunal.

The case had all the attributes of a major one, and can be seen as about as important as the US basing point antitrust case, given the large number of companies that were involved, the length of the legal process, and the intricacies of the statement of objections.

In contrast to the handling of the Japanese case, which involved the MITI and the FTC, the European case has been investigated by a single authority, the EC Commission. The characteristic of the EC Commission is that it deals at the same time with antitrust (as the US FTC), antidumping/countervailing duty (as the US Department of Commerce and the ITC), and the anti-competitive effects of Members' State Aids within the EU. These different procedures are managed by two Directorates within the Commission: General Directorate 4 deals with antitrust and State Aid cases, and General Directorate 1 with international trade issues.

---

1. In 1997.

CHAPTER 10

The European case

Throughout the course of the 1980s, the European cement industry was confronted with the threat of globalisation. It was in this context that the EC Commission decided to intervene. From April 1989 to July 1990, it began investigating, and requesting information on, the competitive behaviour of European cement producers, and carried out searches at the headquarters of European cement companies and the European cement trade associations. The case was by far the biggest ever initiated by the Commission. Overall, 76 cement companies and trade associations were involved. The markets covered by the case were those of the Member States of the EEC, plus those of three other countries, Norway, Sweden and Switzerland. The legal charges were extremely grave (EEC, 1994).[1]

The European case illustrates the contents of the previous chapters: the cement producers' local competitive strategies and the rise of globalisation in the local competitive game; the local producers' responses to globalisation; the Authorities' difficulty in comprehending the meaning and consequences of the globalisation process, as well as regulating the local competitive game that is threatened by market's globalisation.

---

1. The EEC accusation pertained to two separate markets, the grey Portland cement market, and the white cement market (white cement is more expensive). This chapter focuses on the main market, grey Portland cement.

The competition game in Europe in the 1980s

In the early 1980s, two competitive strategies confronted each other in Europe. The first was a continental strategy, which could be characterised as inland and local. The second was a maritime strategy. They conflicted in the mid-1980s.

The inland rivalry model in Europe

Because of the geography of the European continent, cement is primarily shipped by road and rail (although to a lesser extent in the United Kingdom and the Netherlands). The European cement markets are more regionally focused than those in Japan or in the US.

If geography has played a role in favour of the maintenance of local markets, some cement producers endeavoured to move beyond the bounds of their local framework from the 1970s. They sought to take advantage of US shortages, and to settle there, although without much success, as can be illustrated by considering the UK and France.

As islanders, the UK cement producers set up their operations close to harbour locations, by the sea. That was the case with Blue Circle and its Northfleet plant in Kent. In 1972, it was the largest plant in the world (4 million tons), and was the only UK plant capable of exporting. Blue Circle had recently expanded the production capacity of the plant in response to an increase in UK cement demand, but also with the intention of exporting to the US when market conditions were favourable. In 1970, Blue Circle signed an agreement with a large independent RMC company, Maule Industries, Miami, Florida, to supply its Port-Everglades terminal. In 1973, Blue Circle was the second largest exporter to the US, and accounted for 1.1 million tons. The exports were circumscribed to particular and well defined areas. At first, this covered Miami, then Houston, and later involved some attempts in Charleston, and in 1974, New Orleans. Following the oil crisis, the economies of the European Members States deteriorated, while at the same time, cement shortages developed in US markets. Understandably, Blue Circle increased its exports (by 77 per cent in the period 1974-78).

However, from the early 1980s onwards, gambling on exports was a risky game to play: *'Blue Circle decided in 1980 to reduce its exposure to international trading and [...] the 1980 tonnages were way down and for 1981 even lower.'* (*RP,* Duthie and Liduena, April 1982: 37). An international trading representative vividly expressed the opinion of many in the business.[2] *'If, however, I were pressed to give advice to a would-be exporter, I should say it is rather like taking your beautiful secretary out to dinner. Rule 1 - Don't, unless you are sure you know what you are doing and why. Rule 2 - If, notwithstanding Rule 1, you find yourself doing it, keep the frequency low, certainly below 10 percent, say once in two weeks and never on a Sunday. Rule 3 - Have the sense to stop once it starts really hitting your pocket; and Rule 4 - Never get to thinking it is a substitute for home cooking.'* (*RP*, Duthie and Liduena, April 1982: 38).

A similar attempt took place in France at about the same time. At the end of the 1960s, the Lambert group, which had specialised in the plaster business, decided to enter the cement market. It set up a large cement plant in Le Havre, the French harbour at the estuary of the River Seine, which opens into the Channel and the Atlantic Ocean. It aimed to supply the local market, but also wanted to supply the West Indies (particularly the French part) and the US. As with Blue Circle, the Lambert group found it difficult to make the business profitable, and exited the market selling its important asset.

These attempts to expand beyond their traditional markets failed, so, at the end of the 70s, the European cement industry went back to basics, and concentrated on local demand. Olivier Lecerf, the chairman of Lafarge summed up the prevailing view: *'A few years ago the trend was towards larger and larger units. Our experience in Europe and North America is that each plant should be adapted to its immediate market. We have found that a plant with an initial capacity of 500000 tons, that can be doubled if necessary, is very efficient. Very large plants provide some savings because of size, but these are more than offset by the cost of setting up huge distribution networks.'* (*RP*, Ironman, April 1978: 94). As investment policy takes time to materialise in the cement industry, this back to basics policy had an impact throughout the following decades. The competitive framework remained local. It consisted of optimising the size of plants according to locations. The effect was a reduction of the overlapping zones between natural markets, and therefore less direct competitive confrontation. The high level of vertical integration facilitated the stabilisation of competition: *'Most of the producers are vertically integrated. In addition to controlling raw material sources upstream, they own downstream many ready-mix concrete products, who are all cement users, and they often control, directly or indirectly, cement transport firms:*

---

2. A doubtful politically correct expression.

all of this enables them to influence behaviour on demand side.' (EEC, 1994: §12.5).

However, rivalry has been intensive. The means of production and production capacity have been rationalised and optimised according to the local demand levels. Plants have been modernised and costs reduced.[3] The financial surpluses locally gained from higher productivity and the restructuring of market overlaps enabled producers to invest abroad. As multi-market rivalry increased in Europe, European producers invested massively in the US.

The maritime model in Europe

At the end of the 1970s, and in the early 1980s, the largest European cement producers reduced their exposure to exports, and adjusted their production capacity according to the demand in the local markets. They competed as rivals, reducing costs and acquiring international positions. Meantime, Greek producers were adopting a totally different strategy, the maritime strategy.

In 1979, the Greek producer Titan expanded production capacity at its Kamari cement plant to 2.35 million tons. Halkis, another key player, set up two new kilns that increased its production capacity by 2 million tons. In the early 1980s, Heracles General Cement Co. added 1.9 million tons of capacity to its Velos plant for the explicit purpose of exporting. Velos became the largest European plant, with 4.4 million tons. The moves were significant. They added production capacity accounting for a third of Greek cement consumption while Greek consumption was already being supplied from existing capacity. Overall, half of Greek cement production capacity was dedicated to exports. The Greek approach to the market was to supply the Middle East markets which, at that time, did not produce cement in proportion to the oil-driven economic boom that they were experiencing. Greek exports to the Middle East peaked, in 1985, at 7.6 million tons, with Egypt, Algeria and Saudi Arabia accounting for 78 per cent. At that time, Greece was the largest world exporter of cement, with annual revenues from cement exports amounting to $250 millions. Cement

---

3. In France, for example, overall production capacity was 42 million tons in 1974. This had fallen to 30 million tons by 1986. Most plants have been converted from the wet to the dry process (55 per cent of the industry production capacity in 1972, 84 per cent in 1983, 87 per cent in 1990, to be compared with 44 per cent, 56 per cent, 62 per cent in the US), resulting in cost savings in energy consumption in production.

prices were remunerative (in the range of $37-$38 in Egypt, as against $39).

Although buoyant in 1984-85, the Middle East export market began to show signs of weakness. Between 1986 and 1988, it simply collapsed following the failure of the OPEC countries to sustain oil prices, and a downward trend in cement price ensued. The resulting fall in the Greek cement export price ($31 in 1989 for the best cement quality) did not pick up.

The previous chapters emphasised that exports are usually highly concentrated, and considered within a long term perspective. The Greek strategy was no exception to this. It did differ, however, in terms of the scale of operations, with a massive investment plan having been focused on supplying a small number of target markets. The gamble involved in the investment was highly speculative, given that a collapse of the target markets would leave producers with a huge amount of unemployed production capacity.[4] It was shown earlier that the strategy of producers who built significant amounts of capacity in the US in the 1960s was very different. Dundee and Atlantic Cement set up huge plants in order to benefit from economies of scale in production. Alongside this, they developed distribution networks using cement barges and terminal depots. The combination of the economies of scale and their distribution network enabled them to sell in a multitude of distant regional markets, where they only aimed to take a small market share. Their business risk was diversified in two ways. Firstly, the consequences of a local market collapse would not have been fatal for Dundee or Atlantic Cement. Secondly, distant local producers were not able to retaliate in the local market of either plant. By contrast, the Greek producers concentrated their risk on a small number of markets. Presumably, they undertook the venture with the assurance that the government would intervene if the situation turned sour. As a matter of fact, cement exports were one of the main sources of revenue for Greece. In the first few years, the strategy

---

4. The gamble was speculative in two ways. Firstly, it was presumed that the demand for cement in the Middle East was to be sustained over time. Secondly, it was presumed that the Middle East countries would not see any advantage in setting up their own production capacity. Neither presumption held, and the latter was particularly inaccurate. By 1989, Saudi Arabia had 11.8 million tons production capacity at its disposal, and itself exported 1.3 million tons. In fact, cement producers were aware, from the early 1980s, that the Arabic oil countries intended to set up cement plants (*RP*, Duthie and Liduena, April 1982).

proved very successful. However, in 1985/86, economic circumstances changed and the Middle East countries stopped importing cement.

The Greek producers were left with a massive amount of unemployed production capacity and had no hope of finding ready alternative outlets. Under normal economic circumstances, such a strategic failure would have resulted in the market exit of less efficient plants and producers. The production capacity of Halkis and Heracles had to be drastically reduced, and if not, it seemed likely that the companies would have to be declared bankrupt.

But, cement was a key item in the national balance of trade, and the Greek government intervened. Different means of financial support were mobilised, such as the subsidisation of exports and the provision of capital to write off debts. The state aid added up to $180 million.[5]

The situation then became comparable to that in US with regard to the Venezuelan dumping episode.[6] The Venezuelan government, had subsidised cement exports, in the same way as the Greek government, in order to increase his dollar holdings.

However, the institutional and political situation in Europe at that time, was very different to that in the US. Firstly, the Greek government was negotiating to join the European Community. It was a transitional period, with Greece neither a full European Member State nor a non-EC country. With regard to alleged anti-competitive cement imports from Greece, then, the European Commission was in a difficult position. It could not initiate an antidumping procedure against Greece, as Greece was not a non-EC country (antidumping procedures only applied to countries outside the European Community). Nor could it apply state aid procedures (the interdiction of state aids only applied to countries within the European Community) as Greece was not a full Member State of the EC. The only option was a political settlement. *'When Greece joined the Community, its cement industry was receiving a considerable amount of State aid. By Decision n° C/85/1344 of 13 August 1985, the Commission found that Greek aid in the form of export refunds was incompatible with the common market. However, in view of the balance of payments situation in Greece, the Commission decided in Decision 85/594/EEC of*

---

5. Law of 7 August 1986.
6. At the end of the 1980s and the beginning of the 1990s, the European cement producers petitioned the EC against non-EC countries. The main issues were imports from Eastern countries that were dumped at the West German border, and Tunisian exports to Spain.

22 November 1985 (OJ n° L 373, 31.12.1985, p. 9) that the refunds could continue until 31 December 1986. Again in view of the Greek economic situation, the Commission decided in Decision 86/614/EEC of 16 December 1986 (OJ n° L 357, 16.12.1986, p. 28) to amend its Decision of 22 November 1985 by authorising Greece to abolish the aid gradually in four stages, the final stage being scheduled for 1990. The Commission also decided the aid granted by Greece in the form of interest subsidies was incompatible with the common market (Decision 86/187/EEC of 13 November 1985, OJ n° L 136, 23.5.1986, p. 61).' (EEC, 1994: §24.2. note 113).

Subsequently, the Commission conducted an investigation into the recapitalisation of Heracles in 1988. The file was closed in January 1992 without official comment.

Overall, then, in the late 1970s and early 1980s, the European cement industry adopted two contrasting development strategies. Almost all European cement producers chose to follow the inland competition model, which involved the reduction of local market overlap, but the Greek cement producers chose the maritime development model, which involved creating capacity to sell cement in target overseas markets. As the latter strategy failed in the mid-1980s, the European Community cement markets experienced a competitive confrontation between local and global approaches to the market.

The confrontation between local and global inside the EC

In the mid-1980s, Europe provided the best opportunities for new outlets for the Greek cement producers. Given the geography of Europe, and its local demand and market structures, they decided to target the UK and Italy.

The UK and Italy had some interesting features. In both cases, the biggest cities, in other words the largest cement consumption areas, were within easy reach of harbours which had the facilities to deal with cement shipments. Also, their cement industries were highly concentrated. In the UK, three producers (Blue Circle, Rugby Cement, and Castle Cement) accounted for almost all of the market. In Italy, Italcementi, Unicem and Cementir accounted for two thirds of the market. This concentration in production was matched by concentration at the downstream level, in the Ready Mix Concrete industry. RMC and Tarmac, the two largest UK concrete companies, were international companies, operating in many world markets. The large concrete company, Calcestruzzi, was in a similar situation in Italy. In both countries, then, vertical integration was weak, and powerful independent concrete companies were a match for local cement producers. Finally, in the UK, the cement industry officially ran a basing point system of pricing (the basing point system was also assumed to prevail in Italy). This had a number of consequences. Firstly, the level of cement prices was higher in the UK than in other parts of Europe. Secondly, the basing point system only allowed producers to lower all cement prices in a local or regional market in response to selective rebates. Thus, the system was rigid and not very suitable for responding to simultaneous price discounts in various parts of the market.

At the turn of 1985 and 1986, the trading company, Libexim, sent two silo ships to the UK to sell Greek cement. At the same time, Greek producers initiated talks with Calcestruzzi in Italy. The response of UK producers to the threat of Greek cement imports was twofold: they gave up the basing point system in order to meet the selective Greek price cuts; they organised lobbying at the national and European Community levels. In terms of this latter response, the unclear position of Greece vis à vis the European Commission has already been mentioned. This resulted in their lobbying strategy having little effect at the European Community level, in spite of EC investigations into State Aids granted to the Greek industry. At the national level, the lobbying strategy was more effective. The UK government took account of the EC deadlock, and decided to negotiate an import quota directly with the Greek government. It was set at 3 per cent of national consumption.[7] In Italy, the cement producers offered exceptional price discounts to Calcestruzzi in order to prevent Greek producers from entering the Italian market.

Another potential response to the Greek competitive threat would have been to retaliate in the Greek market (the multi-market competition strategy). However, the cost of this strategy was too high. Moreover, the Greek concrete companies were vertically tied to cement producers making entry more difficult. As a result, European cement producers chose to buy cement and clinker[8] from Greek producers, and use their

---

7. On 18 December 1986, an article in the *Financial Times* mentioned an intergovernmental agreement between the UK and Greece limiting Greek cement imports to 2.75 per cent of national cement consumption. Imports were allowed to go to 3 per cent of market consumption in 1989.(i.e. 300000 tons a year); (also see EEC, 1994: §25.47).

8. It has already been mentioned that in some part of the world local cement producers have grinding mills but no kilns, either because they do not have limestone quarries, or because the kilns have been shut down for

distribution networks to sell it in other world markets, notably the US and Africa.

The view of the EC Commission

Throughout the course of its investigations, the Commission seized many documents. They related to three main topics: firstly, exchanges of information among European cement producers, particularly at the level of the European cement trade association, Cembureau; secondly, cross-border trade between Member States (the inland local competition model); finally, the Greek issue.

The Commission considered the documents as making a single antitrust case and provided a global interpretation. It considered that the European cement producers had colluded in order to stabilise competition in the European Community, and had used various means:

1. they had colluded at the national level. The market shares of local competitors were stable over time. This gave a clear indication of collusion.
2. collusion would have been unworkable if the investment strategies of the cement producers had not been co-ordinated. Investments in production capacity that were incompatible with local cement consumption would de-stabilise the markets. Exchanges of information enabled producers to co-ordinate capacity investment policies.
3. as it would not have been possible to perfectly adjust production capacity to consumption at the national level, European cement producers had applied the *'home market rule'* (as the expression appeared in the seized documents). If local production over-capacity arose, a cement plant would refrain from selling beyond the boundary of its Member State, except in the case of a formal order from a foreign competitor. In this manner, the national Member States markets were to be isolated from competitive disruption. Persistent and significant discrepancies between the cement prices of different Member States had not generated cross-border trade. This was a clear indication of mutual respect of the home market rule at the European level.

---

environmental reasons (Florida). In such circumstances, the producers buy clinker on the international market and grind it at the plant location.

4. however, in spite of this respect of the *'home market rule,'* in adverse economic circumstances, local production over-capacity would exist in the short-run, and competitive aggression would be tempting. Because of this, European cement producers had set up export committees, that channelled production surpluses towards overseas destinations. Non-EC markets were targeted in order that exported surpluses were not resold in the markets of EC Member States.

5. this general policy would been applied in the management of Greek production surpluses. After the collapse of Middle East markets, Greek producers had attempted to sell in Member States markets. The European cement producers reacted swiftly, by threatening to retaliate in the home Greek market and collectively attempting to export some of the Greek surplus, particularly to the US.

Two points need being stressed.

The first relates to the alleged role of the European cement trade association, Cembureau. The Commission regarded Cembureau as having been at the heart of this mechanism, and the place where the agreements between the producers were worked out and operated. Cembureau had centrally managed and enforced the *'home market rule,'* referred to in some documents as the *'Cembureau principle.'*

The second point is that the anti-competitive practices (refraining from competing, exchanging information on investment policies, collectively attempting to export Greek surpluses) were all organised and revolved around a single principle. The Commission considered that the practices formed *'an indissoluble whole'* (EEC, 1994: §58.4). Thus, the Greek issue was seen as *'a serious and flagrant application of the Cembureau agreement or principle of not transhipping to home markets.'* (EEC, 1994: §53.1).

The purpose, here, is not to go very deeply into the detail of the case (the Commission's decision runs for 150 pages). The aim is rather to gain some economic insights from the European case, based on the lessons that were drawn in the first and second parts of the book.

Exchanges of information

The Commission investigators seized documents at the headquarters of Cembureau. These documents indicated that the national trade associations fed a Cembureau data base with information about the cement prices that were being charged in their respective national markets. The mentioned prices were average prices calculated from a schedule of f.o.b. prices.

On reflection, this information seems benign. One cannot figure on the cement producers being able to co-ordinate their business strategies on the basis of such data. The debates from US antitrust cases illustrate the minor importance of such information.

While the economics of the industry make it local, markets are regional. Average prices are meaningless. A brief seized by the Commission which related to Spain pointed out: *'The prices have followed a different trend from region to region. It is thus difficult to establish an average price for the whole of the country.'* (EEC, 1994: §16.20).[9]

Moreover the indicated prices are f.o.b. prices. To co-ordinate their pricing strategies, the cement producers would have required more detailed information. They would need to know how to get from f.o.b. prices to delivered prices. As the Commission rightly noted, quoting an economic study from Louis Phlips, it is the publishing of delivered prices together with f.o.b. prices that produces anti-competitive effects. But, none of the documents gave any clue of how delivered prices were established or what they were. It has been seen that in the US basing point antitrust case, transportation costs were vital to a knowledge of what cement prices were being charged to cement buyers. The antitrust authorities had got hold of the railway price lists that were in use in the cement industry, and that were published by the trade association, the Cement Institute. Any cement plant would know which price to charge at any delivery location

---

9. This goes along with the analysis of the US Department of Commerce economists: *'Cement pricing is regional in scope. Prices around the country differ depending on such factors as the supply/demand situation, energy costs, the number of suppliers (including foreign suppliers), the efficiency of local production facilities, the proximity of the suppliers to the market, and type of transportation available.'* (US Department of Commerce, 1987: 43). Similarly, *'Domestic Canadian cement prices also vary considerably among provinces. In most years, Quebec cement prices are below the national average, while Ontario prices are about average. British Columbia and the Prairie provinces have cement prices that are above the national average.'* (*ICR*, Roy, August 1995).

by applying the basing point formula. The situation was similar for the implementation of the basing point system in the European steel industry (Phlips, 1995: 121). However, no data on transportation cost schedules had been found at the headquarters of Cembureau.

Finally, the prices communicated to Cembureau were list prices. But, particularly at times of recession and production over-capacity, list prices neither reflect the economic circumstances nor the likelihood and the dissemination of secret rebates to gain new customers as the economists at the FTC have emphasised (USFTC, 1966a: 58-59).

Given what is known about the competitive processes at work in the cement industry, it is very unlikely that information on cement prices, as picked out from the national trade association correspondence with Cembureau, would suffice for the organisation of a collective colluding scheme among European cement producers. To be effective, the information would have to have been more detailed and precise, and gathered at the regional level. For example, it does not go as far as the information and data published in specialised magazines. The *International Cement Review* published the market prices in the regional markets of Spain, information that Cembureau did not seem able to get from the cement producers. In 1995, cement ton prices were $85 in Madrid, $65 along the Spanish South Coast, and ranged around $55 in Malaga and Motril (*ICR*, anonymous, July 1996). Similarly, the information provided in the annual issues of the *Mineral Yearbook*, published by the US Bureau of Mines (US Department of the Interior) appears to go into more detail than the information disseminated by Cembureau. Actually, the US BofM publishes average mill values per short ton in various districts of the US. In the most significant states, markets are divided into two districts (Southern California, Northern California; Southern Texas, Northern Texas; Eastern Pennsylvania, Western Pennsylvania). As far as it is known, the US antitrust authorities do not see any problem with the publication of these annual reports. Besides, industry magazines provide any reader with detailed information on current prices in the various States of the US. In 1993, Robert Roy wrote a paper on the Florida cement market that gave the price quoted by local producers -$52.66- (*RP*, Roy, November 1993). In 1994, an appraisal of the economic situation in Texas, gave an account of current prices and estimates for that current year (at the time, the annual Mineral Year Book report had not yet been published) (*RP*, Roy, August 1994). On a regular basis, the US magazine, *Rock Products*, investigates the operating costs of US cement plants. Data published includes cement delivery costs per mile and ton (*RP,* Huhta, November 1992).

The Commission had also seized documents in which exports to non EC countries were mentioned. Information was gathered by the export committees. However, once again, information on export volumes to different countries, and average cement export prices does not seem any more sensitive, with regard to competition, than the information published in specialised industry magazines. Similar and more detailed statistics on international trade are published per country in the *International Bulk Journal.* Articles give indications of prices according to destinations, and of shipping and unloading costs (*IBJ,* Beechner, January 1993).[10]

It does not seem as though the export committee documents went any further than collecting data that was otherwise available in official publications and specialised magazines.

Overall, the Commission did not find the detailed and technical information in the documents (that would at least cover how delivered prices were calculated), that would almost certainly be needed to set up and operate a coherent collusive scheme. As they had not provided evidence that such information had been circulating among European Cement producers, the Commission might be suspected of having jumped too easily to conclusions. From an economic perspective, alternative interpretations were possible.

Cross border trade

The Commission thought that over time there had been significant and persistent discrepancies between the production costs of Member State cement producers, and between the cement prices they had charged to customers (EEC, 1994: §11.6, p. 13). From 1981 to 1991, European price discrepancies range as follows:

1. 10 per cent to 20 per cent between France and Germany; Germany, the Netherlands and Belgium; France and Italy; Germany and the UK.

---

10. For example, shipping costs in Mediterranean were $30 to $33 per ton in 1992. Producers that were situated on the coast of the Black Sea had a shipping cost disadvantage of about $2 a ton. Shipping to Western Africa was estimated to cost $15 per ton (7 days). Unloading costs were approximately $10.

2. 30 per cent between Germany and Italy , between Spain, Portugal and Germany;
3. 50 per cent between the Italy and UK , between Spain, Portugal and the UK;
4. 100 per cent between Greece and the UK.11

In view of these production cost and price differences, it was thought that cross-border trade should have developed.

On this particular issue, once again a comparison with the US situation is useful. In chapter 6, it was noted that the difference in average cement prices between different States of the US had moved from 45 per cent in 1978 (a year where the average national price was at a peak -$58.28- in constant dollar value terms) to 60 per cent in 1990 (a year where the average national cement price was close to its lowest level -$41.89- in constant dollar value terms). In Europe, as in the US, differences in prices mirror local market conditions. They do not reflect artificial barriers to entry purposefully erected by producers. Actually, the differences in prices should be greater in Europe than in the US, as geographical characteristics reinforce market localisation. There is no river network comparable to that in the US that could provide the opportunity of unifying European regional markets within larger ensembles. Therefore, pointing out differences in cement prices in the European Member States does not contradict the existence of an ongoing normal competitive process.

In addition, it must be emphasised again that the Commission referred to average Member State f.o.b. cement prices, which do not give a fair account of price competition in local markets. Consider two countries. One has a coastal area (France, for example), and the other is surrounded by mountains with no opening to the sea (Switzerland, for example). They have a common boundary in the mountainous regions. Presumably, the average national price of the former will be lower than that of the latter, as the former average cement price will include cement prices in harbour locations that are influenced by cheap imports. So there will be a significant difference in price between the two countries. However, it is very likely that on either side of the boundary, in both inland mountainous locations, the cement price is not that different. In such circumstances there is no reason for cross-border trade to develop.

---

11. Greece will be analysed separately since the setting up of massive greek production capacity to export to the Middle East, at the end of the 1970, had a specific impact aver the greek domestic cement production costs and prices.

Two other factors have certainly influenced the fact that differences in prices between the Member States, however limited, had not led to cross-border trade in the short run.

The first factor has already been touched upon. In the 1970s, the European cement producers chose the inland local market strategy. This aims at adjusting production capacity to local market demand.

The second factor relates to the economic circumstances of the day. In contrast to the US, in the 1980s, the European economy was sluggish. The Commission took account of economic circumstances when fining the European cement producers *'The Community industry was having difficulty in overcoming the bad economic situation.'* (EEC, 1994: §65.6)]. But paradoxically, the Commission did not take economic circumstances into account in their analysis of the case. Yet, it is commonly agreed that in bad economic situations:

1. Cement prices are rigid.[12] The Commission itself agreed with this. *'Demand is relatively rigid even when alternative prices are available. Consequently, the traditional solution of cutting prices when sales are falling is not a very viable one for producers, since the cement industry in itself can have only a very small influence on the factors determining demand, which are a reflection of the general state of the economy.'* (EEC, 1994: §8.4). However, they disregarded this fact when reaching their conclusions.

2. Competitive aggressions are unlikely. On the one hand, European markets are regional and traditional, and as a result, any price aggression would be quickly detected.[13] The arrival of cement shipments from other Member States would immediately be spotted, particularly in markets such as France where cement producers are vertically integrated into concrete production. On the other hand, the threat of swift retaliation in a multi-market competitive game is credible, as European producers face each other in many non-EC markets. Hence, European producers were cautious about aggressive price rebates. In their European operations, they used to prefer a geographical self-containment

---

12. The rigidity of prices in bad economic circumstances is a well-known phenomenon, even in the US (Carlton, 1986).

13. In each period, except when new kilns and plants were set up, it was common knowledge, within the industry, which regional markets and customers a cement plant supplied. On this issue, see, for example, Kamerschen (1974) on the RMC Memphis market.

policy, comparable to policies that have been implemented in the US.[14] Also, the cultural differences between Member States (differences in language, and business practices concerning cement quality and colour, for instance) are additional brakes to cross-border expansion in recession periods.

But once the economy recovers, the competitive process revives. The recovery creates uncertainties in the local market situation. It makes price competition less visible and retaliation more difficult (see Ch. 3, and Rotemberg and Saloner, 1986; Rosenbaum, 1986). Still, the cement producers that are, or want to be, engaged in the local competitive game, act on the basis of a long term rationale, and define their investment policy accordingly. In the case of the inland model, the conquest of a neighbouring market usually requires an investment in production and distribution facilities, with cement being conveyed by rail rather than truck.[15] For example, this was the strategy adopted by Cemex when targeting Southern US markets (specific investments in cement plants in the North of Mexico, and deliveries to the US by rail towards San Diego, El Paso, and even Albuquerque). Ciments Français adopted a similar strategy in the early 1990s, when they acquired the CCB plant in Belgium, situated close to the French/Belgian border. They shut down their obsolete plants in the Paris area, and transported cement from Belgium to Paris by rail. At that time, French cement imports were about 400000 tons. They jumped to 1.3 million tons in 1991, 1 million tons of which came from Belgium. The search for inland market expansion fit into a rationalisation and restructuring policy, and therefore into a long term business strategy.

In the 1980s, neither the economic circumstances, the structure of cement industry, nor the political context suited the rise of price aggression when there was short-term new entry into neighbouring markets. In this regard, the only piece of evidence that the Commission gave was that differences in cement prices between Member States were frequently steady over time.[16] It has been shown that this type of evidence

---

14. See the 1968 Kaiser Cement memorandum quoted in Chapter 2: '*As you are aware, though Oregon Portland (and Idaho Portland could have sold in the same area, they have refrained from doing so by creating an imaginary boundary line...*'
15. "border markets" trade accounted for 16 per cent of international cement trade in 1982, and mostly occurred by rail (*RP*, Duthie and Liduena, April 1982).
16. The Commission also provided pieces of evidence on infringements of European competition legislation. However, it is not the purpose of this book

is fairly unconvincing. But the Commission should have asserted its findings by studying competition at the local level, and inquired whether rather than explicit collusion, the absence of cross-border trade was more likely the result of a competitive process within a restrictive vertically integrated oligopoly engaged in spatial competition. The Commission itself has underlined the principles that should have guided such an analysis. *'In the light of what has been stated above regarding economies of scale, production costs, freight costs and the methods for adding freight costs to the cost price, it may be said generally that, in a competitive system, the distance at which cement may be sold depends on a number of factors such as the size of the production plant, the degree of utilisation of production capacity, production costs, the means of transport used and the cost of each means of transport, and the prices charged on the various markets.'* (EEC, 1994: §11.3).[17] Thus, a proper economic analysis testing the relevance of the Commission's interpretation was not carried out, probably due to time constraints that the Commission was under. The decision did not disclose data or information about the utilisation of capacity either side of Member State boundaries, about local demand conditions, or about distribution networks.

The Greek case

In the mid 1980s, Greek cement producers were almost bankrupt. The Greek government re-capitalised and subsidised the industry. The producers had to find new outlets for their production capacity. The situation was quite similar to the US in the 1990s. In the US this triggered antidumping and countervailing procedures. Injured local producers gathered and exchanged information in order to make their case, and lobbied federal departments. The European producers set up a task force to gather the available information, and argue their case before the Commission. Within the framework of the European Task Force, counteracting moves were discussed: retaliation by exporting to Greece, a strategy based on a multi-market competition rationale; the setting up of a

---

to discuss whether or not the seized documents were sufficient evidence of guilt from a legal perspective. Here, we simply discuss the significance of the economic content of the documents in the economic reasoning of the Commission.

17. Investment costs in distribution, such as from the building of terminals, and potential retaliation in a multi-market competition game, should be added to the list.

joint trading company that would buy Greek cement and sell it in overseas markets; the lobbying of national governments and the EC Commission. The outcome proved to be disappointing. A few lobbying decisions were taken, but in a legal context, this was blurred by the Greek entry into the European Community.

In its decision report, the Commission interpreted the counteraction to Greek exports as an example of an enforced general principle during the 1980s, the *'home market rule.'* Although the Commission recognised the anti-competitive nature of the financial aid from the Greek government, it refused to regard the Greek exports as anything other than cross-border trade. The Greek affair was considered was considered with the other issues, as mentioned earlier.[18] Its contention is based on two main arguments.

In the first place, the Commission distinguished between the three Greek producers. Halkis and Heracles had been re-capitalised, but Titan had not. As a result, they argued that they could not apply an antidumping procedure to Greece. The argument is fragile. Titan had benefited from financial support with regard to exports, and, above all, there had been no significant restructuring plan in return for the re-capitalisation. Had one taken place, the issue of Greek exports to the European Community would probably have dissolved.

Secondly, the Commission noted that the European cement producers responded collectively to the Greek imports, while only two countries, the UK and Italy, were in the Greek line of fire. In the view of the Commission, this could only be explained if the European cement producers had already been colluding. The argument was that they were used to colluding in EC markets, and acted similarly in the Greek case by consistently applying the *'home market rule,'* and using export committees to get rid of production surpluses in overseas markets. Both forms of market conduct were said to *'form part of a whole'* (EEC, 1994: §57). This would be comparable with the Federal Trade Commission deducing the existence of anti-competitive practices in the local cement markets of Florida, from the existence of the "ad hoc committee" of the US cement producers of Florida, which was set up to make their case before the ITC and the DoC. Of course, the AD/CDV procedures did imply that competitors should gather and exchange information, but this did not automatically indicate the presence of local anti-competitive agreements.

---

18. The Commission referred to the issue several times as the *'so-called Greek problem'* (EEC, 1994, in particular §28.15).

The Commission skipped from one set of issues to another without properly addressing the question of what the relevant market was, or its implications. In the Greek case, while the UK and Italy were the easiest targets, other EC countries were also under threat, particularly given the extent of coastal borders (Denmark, France, The Netherlands, Belgium, Portugal and Spain all have a significant coastal border).

Local and global: defining the relevant market

Cement markets are regional in scope. *'Supply, demand, costs, and prices vary, sometimes widely, among regions.'* (US Department of Commerce, 1987: VII). Attempts to consider the competitive issues in a broader context (the US national level) have failed (in antitrust, the Arizona Case; in antidumping, the 1986 Cement Case). The basing point system was an exception. The calculation of delivered prices was based on transportation costs which were dealt with centrally by the Cement Institute. Nothing of this kind had been found in the Cembureau archives. However, the Commission thought that it could cover three separate issues in a single case: cross border trade between inland local markets; exports committees; and the Greek affair. It justified its interpretation by treating the local and the global competitive processes under the same relevant market definition. *'It is evident [from the above] that Europe is the relevant market, consisting of a set of juxtaposed and interdependent markets.'* (EEC, 1994: §11.7).[19]

To determine the relevant market, the Commission made use of the concept of the "ripple effect". This is described as follows: *'All the overlapping markets are interdependent on one another, and any action taken on one market may have an impact on the most distant markets.'* (EEC, 1994, §11.7).[20] With Greece exporting cheap cement to the UK and

---

19. In French the word "juxtaposer" means placing things next to others without them being dependent on one another. The French expression "juxtaposés et interdépendants", which was used in the Decision of the Commission, is as contradictory as speaking of a square circle. It is probably the first time in a European competition case that the relevant market was so ill-defined. In a way, this indicates that the Commission were not at ease in their efforts to articulate the local and global dimensions of cement markets.

20. Commissioner Seeley G. Lodwick, a member of the US International Trade Commission, has given a more technical and detailed definition of the ripple effect. *'Even when some domestic producers are not in the near vicinity of a source of a significant subject imports, this does not mean that there is no basis*

Italy, other European producers were under threat from the ripple effect, so they mobilised and set up the European Task Force.

Two problems arise from the interpretation of the Commission.

In the case of inland locked markets, a competitive disruption can certainly materialise when demand falls. However, it will remain local and will not propagate. The high transportation costs limit the extent of the ripple effect. An inland cement plant facing aggressive price competition would try to shift part of their production to neighbouring markets, but this shift would be limited due to the cost of trucking. The ripple effect would be all the more limited if the natural market of the plant does not overlap with that of their competitors (which would be the case if, in the past, restructuring strategies had been adopted by the producers), and where the market is highly vertically integrated.

The Commission argued that, overall, the inland local market disruption should drag the other neighbouring markets in its path. But, the Commission only offered one example of such a situation, concerning cross-border issues between France and Germany. In that particular case, one will note that the ripple effect was limited in scope and that a cement producer referred to the observed market disruption as "limited to the Lower Rhine and Moselle" (two French districts out of 95 in mainland France - here district refers to the administrative division of the French territory, the département), but that it could spread to Moselle and Vosges (two other French districts).[21] Indeed, it would be nonsensical to presume

---

for a causation argument, based upon the effect of some domestic producers shifting shipments away from areas where subject imports compete, a phenomenon referred to as "the ripple effect". These "displaced" shipments that are shifted away the geographic region in which subject imports compete then impact the surrounding geographic areas. Producers in the surrounding areas must then shift their shipments away from the "displaced" domestic shipments or face price declines in their area. The net effect of lower subject imports prices through the whole region after all the adjustments by domestic producers will result in lower domestic prices or reduced US shipments in the entire region.' (USITC, 1990: 66).

21. *'Should this situation, which is limited to the Lower Rhine and Moselle, spread to the Meurthe et Moselle or Vosges regions, it would have particularly serious consequences in a market experiencing full recession.'* (EEC, 1994: 22.1) But the Lower Rhine covers 4786 km^2, and the Moselle 6214 km^2. Together the Meurthe and Moselle account for 5280 km^2, and the Vosges for 5903 km^2. Overall, the four districts cover a total surface area of 22183 km^2. France covers 550000 km^2. The relevant market quoted as possibly experiencing serious consequences, accounted for 4 per cent of the French territory. The

that the ripple effect could disseminate throughout the European market as a whole, because, as stated by the Commission, European regional markets are juxtaposed and also interdependent. Inland border markets, therefore, have to be taken in isolation if there is to be a robust competitive assessment. There are no legitimate economic grounds for considering that the border markets of Europe are truly interdependent.

A similar criticism can be made with regard to the Greek affair. The Greek producers could only sell in the European market by shipping cement. The Greek cement had to be unloaded in harbour terminals. Once unloaded, cement would be delivered to the customer by truck, so trucking costs would limit the delivery zone.[22] The relevant market with regard to Greek cement, then, covered the coastal regions of EC Member States. It must be stressed, though, that the harbour terminal would have to be within the proximity of a large cement consumption area, that is, a large urban area.[23] Given this, the ease of penetrating the market hinges on the degree of vertical integration that prevails in the industry. If the largest regional concrete firms are subsidiaries of cement producers, it is unlikely that they will buy the cheap imports. Likewise, as the exporter has to unload cement at a terminal, and ensure delivery to the customer by truck, vertical integration in trucking would also be important. The Commission noted that European cement producers *'often control, directly or indirectly, cement transport firms.'* (EEC, 1994: §12.5).[24] The relevant

---

market disruption by the ripple effect would, therefore, have to have been circumscribed in a very limited area.

22. It has been stated that deliveries from a terminal depot rarely occur outside a radius of 100 mile (USITC, 1990: 13-14).

23. As the vice-chairman of Atlantic Cement has argued, a distinction should be introduced between concentrated high tonnage volume and scattered high tonnage volume: *'While perhaps half of the balance [of cement work] is done by contractors buying for state highway work, it is work that is scattered. It is not concentrated. Work on highway jobs may be 75 mile away. It is not the concentrated, high volume tonnage that is easily accessible for the Atlantic Cement Company, for example, and its terminals. It forces us into different selling operations -with added transport costs, smaller customers and more salesmen.'* (US Federal Trade Commission, 1966b: 466).

24. There is a fundamental difference between Europe and the US in this regard. The entry of foreign imports into the Florida market was made easier by the existence of large independent RMC companies which controlled most of the trucking. *'The actual hauling of Portland cement to end users is generally performed by independent common carriers or by subsidiary trucking firms of*

market in the Greek case, therefore, covered the regional harbour markets throughout Europe.[25] As the Commission acknowledged, local market conditions would determine how vulnerable producers would be to cement imports (EEC, 1994: §56.1). Cheap cement imports have a "ripple effect" in the neighbouring inland markets of regional harbours, but this is limited by transportation costs, the extent of inland overlapping markets, and the degree of vertical integration in the concrete industry and in trucking. For example, the ripple effect would probably have been at a minimum in France, given that all of these limitations are important in the French cement market. Cheap imports, then, would probably have only spread to districts close to the point of market entry.

This economic analysis leads us to identify two types of relevant markets: the inland borders markets (France/Germany, Portugal/Spain, Italy/France, etc); and, with regard to Greek imports, the regional harbour markets. Of course, the ripple effect is effective, but to different degrees, depending on the particular market conditions. It is certainly not effective throughout the whole of the European market. The relevant market, then, cannot be the whole of Europe, consisting, as argued by the Commission, of a set of juxtaposed and interdependent markets. The globalisation of markets has not meant that the local dimensions have been removed. Certainly, the Commission was aware of the importance of the local dimensions of the cement markets. But probably also, the Commission has been bound to consider European markets as forming part of a whole in order to lodge a credible complaint and to sue the cement producers on the basis of a particular infringement of Article 85 of the Treaty of Rome. In other words, their conduct was led by practical and legal issues.[26]

---

ready-mix companies. Some ready-mix companies have trucks and pick-up the Portland cement at the plant for their basic needs.' (USITC, 1991b: A-55).

25. Most European countries have harbours with facilities to accomodate cement ships. The whole European cement industry was, therefore, under threat from Greek cement imports.

26. On this issue, the Commission adopted a paradoxical position. In the course of its actions, it dropped the accusation relating to national markets, that of the collusion of cement producers within the limits of their home Member State market. Only anti-competitive practices against the Greek producers remained. But, according to the Commission's definition of the relevant market, the regional European markets were interdependent, and an imbalance in one market, given the ripple effect, could have a knock-on effect in *'the most distant markets.'* Since the allegations were dropped at the national level, the Commission would have to give evidence that an imbalance, say between the border markets of Spain and Portugal, could spread, say, to Denmark -a distant

Our purpose is not to assess whether or not the legal approach of the Commission was legitimate. The aim is, rather, to give an economic analysis of the case. Probably for the first time in its history, a competition policy authority had to draw a line between what should be permitted with regard to the competitive conduct of an oligopoly that was engaged in a process of spatial competition but was experiencing the globalisation of its traditional markets, and what should be considered as anti-competitive and unlawful in such circumstances. From an economic perspective, dealing with such an issue requires the simultaneous study of:

1. how the markets were operating (for instance, in terms of multipoint competition and potential retaliation)?
2. what the economic circumstances were (rates of capacity utilisation, local demand fluctuations, investment policies)?
3. what the conditions of the globalisation process were, and what market globalisation means?
4. moreover, what was the impact on social welfare?[27]

Of course, it would have required numerous and detailed investigations to propose a consistent economic analysis. In the European case, the weight of the legal approach seems to have overwhelmed the economic analysis by far. Such an ourtcome is disappointing with regard to the progress of the globalisation process in most industries. Thus there is a need to

---

market- without having to go through France, Belgium, Germany, or the Netherlands. The Commission's rationale would then be based on a sort of "jumping ripple effect" that operated over the boundaries of the European Members States.

27. For example, the Commission did not debate the issue of cross-hauling. The development of cross border trade implied an increase in trucking in Europe. For example, suppose that cross-border trade in cement between France and Italy intensified. The road network between the two countries is already saturated. What about the Summer holiday periods when cement trucks would add to tourists' traffic jams? Would the cross border trade really be profitable, and optimise social welfare? These issues are not touched upon. The Swiss competition authorities did tackle them. Their decision was to authorise a certain amount of co-ordination in the industry, in so far as it limited trucking to the benefit of rail transportation, which was less costly and more advantageous as regards welfare (Kartellkommission, 1993).

develop and discuss economic tools to regulate the new competitive environment.[28]

---

28. As it stands, the European cement producers have lodged an appeal to the European First Instance Tribunal.

CONCLUSION

The word globalisation has been extensively used since the 1980s, but as Sylvia Ostry rightly points out, *'no one definition exists'* (Ostry, 1996, p. 333). In the economic literature, it is embodied by a series of facts and analyses.

There has been the tightening of trade and financial linkages between countries. Financial markets have been liberalised and interconnected, allowing for the easy access of capital which circulates freely from country to country at a speed never before experienced.

At the micro level, the firm and the consumer seem also to be becoming global. Beyond differences in taste, a convergence in national consumption appears to be at work, at least with regard to specific brands and products. In terms of firms, new entities are developing that are not only multinational but organised networks, deliberately scattering their functional and production departments according to the available sites of excellence and know-how across countries (Ohmae, 1995).

Thus, globalisation, though an imprecise concept,[1] primarily refers to the scale of the increase in internationalisation with regard to trade, direct foreign investment, capital mobility, and the progress of information technology. But it also refers to the opinion of a crisis in the policies elaborated and formulated by Nation States (Ostry, 1996). The emergence of so-called trading blocks such as NAFTA, the EU, and Southern American and Asian markets, at the same time as the prosperity of particular regional markets (California, Catalogna, etc) that are smaller units than countries, seems to indicate that the level of the Nation State is becoming less relevant when attempting to formulate proper political economic answers. Is it conceivable that Nation States can influence, or

---

1. Some authors even suggest that the concept makes no sense. See, for example, Cohen (1996).

govern this globalisation of the economy, and if so, how? What would the proper level of action be?

The aim of this book has been to give more focused and rigorous insights into the precise the concept of globalisation, and to examine issues relating to its regulation. Our approach has been to give a dynamic and micro-economic perspective on the changes that have occurred in a particular market, that of cement. The cement industry has traditionally been considered a local industry, and has been studied as such by economists. However, the 1980s saw its globalisation.

The contribution of the historical perspective to the understanding of markets globalisation

The globalisation of cement markets can be looked upon as the competitive linkage of local markets with distant ones. The globalisation of a local market is revealed through the alterations made to the price system. The coherence of the local price system is drastically disrupted by changes that occur in distant markets. International trade is, at best, an imperfect measure of the globalisation of markets.[2]

Increases in trade between countries comes within the scope of internationalisation. Large producers import to and export from their local markets. They control the trade from overseas sources. It has been illustrated how, in the 1970s, US producers had organised their distribution networks and started to import cement when facing shortages, and take advantage of differences in production costs between countries. In a sense, it was as if the US industry had de-localised part of its production facilities abroad.

Obviously, the globalisation of cement markets which occurred in the 1980s has been characterised by a significant increase in international trade. The leap has been dramatic: 22 million tons in 1970 (a quarter of US cement consumption); 80 million tons in 1980; 95 million tons in 1995 (roughly equal to US national cement consumption). But these new record levels have hidden a fundamental difference from the previous period.

New economic agents, the traders, have emerged and prospered. They have detected the differences in cement prices in world markets, and made the most of differences in growth rates and currency fluctuations between

---

2.   A local market is said to be part of a global market if its price equilibrium (but also, the availability of new products and technology) depends on the price equilibrium (and the availability of new products and technology) in a distant market.

distant local markets. They have also used available distribution networks to their benefit, while setting up parallel distribution systems. They have innovated in making new cement loading and unloading systems operational, and have invested in silo ships. In doing so, they generated new trade that was not under the control of incumbent local producers. The latter had no other choice than to follow this lead, and to start thinking with a global perspective, and no longer in terms of the management of independent local market equilibria.

Traders themselves have endeavoured to enter the local competitive game smoothly. At first, they did not seek to globalise cement markets. In fact, the technical systems which allow long haul cement trading were developed to supply a particular market, the Middle East region, which was booming due to oil revenues. At this time, the Arabic countries did not have significant cement capacity production to match demand. The traders organised themselves to supply these markets.

Some years later, the oil price dropped and the Arabic peninsula economy went into recession. Cement demand fell as new domestic production capacity was becoming operational. This new situation created a massive imbalance in international cement trade which had repercussions in US, European and even Japanese markets. From this time onwards, differences in growth and currency rates between countries were to be systematically exploited. Even when international trade is apparently small, the globalisation of markets acts as a threat to local markets. Distant local markets can, therefore, be linked even without significant trade occuring between them.

In extreme cases, trade between countries may be significant without the globalisation of markets occurring. In such situations, incumbent producers control the flow of imports and exports in their local markets, taking advantage of price differentials (for example, de-localising their production units). Conversely, globalisation may occur without significant international trade. The possibility of such trade, as a threat to the incumbent producers, weighs on the local market price equilibrium and de facto produces the interconnection of markets.

From the cement case study, salient points deserve to be emphasised.

The globalisation of markets is a sudden process which competitively links distant markets. It is made operational by the development of distribution networks which shape the boundaries of local markets, and the existence of independent purchasing power not controlled by incumbent local producers, guaranteeing them an outlet for entry. These two dimensions determine the potential exposure to globalisation of a particular market.

Globalisation comes into effect when transportation costs, currency rate fluctuations and divergence in growth rates across distant markets make an arbitrage trade profitable.

Geographical differences, product differentiation, divergence in consumer tastes (Usunier, 1996), and the supply of quality services attached to the sale of a good offer relative protection against globalisation. Sustained price differences between markets, and stability of the market shares of local incumbent producers over time, are indicators of the relative "localisation" of markets.

Usually, globalisation occurs with the advent of a chaotic local market regime. *Ex ante,* the local market price system is driven by the confrontation of local economic circumstances with the long term view of the business held by incumbent producers. Under conditions of globalisation, tacit agreement over the price system collapses, and entrants (traders in the case of the cement industry) introduce a new competitive rationale.[3] Price discounts multiply, and the conditions within which prices are set become opaque. Local producers have little knowledge of the cost functions of the entrants or the distant market producers, and therefore of their price reaction curves. The local price system loses its long entrenched coherence. Sometimes the incumbent producers simply do not know which distant local market they are competitively linked with.

Finally, the globalisation process is primarily a one way process. The incumbent producers who witness the globalisation of their local market rarely have the means to retaliate in the distant market which is the source of the competitive disruption. In the case of cement, back hauling generates this type of asymmetry between local and distant market, but consumer tastes, and distribution systems may also reinforce it. Besides, in terms of dynamics, the distant market which is the source of the globalisation changes over time. The globalisation process therefore refers to changing competitive linkages between local and distant markets.

---

3. The competitive rationale can be based on cost saving and favourable exchange rates in other countries. Low cost production from delocalised units shipped to local distant markets are part of the globalisation process.

Strategic responses to globalisation

Can the globalisation process be reversed?

The 1980s witnessed a surge in the globalisation of cement markets. This happened at roughly the same time in the different parts of the world. In the Pacific zone, the Japanese and Korean cement markets have been competitively linked. In Europe, the UK and Italian markets have been flooded with Greek cement. In the US, the Eastern, South Eastern and Western markets had a similar experience, with imports of cement from Mexico, and more distantly from Venezuela and Japan.

The issue of whether the globalisation process can be reversed can be considered in terms of two questions.

If the factors responsible for globalisation reverse (i.e. - differences in growth and currency rates) will the process come to a halt?

Are there effective strategies that incumbent firms can adopt to halt the globalisation process, or at least to alleviate its impact?

The cement case study give some insights into these questions.

As a general rule, producers export when domestic demand falls and stop doing so when it increases. The Korean cement industry, which severely hit the Japanese markets from the mid 1980s, stopped exporting to Japan at the beginning of the 1990s when Korean domestic cement demand surged.[4] In addition, business with Japan was less attractive due to lower domestic Japanese cement prices and a weaker yen.

In the US, the imports accounted for 23.6 per cent of the domestic consumption in 1988. By 1993, they had dropped to 9.9 per cent.[5] As Robert Roy noted *'Nowadays, economic conditions have more or less returned to the earlier conditions as far as import competitiveness is concerned [...] Cement traders are facing reduced quantities available, higher prices, higher freight rates, and a weaker dollar.'*[6]

International trade, which had reached 80 million tons in 1980, dropped to 65 million tons in 1987 due to the fall in oil prices and to the setting up of new production capacity in the Middle East and the US, traditionally significant importing zones (*WC*, Hanrahan, 1996).

But this halt only expresses a short term reversal of the globalisation process. Later, it may in turn be propitious to an increase in globalisation, as the threat still remains even if the short term conditions are no longer

---

4. In 1994, Korean cement producers even imported 2.17 million tons of Japanese cement due to domestic shortages.
5. Obviously, the effect of the antidumping policy has to be taken into account.
6. (*ICR*, Roy, May 1985: 53)

satisfied. The impact of the conditions necessary for globalisation ceasing to be met simply illustrates the dynamic instability of the links between distant markets. In the first half of the 1980s, Spain plunged into economic recession. Spanish cement consumption dropped from nearly 20 million tons in 1980 to 16 million tons in 1984. Over the period, Spanish cement exports exceeded 11 million tons each year, (more than half domestic consumption), and reached 13 million tons in 1983. There were no cement imports. Ten years later, the situation was entirely reversed. By the first three years of the 1990s, Spanish cement exports had declined to an average of 2 million tons per year and imports had started to penetrate the Spanish markets. They picked up at the same level as exports while the annual domestic consumption reached record levels of nearly 29 million tons. So, Spain which had been an exporting country in the 1980s - and was the world first exporter in 1983 - became an importing country in the first years of the 1990s as the domestic consumption and the peseta got stronger.[7] Thus the role of Spain in the globalisation of the cement markets had dramatically changed over time. It is not so much the transitory character of the markets globalisation then, that is telling but the adjustment of the globalisation process to changes in both the targeted and the competitive influencing distant markets.

In a dynamic perspective, local incumbent producers exercise little power over currency rates and local economic growth rate fluctuations. Nevertheless, they have at hand strategic responses to curb the effect of globalisation or else to gain a partial control over the globalisation process.

There are five main strategic responses available to incumbent producers: to rationalise excess capacity and improve the productivity of plants in local markets that are politically exposed to the effects of globalisation, in order to reduce differences in competitiveness between them and distant markets; to differentiate the product or service in order to re-localise the market; to take over the traders or to incorporate the trading function into their activities; to create the means for retaliation in distant markets, and develop multi-market solidarity and co-operation among producers; to take control of distribution networks and of the independent cement purchasing power in local markets.

Disposing of excess capacity and modernising plants is the engineer's response to globalisation. It enables low-cost production and therefore resistance to low price imports entry. This type of strategy is available, but

---

7.   *European Annual Review,* n° 16, 1993 (p.49); n° 17, 1994 (p.49).

within limits, particularly if it is assumed that the local market is already highly competitive and in line with local economic circumstances. The incumbent producers may be led to de-localise their production units in order to maintain their market share. The adjustment to the global environment is all the more brutal since the local competitive game, which had previously been based on rivalry, had postponed the restructuring of the industry.

The second strategic response is to re-localise the market by differentiating the product and the services attached to its consumption, or improving its quality. In the cement industry, such a strategy has a limited impact, although cement standards, speed and security of supply, just in time delivery and assistance to customers are not negligible.

The third strategic response is to internalise the arbitraging function. Rather than undergoing the globalisation process, incumbent firms enter the trading market or acquire existing trading firms with a view to channelling and diverting potential threats from globalisation. Such strategy allows producers to collect the profit of the trading activity.

The firm would then become global, with particular characteristics that make it distinct from international firms. The latter are focused on the partitioning of markets, and the search for profitable niches. By contrast, the global firm has to reconcile the international long term approach based on market partitioning with short term opportunistic behaviour based on swift arbitrage, where actions are taken according to the difference in economic circumstances between countries without concern for consequences in the local markets.

The fourth strategic response to globalisation is to create the means of retaliation in distant markets, and to develop multi-market solidarity and co-operation among producers. This strategy seeks to restore a competitive balance between producers, and enables the re-localisation of the market. However, a return to a stabilised local market based upon a multi-market competitive rationale is likely to create "overflow markets" in other areas where trading surpluses will be directed. In these latter markets, price competition will be fierce and erractic making life even more difficult for the affected local producers.

The fifth strategic response available to cement producers is to take control of distribution networks, and to discipline or acquire downstream independent purchasing power. Local cement producers may take financial holdings in, or acquire, coastal and inland terminals. This has been the case in the UK, where the leading producers (Blue Circle, Castle and Rugby) own 8 out of 20 cement terminals. UK producers have also been major importers, when globalisation of their local markets has occurred, importing 2.5 million tons out of a total 3.8 million tons imports. By 1996, imports had reduced to a mere 0.8 million tons.

Producers could also develop vertical links with their customers, or even take them over. In the case of global firms, control of trading combined with the development of downstream vertical links can lead to the use of globalisation as a weapon against itself. Thus, Japanese cement producers made profits by trading Korean cement, and channelling it through their distribution networks (Tilton, 1996).

The degree of vertical integration is crucial in terms of exposure to globalisation. In Europe, the Italian and British cement markets are characterised by powerful independent downstream buyers. They have been more vulnerable to imports from Greece, than other cement markets, such as the French, where vertical integration between cement and concrete producers is high. By the same token, the ban on vertical integration imposed by the FTC in the US facilitated the globalisation of US cement markets in the 1980s. But vertically integrated firms also have to manage and deal with a contradiction: seizing short term opportunities via the distribution network and whilst holding a long term view with regard to the cement production business. The global firm organised as a network, is therefore a firm in a state of permanent internal conflict.

The five strategies mentioned have been used by cement producers to curb the effects of market globalisation in the mid 1980s. Producers have also mobilised institutional strategies, trying in particular, to get antidumping sanctions and imports quotas, in order to halt and regulate the globalisation process.

Regulating the market at a time of globalisation

Three types of regulatory policies impact on the functioning of markets: competition or antitrust policy, either at the national level or at the level of an enlarged integrated market (eg Europe); national policies that shape competition in local markets by dealing with the effects of international trade; supranational agreements with regard to barriers to trade.

Competition policy supports the globalisation of markets in several ways. Its aim is to intensify competition in local markets. It has already been stressed that by opposing vertical integration between cement producers and concrete firms, and therefore maintaining independent downstream purchasing power, the FTC facilitated the entry of cement imports into the US markets. Similarly, the FTC has been keen on limiting concentration in local markets while it agreed to let European producers take over US cement producers as the former were regarded as new entrants. By contrast, other national policies have had the effect of stabilising competition in local markets. This was the case with the industry restructuring policy initiated by MITI and jointly managed by the Japanese cement producers.

Other trade policies (antidumping, state aids, import quotas) slow down the globalisation process. They prohibit particular trade practices that would usually be deemed competitive in a larger integrated market. In most cases, they have been regarded as helping co-ordination between incumbent local producers and protecting them from the price competition of distant markets (Hindley and Messerlin, 1997). They may also outweigh the competitive distortion produced by subsidisation to exports that are commonly used by some Nation State governments. They may sometimes reverse the globalisation process, as happened in the US with antidumping policy.

At a supranational level, trade policy under the GATT agreements interferes with the competition and antidumping policy. It seeks to curb their negative impact on international trade. Thus, Mexican cement producers have appealed before the World Trade Organisation against the duty sanctions imposed by the US ITC.

The regulation of the globalisation process is therefore particularly complex. Competition at the local, national, and integrated single market levels, is regulated by the interplay of competition and industrial policies, in the same way that trade links between local and distant markets are regulated by the interplay of trade policies either at the national or integrated single market level. These policies are managed by different institutions which have their own agendas. Some support the globalisation process: antitrust authorities, the WTO. Others interfere with it and de facto slow it down, such as with the antidumping policy.[8]

The issue of regulating globalisation revolves around five main points that have been at the heart of the analysis and that the diverse trade and competition institutions find hard to deal with.

The first point is about the definition of the relevant market when considering a competitive assessment at a time of globalisation. In the first

---

8. Governments themselves can intervene directly to slow down the globalisation process (as the UK and Japanese governments did by negotiating imports quotas) or to speed it up (as did the Greek and the Venezuelan governments by subsidising the national producers).

place, globalisation does not ipso facto mean that the relevant market is worldwide for all industries. Secondly, globalisation of markets introduces the notion of a local market that is competitively, or under the threat of being competitively, linked to distant markets. Therefore, the relevant geographical market is not necessarily the local market plus the contiguous markets which shape an enlarged trading zone, whether it be a national market (as in the US), a single integrated market (as in Europe), or a trading block (such as South East Asia). The case of the cement industry is particularly telling in this regard. The globalisation of US cement markets illustrates that a clear distinction needs to be made according to the degree to which the local markets are potentially exposed to competition from distant markets. The West-Centre local US markets are landlocked and little threatened by the globalisation of cement markets. However, producers located in the Mississippi basin and its river system, the coastal markets (Florida, California), and the Great Lakes area are vulnerable to imports that may come from Canada, South America, Europe and Asia. The antitrust and antidumping authorities have usually made this distinction when reaching a decision. By contrast, the European Commission has not made such a distinction with regard to European coastal markets vulnerable to Greek imports (mainly in the UK and Italy due to the existence of independent concrete buying power) and European inland markets.

The relationship between local and global competition is an issue in all industries. The new information technologies, the progress in transportation logistics may alter significantly the supply chain and the potential exposure to globalisation in many sectors. The definition of the relevant market should therefore include these changes in the competitive assessment and in particular should characterise the exposure to globalisation of the local markets.

The second point, linked to the previous one, relates to the vertical dimension of competition. The relationship between producers and distributors are, as it has been stressed, at the heart of globalisation and localisation process. How to deal with vertical restraints? How to assess their competitive impacts? Economists, at least in their theoretical field, seem to be less convinced of the anti competitive and foreclosure effect of vertical links. But, little empirical studies have been carried out on that issue.

The third point is on multi-market competition which, there again, has received insufficient attention. The cement case indicates that it is an essential part of the competitive game. But the outcome is unclear. The multi-market rivalry seems to help, stabilising competition in particular local markets and at the same time, takes part in the development of what has been referred to as "overflow" markets. These overflow markets are in a sense the opposite of Marshallian districts. They are areas where local production is no longer given a chance to develop in the long run. The larger multi-market producers have an edge over the smaller monomarket producers as they are more likely to be able to develop credible and effective strategies in response to the globalisation of markets. It is the case, even if in the local market, the large multi-market producer finds it hard to discipline recalcitrant mono market producers in ordre to stabilise the market.

The fourth point focuses on the degree of rivalry in a multi-market oligopoly. The antitrust authorities are used to considering competition primarily in terms of price and volume. The issue of rivalry is generally left aside although it is to be acknowledged that it is not easy to handle. How should a fair account of the degree of rivalry between multi-market producers that compete in production, distribution, R&D, trading, preemption of sites, acquisitions be given?

Finally, stands the regulatory issue of the welfare impacts of globalisation. The globalisation of markets may produce wastes of resources and pollution. In the cement industry, cross hauling and the increase in transportation have in the past been assessed by the UK Restrictive Practices Court and the Swiss Kartelkommission, where they were found sufficiently damaging that the reduction of price competition between producers was allowed as a trade-off against positive welfare impacts.

From another angle, the globalisation of markets may also prove detrimental to competition when it results in a chaotic market. In such circumstances, prices stop playing their fundamental role as an economic signal with regard to investment. In a chaotic market, economic rationality is put into brackets. The fluctuations of currency rates bear part of the responsibility for this type of competitive outcome. Because of short term fluctuations, local markets are suddenly globalised and are likely to remain so due to the threat of globalisation, preventing producers from investing in their industry with confidence. How therefore should artificial sources of markets globalisation be regulated? Is it acceptable to let "overflow markets" develop for the sake of competition?

The regulation of globalisation is only at its early stages.

POSTFACE

by F.M. Scherer
Harvard University

Globalization and Regulation of the Cement Industry

The portland cement industry has been a perennial focus of controversy among economists and competition policy authorities - a concern disproportionate to the industry's relatively small size. Several characteristics explain this attention. Its physical capital intensity is atypically high among manufacturing industries, and the capital sunk in cement plants has no viable alternative uses. The variable cost curve is L–shaped; incremental cement production costs (mainly for energy and raw materials) are fairly low relative to minimum average total cost until full capacity utilization on a 24-hours-per day basis is approached. The demand for cement is cyclical and probably quite price-inelastic over plausible price ranges. As a result of these characteristics, economic theory predicts, cement prices will be volatile under purely competitive price-setting - so much so, cement industry advocates have long claimed, that unfettered competition would be "chaotic" or "ruinous".

Except for the fact that it is relatively inelastic supply functions, rather than demand functions, that oscillate over time, the supply of staple crops such as wheat, maize, and sugar beets experiences analogously unstable pricing under competition and comparable difficulties adjusting capacity to demand.[1] Most industrialized nations have developed elaborate governmental schemes for mitigating the competitive fluctuation of staple agricultural product prices. But the cement industry employs far fewer persons than agriculture, so its political clout is negligible. To deal with their problem individualistically, the cement producers have evolved price-setting institutions, ranging from outright cartel arrangements to "open price" reporting and tit-for-tat recognition of mutual interdependence, which have repeatedly drawn challenges from national and supranational competition policy authorities.

Cement has another fairly unique characteristic - the high cost of shipping finished product from cement mills to users by traditional transportation media. Among the 101 U.S. manufacturing industries for which my colleague Dennis Murphy computed composite 1963 transport cost indices on a standardized 350 mile (564 kilometer) shipment, Portland cement had the second-highest index: 51.5 cents per dollar of f.o.b. plant product value.[2] Only industrial gases had a higher index (at 70 cents per dollar of product value). The unweighted average over 101 industries was 5.45 cents, the median 2.61 cents. High outbound transportation costs normally mean that markets for the product are severely localized. That plus compelling economies of scale at the plant level imply that the number of cement producers confronting one another rivalrously in the typical market is small. Portland cement is the quintessential spatial oligopoly. Intellectually, pricing in spatial oligopolies is one of the most difficult and complex problems addressed by economic theorists.[3]

Nevertheless, cement shipments are not always limited to short radii by the high cost of traditional overland media. In recent decades, efficient water transport alternatives - at first, specialized river barges, and then large ocean-going "floating silos" - have been developed, making it possible economically to ship cement thousands of kilometers from the production source. Partly because seaside locations often contain a trove of sea shells rich in the calcium carbonate needed to make cement and

1. See e.g F. M. Scherer (1996), *Industry Structure, Strategy, and Public Policy.* New York: Harper Collins, pp. 18-22.
2. F. M. Scherer, Alan Beckenstein, Erich Kaufer, and R. D. Murphy (1975), *The Economics of Multi-Plant Operation: An International Comparisons Analysis.* Cambridge (MA), Harvard University Press, pp. 429-432.
3. See Melvin L. Greenhut, George Norman, and Chao-Shun Hung (1987), *The Economics of Imperfect Competition: A Spatial Approach.* Cambridge (U.K), Cambridge University Press.

partly for strategic reasons, large new cement plants have been built where the output could be loaded onto ocean-going vessels. The resulting shipments have transformed cement into a globalized industry, side-by-side, to be sure, with local markets where geographic conditions require overland transport. This industrial structure transformation provides a central theme for the analysis presented here by Messrs. Dumez and Jeunemaître.

The globalization of cement shipments sent shock waves into coastal cement markets, triggering numerous behavioral and public policy adaptations. Such shocks should by no means be viewed as intrinsically undesirable. When business cycle peaks are unsynchronized across major industrial nations (as they have for the most part been since 1973), shipments of cement to nations experiencing boom demand from recession-impacted nations can make it possible for the world as a whole to satisfy its cement demands with less total capacity, thereby sparing resources for alternative uses. But national authorities resent imports that injure their local producers, so they have sometimes responded by erecting trade barriers to curb cement import flows. Even more unwelcome may have been a hysteresis effect identified by the authors of this volume. Once imports gained a foothold in new national markets during demand peaks, they persisted after demand ebbed. And to capitalize on the transformations wrought by long-distance cement shipping, cement producers that once operated mainly within a single nation have through merger and green-field plant construction become multinationals, meeting one another as rivals in a host of national and local markets. How multi-market contact affects the pricing and investment behavior of oligopolistic rivals is another difficult problem on which economic theorists have not yet achieved definitive insights.

The specific impetus to the writing of this book appears to have been the decision of the European Community Commission in November 1994 to levy fines totalling ECU 248 million against 42 cement-producing enterprises for alleged violations of Community competition policies.[4] Among the numerous cement company actions cited as violating Article 85 of the Treaty of Rome, special attention was devoted to a series of measures taken in response to the problem posed by Greek cement producers. They had expanded their capacity at seaside mills to meet the

---

4. "Commission Decision of 30 November 1994", Cases IV/33.126 and 33.322 - Cement, *Official Journal of the European Communities,* vol. 37 (30 December 1994), pp. 1-158.

voracious cement demands of Middle Eastern OPEC lands following the petroleum price increases of 1973-74 and 1979-82. But when petroleum prices collapsed in 1985 and 1986, so also did Middle Eastern cement demand, leaving Greek producers with a huge overhang of excess capacity. As the Greek firms began shipping cement to Italy and the United Kingdom and threatened inroads into other European coastal markets, northern European cement makers linked up as what I have elsewhere called "dancing partners" with Greek firms, diverting the Greek supplies to Africa and North America and thereby alleviating the threat of price erosion in their European home markets.

This historical episode is critically analyzed by the authors. But their investigation sweeps much more widely. They provide rich insights into circumstances and reactions attending the penetration of Korean and Taiwanese cement makers into the traditionally protected Japanese homeland, the growth of cement exports from Mexico and Venezuela into the United States, the half-century history of complaints by U.S. antitrust authorities against the pricing practices, first under a basing point system and later through alleged collusion, of domestic cement makers; and the similar complaints (with a rather different outcome) against United Kingdom cement makers.

My own analysis from an American perspective of the solutions European cement producers devised for the "Greek problem" reaches somewhat more negative conclusions than those of the authors.[5] Nevertheless, I concur strongly in one of their principal conclusions. The Commission's decision, although rich in documentary excerpts from subpoenaed materials, is largely devoid of careful economic analysis on matters that cry out for such inquiry. Although I cannot claim expertise on European Community competition policy matters, I suspect that the flaw lies in the procedures followed by the Commission's Directorate General IV (holding the competition policy portfolio). My first detailed insights into the EC cement action came at a conference convened in Paris during January 1996, at which a thoroughgoing discussion of cement industry pricing in geographic space occurred. There was talk of using the participating economists' findings in appeals to the European Court of Justice. But the Commission's decision was already a fait accompli, apparently based upon little prior presentation of economic arguments

---

5. F. M. Scherer (1997), "International Trade and Competition Policy", in Einar Hope, editor, *Competition Policy for an Integrated World Economy.* Northhampton, U.K., Routledge.

either for or against the cement makers' conduct. One is reminded of *Alice's Adventures in Wonderland*: first the verdict, then the trial. Furthermore, I was told by an EC competition policy official that any economic defenses mounted at the Court of Justice level would be too little and too late. Clearly, the Commission needs to establish procedures that join contested economic issues at an earlier decision-making phase.

There is also much to be said for making the Commission's deliberative proceedings more transparent. During the summer of 1997 I was surprised, for example, to learn from a knowledgeable confidential source that an American economist had prepared on behalf of Airbus Industrie a brief to the Commission alleging anticompetitive consequences from Boeing's acquisition of the McDonnell-Douglas Corporation. I cannot say whether his arguments were right or wrong. But what is significant is that their existence was not mentioned in any of the extensive press coverage on that dispute.

In Chapter 5, the authors advance the hypothesis that the visible lack of dynamism among U.S. portland cement producers, leading inter alia to mergers that left two-thirds of U.S. cement-making capacity in the hands of foreign companies, resulted from "heavy-handed" antitrust policy. European companies, on the other hand, operated for the most part in a more tolerant competition policy environment and, the authors suggest, exhibited much greater dynamism, among others things as the leading acquirers and builders of U.S. cement capacity. The causal conjecture is provocative, but I am not certain that it is supported. My own research suggests three alternative hypotheses.[6] First, at least until the early 1950s, the U.S. industry operated in a cocoon of restrictive practices that emphasized "soft" inter-firm competition. Many of the executives who made, or failed to make, key strategic investment decisions during the 1960s and 1970s grew up in that sheltered club-like environment, which was hardly conducive to the emergence of aggressive entrepreneurship. Second, the plants inherited by those executives were for the most part optimized to highly localized markets. It was hard to modernize them, and existing plant locations were often ill-suited to the construction of much larger new plants exploiting long-distance transportation routes such as

---

6. See e.g. F. M. Scherer, Alan Beckenstein, Erich Kaufer, and R. D. Murphy (1975), *The Economics of Multi-Plant Operation: An International Comparisons Analysis*. Cambridge (MA), Harvard University Press, pp. 429-432; see also David J. Ravenscraft and F. M. Scherer (1987), *Mergers, Sell-Offs, and Economic Efficiency*. Washington: Brookings Institution, pp. 263-266.

rivers and coastlines. Under the circumstances, relying on imports to satisfy occasional peak demand surges was an attractive strategy. And third, the cement industry, very much like the steel industry,[7] found itself during the 1970s and 1980s in an environment of almost persistently stagnant demand growth. The interstate highway building program had peaked and declined, and business capacity additions emphasized new equipment rather than green-field plant construction. The U.S. cement industry's peak 1973 output level has not been matched since then. It is not surprising therefore that the most dynamic new investments came from European companies such as Holderbank at Dundee and Clarksville (whose executives I interviewed at the time of the Clarksville project). It is also not surprising, given the industry's depressed profitability, that company managers in effect gave up and sold out to European firms, whose leaders retained adrenalin surges from meeting the needs of a home economy that sustained vigorous growth at least up to the oil shocks of 1973. Before one can confidently conclude that heavy-handed antitrust actions precipitated U.S. industry leaders' failure of nerve, a more careful investigation exploring inter alia the industry's pathological sociology is needed.

---

7. See e.g F. M. Scherer (1996), *Industry Structure, Strategy, and Public Policy.* New York: HarperCollins, pp. 182-192.

BIBLIOGRAPHY

Allen Bruce T. (1971) 'Vertical integration and market foreclosure: the case of cement and concrete', *The Journal of Law and Economics*, n° 4, pp. 251-274.

Allen Bruce T. (1972) 'Vertical foreclosure in the cement industry: a reply', *The Journal of Law and Economics*, october, vol. XV, n° 2, pp. 467-471.

Allen Bruce T. (1978) 'On not being "stuck in cement"', *Industrial Organization Review*, vol. 6, p. 60-70.

Allen Bruce T. (1993) 'Foreign Owners and American Cement: Old Cartel Hands, or New Kids on the Blocks?', *Review of Industrial Organization*, vol. 8, pp. 697-715.

Aranoff Gerald (1991) 'John M. Clark's Concept of Too Strong Competition: The U.S. Cement Industry as a Possible case', *Eastern Economic Journal*, vol. XVII, n° 1, January/March, pp. 45-60.

d'Aspremont Claude, Encaoua David and Ponssard Jean-Pierre (1999) 'Politique de la concurrence et théorie des jeux. Quelques réflexions à partir de l'industrie cimentière', *Revue d'Économie Politique*, vol. 109, n° 1, janvier/février, pp. 35-58.

Axelrod Robert (1984) *The Evolution of Cooperation*. New York, Basic Books.

Bairoch Paul (1996) 'Globalization Myths and Realities. One Century of External Trade and Foreign Investment', *in* Boyer and Drache, 1996, pp. 173-192.

Baum Joel A.C. and Korn Helaine J. (1996) 'Competitive Dynamics of Interfirm Rivalry', *Academy of Management Journal*, vol. 39, n° 2, pp. 255-291.

Beacham A. (1962) 'Some thoughts on the cement judgment', *The Economic Journal*, June, pp. 335-343.

Benson Bruce L., Greenhut Melvin L., and Norman George (1990) 'On the Basing-Point System', *The American Economic Review*, vol. 80, n° 4, June, pp. 584-588.

Benson Bruce L., Greenhut Melvin L., and Norman George (1990) 'On the Basing-Point System: Reply', *The American Economic Review,* vol. 80, n° 4, September, pp. 963-967.

Berger Suzanne and Dore Ronald (1996) *National Diversity and Global Capitalism.* Ithaca (NY), Cornell University Press.

Bernheim Douglas B. and Whinston Michael D. (1990): 'Multi-market Contact and Collusive Behavior', *Rand Journal of Economics,* vol. 21, n° 1, Spring, pp. 1-26.

Bhagwati Jagdish (1990) *Protectionism.* Cambridge (Mass.), The M.I.T. Press, 4th ed. (1st ed. 1988).

Boyer Robert and Drache Daniel (1996) *States Against Markets. The Limits of Globalization.* London and New York, Routledge.

Bundeskartellamt (1988) B1-253100-A-30/88-4, decision of 12 September.

Carlton Dennis W. (1983) 'A Reexamination of Delivered Pricing Systems', *Journal of Law and Economics,* vol. XXVI, April, pp. 51-70.

Carlton Dennis W. (1986) 'The Rigidity of Prices', *The American Economic Review,* September, pp.637-658.

Chandler Alfred Jr (1990) *Scale and Scope. The dynamics of Industrial capitalism.* Cambridge (MA), Harvard University Press.

Chen Ming-Jer and Miller Danny (1994) 'Competitive Attack, Retaliation and Performance: an Expectancy-Valence Framework', *Strategic Management Journal,* vol. 15, n° 2, pp. 85-102.

Clark J.M. (1938) 'Basing point of methods of price quoting', *Canadian Journal of Economics and Political Science,* November, vol. IV, n° 4, pp. 477-489.

Clark J.M. (1949) 'The law and Economics of Basing Points: Appraisal and Proposals', *The American Economic Review,* vol. XXXIX, n° 2, pp. 430-447.

Clark J.M. (1940) 'Toward a Concept of Workable Competition', *The American Economic Review,* vol XXX, n° 2, June, pp. 241-256.

Cohen Elie (1996) *La tentation hexagonale. La souveraineté à l'épreuve de la mondialisation.* Paris, Arthème Fayard.

Collomb Bertrand and Ponssard Jean-Pierre (1984) 'Creative management in mature capital intensive industries. The case of cement', in A. Charnes and WW. Cooper (ed): *Creative and innovative management.* Cambridge, Ballinger.

Collomb Bertrand (1993) 'L'industrie européenne du ciment au XXe siècle', *Entreprises et histoire,* n° 3, pp. 97-111.

Comanor William S. (ed.) (1990) *Competition policy in Europe and North America: economic issues and institutions.* Chur (CF), Harwood.

Congressional Budget Office (Congress of the United States) (1994) *How the GATT Affects U.S. Antidumping and Countervailing-Duty Policy.* Washington D.C., Congressional Budget Office, September.

Dam Kenneth W. and Shultz George G. (1977) 'Reflections on wage and price controls', *Industrial and Labor Relations Review,* vol. 30, January.

Dumez H. and Jeunemaître A. (1988) 'Une théorie du contrôle des prix aux USA', *Chroniques d'Actualité de la SEDEIS,* tome XXXVII, n° 4, 15 avril, pp. 163-170.

Dumez H. and Jeunemaître A. (1989) *Diriger l'économie. L'Etat et les prix en France (1936-1986).* Paris, L'Harmattan.

Dumez H. and Jeunemaître A. (1991) *La concurrence en Europe.* Paris, Seuil.

Dumez H. and Jeunemaître A. (1994) 'Political Intervention versus *L'État de Droit Économique:* The Issue of Convergence of Competition Policies in Europe', *Essays in Regulation,* n° 5, pp. 136.

Dumez H. et Jeunemaître A. (1996) 'Information et décision stratégique en situation d'oligopole. Le cas de l'industrie cimentière', *Revue Économique,* vol. 47, n° 4, pp. 995-1012.

EEC (1994) Commission Decision of 30 November 1994 Relating to a Proceeding under article 85 of the EC Treatise (Cases IV/33.126 and 33.322-Cement). *Official Journal of the European Communities,* L343, vol. 37, 30 December, pp. 343/1-343/158.

Fetter Frank Albert (1948) 'Exit basing point pricing', *The American Economic Review,* vol. 38, December, pp. 815-827.

Galbraith John Kenneth (1956) *American Capitalism: the concept of countervailing power.* Boston, Houhton.

Gerard Adams F. and Wechsler Andrew R. (1990) *Conditions of competition and the business cycle for gray portland cement.* Mimeo.

Gould J.R. (1963) 'Some further thoughts on the cement judgment', *The Economic Journal,* June, pp. 352-354.

Green Edward J. and Porter Robert H. (1984) 'Noncooperative collusion under imperfect price information', *Econometrica,* vol. 52, n° 1, January, pp. 87-100.

Haddock David D. (1982) 'Basing-point pricing: competitive vs. collusive theories', *The American Economic Review,* vol. 72, n° 3, June, pp. 289-306.

Haddock David D. (1990) 'On the Basing-Point System: a Comment', *The American Economic Review,* vol. 80, n° 4, September, pp. 957-962.

Harrington Joseph E. Jr (1984) 'Noncooperative behavior by a cartel as an entry-deterring signal', *Rand Journal of Economics,* vol. 15, n° 3, Autumn, pp. 426-433.

Heath J.B. (1963) 'Some further thoughts on the cement judgment', *The Economic Journal,* June, pp. 350-352.

Hindley Brian and Messerlin Patrick (1997) *Antidumping Industrial Policy: Legalized Protection in the WTO and What to Do.* La Vergne (TN), The American Enterprise Institute.

Hotelling H. (1929) 'Stability in competition', *Economic Journal,* vol. 39, pp. 41-57.

Johnson Ronald N. and Parkman Allen (1983) 'Spatial monopoly, Non-zero Profits and Entry Deterrence: the Case of Cement', *Review of Economics and Statistics,* August, vol. 65, n° 3, pp. 431-439.

Johnson Ronald N. and Parkman Allen M. (1987a) 'Spatial competition and vertical integration; Cement and Concrete Revisited: Comment', *The American Economic Review,* September, pp. 750-753.

Johnson Ronald N. et Parkman Allen M. (1987b) 'The Role of Ideas in Antitrust policy Toward Vertical Mergers: Evidence from the FTC Cement-Ready Mixed Concrete Cases', *The Antitrust Bulletin,* Winter, pp. 841-883.

Kamerschen David R. (1974) 'Predatory Pricing, vertical integration and market foreclosure: the case of ready-mix concrete in Memphis', *Industrial Organization Review,* vol. 2, pp. 143-168.

Karnani Aneel and Wernerfelt Birger (1985) 'Multipoint competition', *Strategic Management Journal,* vol. 6, pp. 87-96.

Kartellkommission (Schweizerische) und Preisüberwacher (1993) *Die Wettbewerbsverhältnisse auf dem Zementmarkt.* Bern (Switzerland), Eidg. Drucksachen, Dezember.

Kaysen Carl (1949) 'Basing-Point Pricing and Public Policy', *The Quarterly Journal of Economics,* vol. LXIII, August, n° 3, pp. 289-314.

Krugman Paul (1988) *Strategic Trade Policy and the New International Economics.* Cambridge (Mass), The MIT Press.

Krugman Paul (1990) *Rethinking International Trade.* Cambridge (Mass), The MIT Press.

Krugman Paul (1991) *Geography and trade.* Cambridge (Mass.), The M.I.T. Press.

Kwoka J.E. and White L.J. (1989) *The antitrust revolution.* Glenview (Ill.), Scott, Foresman and Company.

Lane Frederic C. (1985) *Venice, a maritime republic.* Mass., 1973. Trad. franç., Paris, Flammarion.

Liba Carl J. (1987) 'Cement shipments in the United States', *in* Proceedings of the 23rd International Cement Seminar.

Liebeler Wesley J. (1968) 'Toward a consumer's antitrust law: the Federal Trade Commission and vertical mergers in the cement industry', *UCLA Law Review,* vol. 15, pp. 1153-1202.

Lieberman Marvin B. (1987) 'Excess Capacity as a Barrier to Entry: An Empirical Appraisal', *The Journal of Industrial Economics,* vol. XXXV, n° 4, June, pp. 607-627.

Lima G.P. (1990) 'Concentration and collusion: the Brazilian cement industry', in Colloque 'Fusions, oligopoles et échange international', Aix-en-Provence, CEFI, 21-22 juin.

Lösch A. (1954) *The Economics of Location.* New Haven, Yale University Press.

Loescher Samuel M. (1959) *Imperfect Collusion in the Cement Industry.* Cambridge (MA.), Harvard University Press.

McBride Mark E. (1983) 'Spatial competition and vertical integration: cement and concrete revisited', *American Economic Review,* December, vol. 73, n° 5, pp. 1011-1022.

Machlup Fritz (1949) *The Basing Point System.* Philadelphia, Blakiston.

McGee John S. (1954) 'Cross-hauling - a symptom of incomplete collusion under basing-point systems', *The Southern Economic Journal,* vol. XX, April, n° 4, pp. 369-379.

Malueg David A. (1992) 'Collusive behavior and partial ownership of rivals', *International Review of Industrial Organization,* vol. 10, pp. 27-34.

Meehan James W. JR (1972) 'Vertical foreclosure in the cement industry: a comment', *The Journal of Law and Economics,* octobre, vol. XV, n° 2, pp. 461-465.

Mestmäcker E.J. (1952) *Verbandsstatistiken als Mittel zur Beschränkung des Wettbewerbs in den Vereinigten Staaten und Deutschland.* Frankfurt am Main, (dissertation).

Moomaw Ronald L. (1976) 'Vertical integration, predation and monopolization: the symbiotic relationship between the cement and ready mix concrete industries', *Industrial Organization Review,* vol. 4, pp. 117-119.

Mutoh Hiromichi (1990) 'Adjustment of Japan's Cement Industry under the structural adjustment law', JCER-Rand Conference on Troubled and Restructuring Industries, 5 May.

Ohmae Kenichi (1995) *The End of the Nation-State, the Rise of Regional Economies. How New Engines of Prosperity are Reshaping Global Markets.* The Free Pess.

Ostry Sylvia (1996) 'Policy Approaches to System Friction: Convergence Plus', *in* Berger S. and Dore R., ch. 13, pp. 333-349.

Owen Diane S. (1991) *Transport rate uncertainty and multiple basing point pricing: cement industry behavior in the 1920s and 1930s.* New Haven, Yale University, November.

Patterson W.C. (1993) 'First mover advantage: the opportunity curve', *Journal of management studies,* septembre, vol. 30, n° 5, pp. 759-777.

Peck Merton J. and McGowan John J. (1967) 'Vertical Integration in Cement: a Critical Examination of the FTC Staff Report', *The Antitrust Bulletin,* vol. XII, Summer, p. 505 et sq.

Phlips Louis (1976) *Spatial Pricing and Competition.* Brussels, Commission of the EC, Competition Approximation of legislation Series n° 29.

Phlips Louis (1983) *The Economics of Price Discrimination.* Cambridge/New York, Cambridge University Press.

Phlips Louis (1987) 'Information and collusion', in Hay and Vickers: *The Economics of Market Dominance.* Oxford, Basil Blackwell, ch. 3.

Phlips Louis (1993) 'Parallélisme de comportements et pratiques concertées', *Revue d'économie industrielle,* n° 63, 1er trimestre, pp. 25-44.

Phlips Louis (1995) *Competition Policy: A Game-theoric Perspective.* Cambridge, Cambridge University Press.

Ponssard Jean-Pierre (1995) 'Concurrence stratégique et réglementation de la concurrence dans un oligopole naturel. L'exemple de l'industrie cimentière', *Revue d'Économie Industrielle,* numéro spécial 'Économie industrielle: développements récents', pp. 385-401.

Porter Michael E. and Spence A. Michael (1982) 'The capacity expansion process in a growing oligopoly: the case of corn wet milling', in McGall John J. (ed.): *The economics of information and uncertainty.* Chicago, The University of Chicago Press, pp. 259-316.

Portland Cement Association (PCA) (1992) *US and Canadian Cement Industry: Plant Acquisition and Ownership Report 1974 to Present.* Skokie (Illinois), PCA.

Restrictive Trade Practices Court (1961) *In Re:* Cement Makers' Federation Agreement. 16 march.

Rotemberg J.J. and Saloner G. (1986) 'A supergame-theoretic model of price wars during booms', *American Economic Review,* vol. 76, n° 3, pp. 390-407.

Rosenbaum D.I. (1986) 'A further test of a supergame-theoretic model of price wars during booms', Department of Economics, University of Nebraska, working paper 86-9, October.

Scherer F.M. (1970) *Industrial Pricing. Theory and Evidence.* Chicago, Rand McNally College.

Scherer F.M. (1980) *Industrial Market Structure and Economic Performance.* Chicago, Rand McNally, (Second edition).

Scherer F.M. and Ross D. (1990) *Industrial Market Structure and Economic Performance.* Boston, Houghton Mifflin Co. (Third Edition).

Schmalensee Richard (1988) 'Industrial economics: an overview', *The Economic Journal,* vol. 98, September, pp. 643-681.

Scotchmer Suzanne B. and Thisse Jean-Jacques (1993) 'The implications of space for competition', London, CEPR.

Scotchmer Suzanne B. et Thisse Jacques-François (1993) 'Les implications de l'espace pour la concurrence', *Revue Economique,* vol. 44, numéro 4, juillet, pp. 653-669 *(version française du précédent).*

Selten R. (1973) 'A simple model of imperfect competition where four are few and six are many', *International Journal of Game Theory,* vol. 2, pp. 141-201.

Simon William (1950) *Geographic Pricing Practices (Basing-Point Selling).* Chicago, Callaghan and Company.

Stigler George J. (1961) 'The economics of information', *Journal of Political Economy,* June, n° 69, pp. 213-225.

Stigler George J. (1949) 'A Theory of Delivered Price Systems', *American Economic Review,* vol. 39, December, pp. 1143-59.

Streeten Paul (1996) 'Free and Managed Trade', *in* Berger S. and Dore R., ch. 14, pp. 353-365.

Tanguy Hervé (1987) *L'instrumentation des choix stratégiques. Pour une élaboration interactive de décisions collectives.* Paris, École Polytechnique, Thèse de doctorat en gestion.

Tharakan P.K.M. and Waelbroeck (1994) 'Antidumping and Countervailing Duty Decisions in the E.C and in the U.S. An Experiment in Comparative Political economy', *European Economic Review,* vol. 38, n° 1, January, pp. 171-193.

Thisse J.F. and Vives X. (1988) 'On the strategic choice of spatial price policy', *The American Economic Review,* vol. 78, n° 1, March, pp. 122-137.

Tilton Mark (1996) *Restrained Trade: Cartels in Japan's Basic Materials Industries.* Ithaca, New York: Cornell University Press.

Tushman M.L. and Anderson P. (1986) 'Technological Discontinuities and Organizational Environments', *Administrative Science Quarterly,* vol. 31, pp. 439-465.

Upham Frank K. (1993) 'Privatizing regulation: the implementation of the large scale retail stores law in contemporary Japan', Bellagio, M.I.T. conference on 'Domestic institutions, free trade and the pressures for national convergence: US, Europe, Japan', February 22-26.

US Department of Commerce (1987) *A competitive assessment of the US cement Industry.* Washington DC, July.

US District Court for the District of Arizona (1983) *In Re: cement and concrete antitrust litigation. Appendix D: Plaintiffs' joint narrative summary of litigation and statement of central facts and legal issues.* MDL docket n° 296 PHX-MLR (MS). 7 September.

US Federal Trade Commission (1932) *Report of the Federal Trade Commission on Price Basis Inquiry, the Basing-Point formula and Cement Prices.* Washington.

US Federal Trade Commission (1933) *Cement Industry, Letter from the Chairman of the Federal Trade Commission, Transmitting In Response to Senate Resolution No 448, Seventy-First Congress, A Report Relative to Competitive Conditions in the Cement Industry.* Washington.

US Federal Trade Commission (1966a) *Economic Report on Mergers and Vertical Integration in the Cement Industry. Staff Report to the Federal Trade Commission.* Washington DC, US Government Printing Office, April.

US Federal Trade Commission (1966b) *FTC Public Hearings on Vertical Integration in the Cement Industry.* Washington DC, 12 July 1966.

US Federal Trade Commission (1976) Martin Marietta Corp. et al. 88 FTC 989. D. 9039, December.

US International Trade Commission (1990) *Gray portland cement and cement clinker from Mexico. Final determination.* Washington DC, USITC publication 2305, August.

US International Trade Commission (1991a) *Gray portland cement and cement clinker from Japan. Final determination.* Washington DC, USITC publication 2376, April.

US International Trade Commission (1991b) *Gray Portland Cement and Cement Clinker from Venezuela. Preliminary Determination.* Washington DC, USITC Publication 2400, July.

US International Trade Commission (1995) *The Economic Effects of Antidumping and Countervailing Duty Orders and Suspension Agreements.* Washington, USITC Publication, June.

Usunier Jean-Claude (1996a) *Marketing across Cultures.* Hemel Hempstead, Herts, Prentice-Hall.

Usunier Jean-Claude (1996b) 'Consommation: quand global rime avec local', *Revue Française de Gestion,* n° 110, septembre-octobre, pp. 100-116.

Wade Robert (1996) 'Globalization and Its Limits: Reports of the Death of the National Economy are Greatly Exaggerated', *in* Berger Suzanne and Dore Ronald (1996), ch. 2, pp. 60-88.

Waldman Don E. (1988) 'The inefficiencies of "unsuccessful" price-fixing agreements', *The Antitrust Bulletin,* Spring, pp. 67-93.

Weingast B.R. and Moran M.J. (1983) 'Bureaucratic Discretion or Congressional Control? Regulatory Policymaking by the Federal Trade Commission', *Journal of Political Economy,* vol. 91, pp. 765-800.

Wilk Doris (1968) 'Vertical Integration in Cement Revisited: A Comment on Peck and McGowan', *The Antitrust Bulletin,* pp. 619-647.

Williamson Oliver E. (1985) *The Economic Institutions of Capitalism.* Free Press.

Williamson Peter J. (1994) 'Domination oligopolistique et politique communautaire en matière de concentrations', *Économie Européenne,* n° 57, pp. 143-203.

Rock products

Anonymous (May 1972) 'What cement's future hinges on', *Rock Products,* pp. 105-131.

Bell Joseph N. (August 1956) 'Cement industry expansion - how far?', *Rock Products,* .

Bell Joseph N. (May 1962) 'Revolution in cement distribution', *Rock Products,* pp. 105-109.

Duthie John S. and Liduena G.H. (April 1982) 'World cement markets: Lafarge, Blue Circle share experiences', *Rock Products,* pp. 35-106.

Grancher Roy A. (March 1969) 'What lies in store for the cement industry in 1980?', *Rock Products,* pp. 70-110.

Grancher Roy A. (May 1970) 'Cement: profitless prosperity?', *Rock Products,* pp. 116-133.

Grancher Roy A. (October 1971) 'Cement's second century', *Rock Products,* pp. 100-104.

Grancher Roy A. (December 1972) 'Cycling with cement', *Rock Products,* pp. 66-92.

Grancher Roy A. (May 1973) 'Internationalization of the United States cement industry. How imports and foreign investments are changing the domestic scene', *Rock Products,* pp. 100-145.

Grancher Roy A. (May 1975) 'Will the U.S. cement industry make plans for survival?', *Rock Products,* pp. 106-130.

Grancher Roy A. (August 1976) 'Florida - the cement market', *Rock Products,* pp. 64-65.

Grancher Roy A. (October 1976) 'Into the Valley... of Pennsylvania', *Rock Products,* pp. 74-75.

Grancher Roy A. (November 1976) 'Mississipi River plants', *Rock Products,* pp. 104-105.

Grancher Roy A. (September 1977) 'Penn-Dixie's purgatory', *Rock Products,* pp. 116-126.

Grancher Roy A. (November 1978) 'The cement shortage condition', *Rock Products,* pp. 86-93.

Grancher Roy A. (April 1989) 'What's ahead for U.S Cement?', *Rock Products,* pp. 38-44.

Grancher Roy A. (April 1990) 'Cement: whose boom will it be?', *Rock Products*, pp. 51-91.

Grancher Roy A. (April 1991) 'Changing scene for cement', *Rock Products*, pp. 28-81.

Grancher Roy A. (April 1992) 'Cement's Outlook For Managed Returns', *Rock Products*, pp. 34-74.

Grancher Roy A. (April 1993) 'Cement Producers Gear Up For Recovery', *Rock Products*, pp. 57-59.

Grancher Roy A. (July 1995) 'The stage is set for earning gains', *Rock Products Cement Edition*, pp. 22-24.

Huhta Richard S. (May 1981) 'The trading companies are coming', *Rock Products*, pp. 58-66.

Huhta Richard S. (November 1981) 'Interview: Jim Stewart, Lone Star Industries', *Rock Products*, pp. 65-67.

Huhta Richard S. (April 1982) 'Cement industry restructuring to continue in Europe, U.S', *Rock Products*, pp. 40-41.

Huhta Richard S. (August 1984) 'Redec opens its Texas terminal', *Rock Products*, pp. 34-A-34-C.

Huhta Richard S. (October 1984) 'We tour Japan's cement industry', *Rock Products*, pp. 50-A-50-H.

Huhta Richard S. (November 1984) 'Touring Japan's cement industry', *Rock Products*, , pp. 40-44.

Huhta Richard S. (October 1985) 'The price war scandal', *Rock Products*, p. 11.

Huhta Richard S. (March 1986) 'How sweet it is', *Rock Products*, p. 11.

Huhta Richard S. (March 1988) 'Target: America. Subject: cement', *Rock Products*, pp. 69-71.

Huhta Richard S. (October 1988) 'Who owns whom in US Cement', *Rock Products*, pp. 43-92.

Huhta Richard S. (June 1989) 'Export emphasis shifts to Mexico', *Rock Products*, pp. 60-61.

Huhta Richard S. (February 1990) 'Another look at vertical integration', *Rock Products*, pp. 15-16.

Huhta Richard S. (March 1990) 'Another look at vertical integration', *Rock Products*, pp. 13-14.

Huhta Richard S. (September 1991) 'The shifting winds', *Rock Products*, pp. 11-12.

Huhta Richard S. (October 1991) 'Who owns whom in U.S. cement', *Rock Products*, pp. 44-49.

Huhta Richard S. (April 1992) 'International Cement Review', *Rock Products*, pp. 38-62.

Huhta Richard S. (November 1992) 'Operating Costs of US Cement Plants', *Rock Products*, pp. 29-35.

Huhta Richard S. (April 1993) '1993 International Cement Review', *Rock Products*, pp. 37-55.

Ironman Ralph (May 1973) 'Multinational operation, ever-larger equipment foreseen by Dr A. E. Schrafl', *Rock Products*, pp. 104-152.

Ironman Ralph (August 1977) 'Société des Ciments Français. Part 1', *Rock Products*, pp. 56-60.

Ironman Ralph (October 1977) 'Société des Ciments Français. Part 2', *Rock Products*, pp. 50-53.

Ironman Ralph (April 1978) 'Lafarge. Part 1', *Rock Products*, pp. 86-94.

Ironman Ralph (May 1978) 'Lafarge. Part 2', *Rock Products*, pp. 78-81.

Ironman Ralph (April 1979) 'Holderbank. Part 1', *Rock Products*, pp. 88-95.

Ironman Ralph (June 1979) 'Holderbank. Part 2', *Rock Products*, pp. 64-68.

Ironman Ralph (October 1980) 'A profile of Dyckerhoff', *Rock Products*, pp. 72-78.

Ito Masahide (April 1983) 'World cement exporting: competition is here to stay', *Rock Products*, pp. 42-97.

Luchs Kurt (February 1991) 'Free trade is cement's future', *Rock Products*, pp. 47-50.

Muckley Joseph E. (May 1967) 'Why investors shun cement stock', *Rock Products*, p. 94-96.

Ousterman W. E. Jr. (April 1982) 'Cement's internationalism: is it a bane or a blessing?', *Rock Products*, pp. 115-142.

Rich Robina (April 1983) 'Cement exports', *Rock Products*, p. 40.

Rich Robina (April 1986) 'Floating silos: wave of future?', *Rock Products*, pp. 34-37.

Robertson Joseph L. (October 1986) 'Ore boat turns into silo ship', *Rock Products*, pp. 44-45.

Roehlkepartain Jolene L. (October 1986) 'European cement operating costs', *Rock Products*, pp. 32-34.

Roy Robert (October 1988) 'How I rate U.S. cement plants', *Rock Products*, pp. 39-88.

Shioya Yoichi (May 1973) 'The world's largest cement kilns', *Rock Products*, pp. 112-113.

Stearn Enid W. (August 1966) 'FTC heeds cement industry pleas', *Rock Products*, pp. 69-106.

Stearn Enid W. (July 1971) 'The evolution of Penn-Dixie', *Rock Products*, pp. 67-120.

Stearn Enid W. (June 1973) 'Cement and aggregates ride the water way', *Rock Products*, pp. 67-71.

Stearn Enid W. (June 1973) 'Rock Products and the railroad option', *Rock Products*, pp. 62-104.

Stearn Enid W. (August 1976) 'The cement shipping situation', *Rock Products*, pp. 58-61.

Sterling Harwell R. (April 1968) 'For the Cement Industry: A time of crisis', Part 1, *Rock Products*, p. 60-114.

Sterling Harwell R. (May 1968) 'For the Cement Industry: A time of crisis', Part 2, *Rock Products*, pp. 110-145.

Sweet James S. (October 1966) 'Cement Industry Over-capacity -Myth or Menace? A close look at the cement industry's past record shows continuing over-capacity even in the "good old days"', *Rock Products*, pp. 89-92.

Tak Jeong-Bu (August 1984) 'World's largest cement plant', *Rock Products*, pp. 34-D-34-G.

Toal William D. (November 1993) 'The Cement Industry of Latin America', *Rock Products Cement Edition*, pp. 24-29.

Turley William (September 1995) 'Mexican Mammoth', *Rock Products Cement Edition*, pp. 21-29.

Turley William (November 1993) 'Sanctions having effect on US Cement Imports', *Rock Products Cement Edition*, p. 13.

Uding George E. Jr (April 1986) 'unity needed in cement industry', *Rock Products*, pp. 30-83.

Ullman Fred (April 1989) 'Cement Trade: a global view', *Rock Products*, pp. 34-37.

Ullman Fred (April 1991) 'The Japanese Cement Industry', *Rock Products*, pp. 47-51.

Ullman Fred (April 1990) 'The Mexican situation', *Rock Products*, pp. 36-90.

Ullman Fred (November 1993) 'Small Country, Big Cement Industry', *Rock Products Cement Edition*, pp. 30-33.

Pit and Quarry

Anonyme (July 1968) 'Dundee's barge delivery system', *Pit and Quarry*, pp. 98-158.

Avery William M. (July 1949) 'More cement from Huron', *Pit and Quarry*, pp. 96-100.

Dorn Joseph W. (April 1991) 'Federal laws remedy unfair trade practices in U.S', *Pit and Quarry*, pp. 42-44.

Dorn Joseph (April 1991) 'Update: Cement Antidumping Cases', *Pit and Quarry*, pp. 43-47.

Fujii Mitsuzo (July 1948) 'The portland cement industry in Japan', *Pit and Quarry*, pp. 103-109.

Grancher Roy A. (January 1967) 'The Cement Industry -Quo Vadis?', *Pit and Quarry*, pp. 124-127.

Grancher Roy A. (July 1981) 'U.S. Cement: shortages and $100/ton product', *Pit and Quarry*, pp. 98-102.

Grancher Roy A. (July 1982) 'U.S. Cement: efficient plants for tomorrow's profits', *Pit and Quarry*, pp. 66-70.

Grancher Roy A. (July 1983) 'U.S. Cement: awaiting the promise of the 1980s', *Pit and Quarry*, pp. 76-94.

Grancher Roy A. (July 1984) 'U.S. Cement: recovering as a changed industry', *Pit and Quarry*, pp. 83-88.

Grancher Roy A. (July 1985) 'U.S. Cement: continued recovery at a price', *Pit and Quarry*, pp. CR 26-34.

Grancher Roy A. (July 1986) 'U.S. Cement: the view at mid-decade', *Pit and Quarry*, pp. CR 3-10.

Grancher Roy A. (April 1988) 'U.S. Cement', *Pit and Quarry*, pp. CR 3-12.

Herod Sandy (January 1986) 'U.S. portland cement: status, prospects, projects', *Pit and Quarry*, pp. 48-52.

Herod Buren C. (July 1967) 'Dundee paces industry with history-making plant', *Pit and Quarry*, pp. 96-172.

Levine Sid (July 1977) 'Cement and construction aggregates - production upturn continues', *Pit and Quarry*, pp. 110-149.

Levine Sid (July 1978) 'Cement and concrete continue climb', *Pit and Quarry*, pp. 165-192.

Levine Sid (July 1979) 'Cement industry anticipates steady growth', *Pit and Quarry*, pp. 140-181.

Levine Sid (July 1980) 'Pit and Quarry's annual financial reports round-up', *Pit and Quarry*, pp. 127-172.

Levine Sid (July 1981) 'Annual financial reports round-up', *Pit and Quarry*, pp. 133-159.

Michard Don (July 1987) 'US cement and ROI', *Pit and Quarry*, p. 26.

Mitsuzo Fujii (July 1948) 'The portland cement industry in Japan', *Pit and Quarry*, pp. 103-109.

Trauffer Walter E. (July 1955) 'The Cement shortage', *Pit and Quarry*.

Trauffer Walter E. (July 1956) 'The highway program', *Pit and Quarry*, p. 10.

Trauffer Walter E. (July 1958) 'Construction leads the way', *Pit and Quarry*, p. 10.

Trauffer Walter E. (July 1959) 'A new era for the Cement industry', *Pit and Quarry*, p. 71.

Trauffer Walter E. (July 1961) 'Cement industry progress', *Pit and Quarry*, p. 83.

Trauffer Walter E. (July 1962) 'Cement industry progress', *Pit and Quarry*, p. 87.

Trauffer Walter E. (July 1963) 'Atlantic Cement - water shipment to entire east coast made possible by large-scale production', *Pit and Quarry*, pp. 115-141.

Trauffer Walter E. (July 1965) 'Cement industry progress', *Pit and Quarry*, p. 79.

Trauffer Walter E. (July 1966) 'Cement industry progress', *Pit and Quarry*, p. 87.

Trauffer Walter E. (July 1967) 'Cement industry progress', *Pit and Quarry*, p. 71.

Trauffer Walter E. (July 1968) 'Cement industry progress', *Pit and Quarry*, p. 71.

Utley Harry F. (July 1956) 'Cement-producing capacity soars in Southern California', *Pit and Quarry*, pp. 75-79.

Utley Harry F. (December 1965) 'American Mining Congress and Show: a Record breaker', *Pit and Quarry*, pp. 122-127.

International bulk journal

Beechener Jenny (January 1993) 'Cement trade develops regional focus', *International Bulk Journal*, pp. 16-30.

International cement review

Anonymous (September 1993) 'Company Focus', *International Cement Review*, pp. 16-43.

Anonymous (October 1993) 'Floating Terminals. A New Life for an Old Ship', *International Cement Review*, pp. 28-30.

Anonymous (March 1994) 'Floating terminals', *International Cement Review*, pp. 16-17.

Anonymous (May 1994) 'Costing out the advantage of efficient unloading', *International Cement Review*, pp. 30-34.

Anonymous (June 1996) 'Floating terminals', *International Cement Review*, pp. 64-65.

Anonymous (July 1996) 'Cement and the European trader', *International Cement review*, pp. 20-31.

Anonymous (January 1996) 'Reviewing European cement prices', *International Cement Review*, pp. 26-28.

Bal Muriel (June 1995) 'Cement in France', *International Cement review*, pp. 84-93.

Bal Muriel (November 1995) 'Greece. Fighting the domestic downturn', *International Cement review*, pp. 20-29.

Biege Neal W. (October 1991) 'What's happening in the North American cement industry?', *International Cement Review*, pp. 51-59.

Griffith Spencer (April 1996) 'Important cement law. Cement trade and the new ammendments to the US antidumping law', *International Cement Review*, pp. 28-31.

Hanrahan Steve (February 1997) 'Pacific hot house', *International Cement Review*, pp. 71-76.

Hargreaves David (February 1997) 'In the Heat of the Dragon', *International Cement Review*, pp. 20-29.

Hoelle Thomas (April 1996) 'Lone Star's rich mix', *International Cement Review*, pp. 35-39.

McCaffrey Robert (May 1996) 'Sun sets on Japan's golden age', *International Cement Review*, pp. 20-27.

McCormack David (May 1996) 'The French connection', *International Cement Review*, pp. 51-56.

Nolan Thomas J. (February 1996) 'Company case study. Medusa', *International Cement Review*, pp. 46-50.

Roy Robert (May 1991) 'Coming to America. Will foreign cement stop coming to America?', *International Cement Review*, pp. 25-31.

Roy Robert (June 1993) 'What hope America. Deliberations on the future of the US cement Industry', *International Cement Review*, pp. 47-58.

Roy Robert (November 1993) 'A Climate for Recovery', *International Cement Review*, pp. 14-20.

Roy Robert (December 1993) 'North American Free Trade Is It good for Cement?', *International Cement Review*, pp. 61-63.

Roy Robert (March 1994) 'Steady as she goes!', *International Cement Review*, pp. 86-92.

Roy Robert (August 1994) 'Texas: Lone Star Ascendant', *International Cement Review*, pp. 32-36.

Roy Robert (May 1995) 'World trade and American cement markets', *International Cement Review*, pp. 53-58.

Roy Robert (August 1995) 'Oh Canada!', *International Cement Review*, pp. 24-30.

Roy Robert (April 1996) 'Much ado about nothing. Election years and the US cement industry', *International Cement Review*, pp. 20-26.

Roy Robert (August 1996) 'Following the Delta flow', *International Cement Review*, pp. 62-64.

World cement

Duarte Andrès (December 1995) 'Turmoil in Venezuela?', *World Cement,* pp. 16-24.

Grancher Roy A. (July-August 1984) 'US cement: cyclical recovery has begun', *World Cement.*

Grancher Roy A. (September 1988) 'US cement: the internationalized integrated commodity in transition', *World Cement,* pp. 344-351.

Gunnarson Bernt (November 1996) 'Cement by sea; more maritime terminals in Latin America', *World Cement,* pp. 22-25.

Hanrahan Stephen (1996) 'Prospects for world cement activity', *World Cement Bulk Materials Handling Review,* pp. 2-5.

Witte Greg (march 1996) 'Modernisation by Medusa Cement', *World Cement,* pp. 32-43.

Newspapers

Anonymous (1962) 'Dundee Plants to Raise Cement Price jan. 1 at 2 Michigan Plants', *The Wall Street Journal,* 19 October, p. 16, col. 4.

Anonymous (1967) 'Dundee Solves a Weighty Problem', *Business Week,* 25 November, p. 150.

Anonymous (1962) 'Huron Portland Cement cuts prices, intensifies Price War in Michigan', *The Wall Street Journal,* 4 October, p. 10, col. 3.

Anonymous (1961) 'Marquette Cement Claims Cerro-Newmont Mill Would Glut Market', *The Wall Street Journal,* 22 March, p. 17, col. 2.

Anonymous (1963) 'Marquette Cement says '63 profit to trail '62', *The Wall Street Journal,* 27 May, p. 7, col. 2.

Aubin Dominique (1993) 'Pour contrer les importations grecques, Calcia veut se développer sur le port de Rouen', *Les Échos,* mardi 28 septembre.

Bommel Sylvie (1992) 'Les cimenteries n'ont plus de secrets', *L'usine nouvelle,* n° 2376, 3 September.

Welles Chris (1984a) 'Cement case: inside look at business', *Los Angeles Times,* Sunday August 5.

Welles Chris (1984b) 'Foreign Cement Firms on U.S. buying Spree', *Los Angeles Times,* August 6, p. VI-1.

INDEX